Images from Paradise

Images from Paradise

The Visual Communication of the European Union's Federalist Utopia

Eszter Salgó

berghahn
NEW YORK • OXFORD
www.berghahnbooks.com

Published in 2017 by

Berghahn Books

www.berghahnbooks.com

Library of Congress Cataloging-in-Publication Data

Names: Salgo, Eszter, author.
Title: Images from paradise : the visual communication of the European Union's federalist utopia / Eszter Salgo.
Description: New York : Berghahn Books, 2017. | Includes bibliographical references and index.
Identifiers: LCCN 2017014734 (print) | LCCN 2017032605 (ebook) | ISBN 9781785336195 (e-book) | ISBN 9781785336188 (hardback : alk. paper)
Subjects: LCSH: European Union—Marketing. | Visual communication—Political aspects—European Union countries.
Classification: LCC JN30 (ebook) | LCC JN30 .S25 2017 (print) | DDC 341.242/2014—dc23
LC record available at https://lccn.loc.gov/2017014734

British Library Cataloguing in Publication Data

A catalogue record for this book is available from the British Library

ISBN 978-1-78533-618-8 (hardback)
ISBN 978-1-78533-619-5 (ebook)

Under the influence of the Ancient
This story is fantastic
to recount
A ghost story for truly adult people

A. Warburg, Mnemosyne
2 July 1929

Contents

Acknowledgements

Many thanks to Leah Marin for all her precision, diligence, and patience on proofreading and for her friendly and wise remarks (including her hint about Europa walking on the Yellow Brick Road toward the Emerald city). I owe a particular debt to Alessandra Pirolli for her meticulous editing of the bibliography and for her thoughts on the videos launched by the European Union during the 2014 electoral campaign. My gratitude goes to Timothy Martin, who helped me think of the Eurovision Song Contestl (and in particular of Conchita Wurst's performance) in a new way. Many thanks to the anonymous peer reviewers who made important suggestions for improving my arguments.

I am grateful to Berghahn Books for embracing my project; to Sasha Puchalski, Rebecca Rom-Frank, Burke Gerstenschlager, Marion Berghahn for their kind and precious support and to Ryan Masteller for his extremely thorough job on the manuscript. I dedicate this book to my family—Antonio, Fiamma, and Lara—whose love, playfulness, and imagination have been vital for me.

Introduction

The (Long-Desired) Rebirth of Europe's "Fantastic Family"

On 1 January 2002 several commentators and policy-makers depicted the advent of the euro in European citizens' daily lives as a historic moment, a transcendental step forward in the history of European unification, the dawn of a new era. The elimination of the national currencies and the consecration of the euro as the "holy icon" of the integration process were represented in a way to conjure up the atmosphere of a sacred initiation ritual. Videos and reports were released that testified to the ecstasy of millions of people gathering in the streets of European cities, rejoicing at the *birth* of the common currency, touching for the first time Europe's hottest totem, and staging special celebrations. The atmosphere of cosmic resurrection of the "European family" was further reinforced by the feeling many shared that, as a result of the magic moments of transformation, reunification was occurring.

The sensation of a new beginning was transmitted, for instance, through the cover image of *Europe* magazine (published monthly by the Delegation of the European Commission in Washington), which portrayed the common currency as a lovely newborn baby actively participating in the celebration of its own birth. In the picture, the infant sits comfortably and displays a high level of satisfaction. He is wearing the black hat of an illusionist, alluding perhaps to the magic force that allowed for his birth, and a blue ribbon with the golden symbol of the euro, referring presumably to the EU's colors—blue and gold. The baby is paunchy; his flab may evoke Cesare Ripa's Europa holding a cornucopia as a symbol of fertility, abundance, and prosperity. Inside the magazine, an illustration of another, even fleshier, baby standing on a heap of euro coins and holding in his left hand a pack of banknotes as if they were bays of victory reinforces the importance of the European Union's cosmic triumph. More than as a newborn baby, he is portrayed as a miniature senator from ancient Greece, reflecting perhaps the tradition of identifying Classical Greece as the cradle of the European integration process. His right hand rests on his hip in the classic power pose. His smile conveys a strong sense of satisfaction, provoked, maybe, by the fulfillment of an archaic and universal yearning.

The colorful whistle in the baby's mouth on the cover might evoke in readers the celebrations that took place in twelve European countries and help them reexperience the atmosphere of the collective revelry. The date 1 January 2002, when the virtual currency turned into reality (removing the uncertainty for those who had doubts about its very existence), assumed for many a cosmic dimension: this special moment was seen as the well-deserved proceeding of Europe's most frenetic Christmas, providing the right motive to transform traditional New Year's parties into special gatherings celebrating the birth of a special child. Many perceived the event as a *European* carnival (in a Bakhtinian sense) that was giving birth to a *European* public space, replacing the dominant culture of a bureaucratic and elitist organization with a democratic atmosphere marked by freedom, equality, abundance, and playfulness. This (supposedly) provoked in more than 300 million European citizens an intense feeling of wholeness, unity, metamorphosis, and rebirth, and renewed their sensation of being part of a collective body. Through these moments of transcendence, the golden age was experienced in thought, on the emotional level, and enacted by the body. The prophecy of the Cumaean Sibyl (the announcement that had been made in Maastricht at the end of a great historical cycle of European integration) was fulfilled in solemn tones; Saturnia reappeared on earth with the advent of a *puer aeternus*.

Similar to the Virgilian *puer,* the European Central Bank's *puer* was of course not a real human being but a (real) political function: it represented (and still represents) the regenerating dream of an all-powerful Europe. As we can learn from the various reportage sources, bureaucrats persevered and managed to win the "psychological battle of the first day" (Solbes 2001/2002: 17); the European Central Bank (ECB) accomplished "the most ambitious experiment in the history of money," the greatest shift in European identity (Coman 2001). As a result of a heroic struggle, Europeans could both discover a "new way of being in Europe" and experience a feeling of being "at home throughout Europe" (Duisenberg 2001). As European Commission president Romani Prodi observed, EU citizens realized that the euro notes and coins in their pockets were a "concrete sign of the great political undertaking of building a united Europe" and were becoming a key element in their "sense of shared European identity and common destiny" (2002). Federalists transfigured the 2002 launching of the euro into an act of redemption that had brought about a metastasis: the "old" world was thus "over"; life had only now become truly real.

Yet no fireworks were launched for the "child's" tenth birthday. In 2012, the E-day seemed to evoke the V-day of Beppe Grillo's Five Star Movement—the mild voices celebrating European federalism were overshadowed by populist and nationalist forces shouting *vaffanculo* and promising *vendetta.* By now, the euro has come to be seen as a huge betrayal: the Eurozone is associated with recession and stagnation rather than with prosperity, with the imminent possibility of painful disintegration rather than joyful unity, with death rather than with birth, with mourning (the loss of a dream) rather than with the jubilation of resurrection. As a result of the unfulfilled expectations of perfect unity and pleasure, the ecstasy has gradually faded; the euro has failed to conjure up in citizens a strong affective attachment. The loss of eschatological dreams has triggered Europeans' disenchantment with the new *home* and reinforced their nostalgia for their old *homes* (the cozy environment of nation-state *families* with all their indispensable components, including the national currency).

ECB president Mario Draghi had to intervene to end what came to be seen by many as Europe's "psychological crisis," to heal the wounds provoked by the trauma of the lost illusion. He recognized that in order to create warm feelings toward the European currency, the time had come to replace the euro's sterile and neutral design with fertile and evocative imagery to prove, also, through visual representation that the euro's bridges lead somewhere and its windows open onto the horizon of a new day. He arrived at the conclusion that a new European icon and a fascinating fable about Europe must take the place of national icons and romantic narratives about the nations' birth and evolution. In 2012 the moment was ripe, he felt, to reaffirm the euro as the "holy icon" of the united and prosperous "European family," to replicate the transcendental moment of creation of 2002, and to make European citizens reexperience the magic feeling of transformation, rebirth, and reunification. Since the euro's launch, transcendental attributes have been assigned to the common currency. Described in mystical terms and represented through awe-inspiring images, the euro was seen as a sacred link connecting Europeans to each other and to paradise.

Citizens' belief in the euro's *transformative* and *resurrective* power, however, has gradually diminished, prompting Mario Draghi to endorse (discreetly) the recommendation made by a committee of experts of the European Community in 1993: "Mother Europe must protect her children" (De Clercq 1993: 24). Super Mario seems to have recognized the need to complement the celebration of Europe's *pater familias* with a fest for the organization's "founding mother." The ECB president adopted a new communication policy proffering a different way of ingraining the meaning (and the promise) of the European Union in people's minds. To reach out to people's hearts and fantasies, the much-celebrated hero of the euro crisis came out with a (seemingly) new cosmogony project. In November 2012, the European Central Bank announced that the watermark and hologram would display a portrait of Europa in a blinding array of blue-purple-green on one side of each banknote of the new Europa series. The representation of Europa's fascinating but almost forgotten tale became the special gift to commemorate the tenth anniversary of the euro. It is the seductive face of the mythological princess, the sacred gaze of Europe's mother goddess that we encounter when tilting the banknote to the sunshine.

The ECB could have chosen from thousands of artistic representations of the Europa myth. In the end, an image adorning an approximately two-thousand-year-old vase found in southern Italy, and exhibited today in the Louvre, was selected. Why did Mario Draghi decide to ornament the new euro series with the portrait of Europa? Why did he borrow an image from a Greek *krater*? Why doesn't Dionysus adorn the imagery of the banknotes too (if the god of wine appears on the reverse of the vase)? What goals of the ECB are sealed in this mysterious image and in its evocative representations?

The scarce consideration of the federalist vision of the European Union, as a special space where the promised land of paradise will soon materialize, reveals academics' and policy-makers' disregard of the key role that imagination and fantasy, sacred and profane, play in the top-down construction of the (utopian) idea of Europe. At the heart of this book is not the attempt to solve a mystery but to invent (another) mysterious story. The initial inspiration came not from a "fantastic binomio," as in my previous book (Salgó 2014), but from an image. Nevertheless, my goal has remained the same: I am still keen on following Gianni Rodari's advice (1973/2010) to enter reality from the window. I will ask my readers to engage with the European Union's institutional visual narratives (expressed though banknote iconography and official videos) in the realm of imagination, to participate in a play, and to give birth to new stories about Europe.

Based on the conviction that we perceive reality through imagination and unconscious fantasy and that political communities are tied together by emotional bonds (including both conscious and unconscious elements), this book examines the European Union as a "fantasy community" (a state of mind rather than an objective, external reality, visionary and real at the same time) and Eurofederalism as a project of *palingenesis,* a political "doctrine of salvation" driven by the eschatological dream of creating a new, idyllic Europe through the transformation sion's extensive 'investment' in the normative 'distribution of [familial] affections' among its members, as well as its enormous interest in creating multiple microsites of intimate space is best exemplified by the institution of twinning" (2008: 73). For me, among the most important attempts to fill the emotional gap the EU suffers from would be to highlight the Commission's portrayal of the Eurozone through the metaphor of the European family; the ECB's decision to ornament the symbol of a united and prosperous European family, and its most beloved "child," the euro, with the pictorial metaphor of Europe's "mother"; the advertising campaign aimed at reinforcing these fantasies (and implicit promises) and the videos launched to prepare the act of communion that was to take place in occasion of the 2014 elections to the European Parliament.

The transition to monetary union lacked "humanity" and "intimacy" according to the report "Reflection on Information and Communication Policy of the European Community" (De Clercq 1993). The "intimization of politics" (Ringmar 1998), which was an outcome of the French Revolution and served as an engine for establishing a democratic public space where politics would be based on the authentic relations among actors, came to be seen by the European Union as a useful strategy to enhance popular attachment to the organization. European politics of intimacy has been following the model adopted during the nineteenth-century process of nation-state building. Since the tropes of familial ties had not contributed to transform the Eurozone into the intimate space of a European home, the ECB had to invest in the enterprise of taking Europeans on a journey to the maternal womb, back to the era of omnipotence. Independently, whether we see Europa's portrait through the mirror image of Winnicott's mother or through the Lacanian gaze, the initiative can be interpreted as Draghi's attempt to offer, through the visual representation of the idyllic mother-child relationship, the symbolic illustration of the maximum level of intimacy that could be reached between the euro and the citizens. The taking of possession of the mother by the child (symbolized by their reencounter on the euro banknotes) nurtures the hope that the return to aradise can be accomplished, the European "art of unification" can be completed, and common currency can finally become the holy icon of Europe's newborn fantastic family.

In the fantasies of many Europeans, the golden era is associated with the last decades before the outbreak of the First World War. Stefan Zweig writes about Vienna in *The World of Yesterday*: "We shouted with joy when Blériot flew over the Channel as if he had been our own hero … a European community spirit, a European national consciousness was coming to being" (1943/1964: 196). In the imagination of many, the First World War is equated with Europeans' expulsion from paradise and signals the beginning of an era characterized by a strong sense of nostalgia for the lost Garden of Eden. According to Heinrich Mann, to accomplish a return to the much-desired state of wholeness and serenity, "we Europeans must build our own church … For our church depends upon our unshakable belief. The belief is Europe, the doctrine of salvation is its unity" (cited by Orluc 2000: 135).

This book will examine European federalism as a political doctrine of salvation, driven by the paradise myth, and the fantasy of a redemptive end characterized by the transformation of the United States of Europe from dream into reality. Since its beginning, the European integration project's undeclared goal has been to accomplish the project of *palingenesis*—to create a *new* Europe, return to *illud tempus,* rediscover the sacred, and to reexperience idyllic feelings. The term *integration* has the same roots as *entire*; it comes from the Latin *integer,* meaning intact, untouched, whole, complete, impeccable. *Integrare* means to restore or make whole, while *integration* refers to processes of unification of separate units. Following its etymological roots, the European integration process could be seen as the par excellence example for the European "art of unification," consisting in the remaking of Europe's fantastic family as a whole and providing a *new* home for *reborn* Europeans.

Symbolic activity can be seen as the most important means of bringing things together, both intellectually and emotionally, thus overcoming isolation and even individuality (Walzer 1967: 194). Supranational policy-makers have identified in symbol politics the ideal tool to reunify European citizens in a strong emotional community. The belief that the EU needs new myths, symbols, and rituals in order to change the nature of familial relationships, reinforce citizens' loyalty to the EU, and attribute transcendental qualities to the organization lies at the base of the federalist agenda and constitutes the main object of inquiry in this book.

With *Images Europe,* Luisa Passerini aims to subvert the traditional interpretations of myth and symbols and find Europeanness hidden in images (2003b). Considering images, in particular moving images, as privileged sites of the imaginary, she analyzes their connections with the unconscious in relation to the Europa myth. Her conclusion suggests that we cannot define ourselves as European without questioning not only our cultural heritage but also our own intimate feelings and attitudes (Passerini 2003a: 27). Jacques-René Rabier contributes to this idea when he points out that the recent renaissance of the various versions of the Europa myth relates both to "mundane factors" and to "phenomena of a psychological nature" (2003: 76). He himself explores the former and leaves the latter to others. With this book, I seek to respond to his invitation and bring in psychoanalytical and anthropological perspectives, along with elements of art theory, film, and communication studies, to explore some of the most novel elements of the European Union's symbol politics, including the revival of the fable of the Phoenician princess. My hope is to show that the reappearance and the various uses of the image of Europa reflect a widespread nostalgia for the golden age, a heartfelt yearning for transformation and rebirth, and the European elite's promise of fulfilling these paradise dreams.

Though the 2007 Berlin declaration officially stated that the dream of earlier generations (a peaceful, prosperous, and unified Europe) had become a reality, today, notwithstanding official celebrations of (alleged) triumphs, the European political elite are seen by many as the "mother of our problems" rather than actors performing the functions of the loving and nurturing *mater familias*. The European Union's failure to fire people's dreams is a self-evident proposition. The collective imaginary is tied to nationalisms and local roots; the European imaginary is weak to reawaken passions for a different, supranational project. Yet EU institutions have not given up the hope of challenging the grip that nationalism continues to hold on the modern imagination. They still aim to take possession of Europeans' fantasies, invent a European culture, promote a new sense of Europeanness that would transcend parochial and nationalistic loyalties, and guarantee a higher level of consciousness based on (unconditional) loyalty to federal Europe. Several questions arise spontaneously: Is it still possible to resurrect the paradise myth? How to appeal to European citizens' emotions? How to make people believe in and feel thrilled about their European family and about the construction of their new European house? How to turn the EU into an intimate space offering a home-feeling? How to transform the nightmare of "a corpse whose hair and nails, wealth, and cumulative knowledge are still growing, but the rest is dead" (Heller 1988: 154) into the paradise dream of a magic land of peace, prosperity, and pleasure?

As George Soros states, "we need to do whatever we can to … preserve the European Union as the fantastic object that it used to be," because the future of Europe depends on the revitalization of the dream (2012). For Heller, a true metamorphosis requires a "cultural backing, a brand-new cultural mythology" (1988: 148).

One of the results of Jose Manuel Barroso's two-term presidency of the European Commission has been the turning of the "United States of Europe (USE)," "democratic federation of states," "European family," "house of the European family," and "irreversible euro" into "symbolic taboos." From Ian Manners's perspective, "symbolic taboos" include those phrases and sayings that are instantly recognizable as the central discourse around which EU politics and policies revolve; they provide a series of inviolable and sacrosanct understandings about what the EU is and what it does (2006). The USE, already a heartfelt desire of many intellectuals and policy-makers in the twentieth century and which was a vision that had been triumphant at the level of political imagination but had always failed to become institutionalized, has reemerged as a powerful state of expectation. The United States of Europe is portrayed as a political utopia with strong mythical connotations. Its advocates are driven by the (omnipotent) fantasy of constructing an idyllic community and by the desire to return to the (fantasized) golden age. Their plans are disguised cosmogonic projects: Eurofederalists strive to repeat the moment of creation by transforming Chaos into Cosmos and also to be recognized as founding fathers of a new European democracy. The word *crisis* comes from a Latin word *cerno* that means "to separate." Following the 2008 *crisis* (that caused the fragmentation of the European family into several separate pieces), the European Commission set out to create a "new faith" in order to help renew the principles of political life, form a European identity and (re)create Europe's fantastic family. The supranational elite's utopia turned into the official soteriology—a federation of nation-states came to be represented as the only salvation, the only way for Europeans to transcend the chaos provoked by the crisis and reconquer the lost idyll. If Europe is to avoid collapse and triumph over those forces that seek to bring back the past, says the mantra of the new political religion, it has no choice but to continue on the path of ever-closer union. The United States of Europe has become the sacred dogma that is to guide Europe's new visionary leaders in their heroic trials toward redemption and assist citizens in leaving behind today's overwhelming conditions. Turning the dream into reality has become a holy mission and a moral duty. The supranational elite have constructed a new symbolic world (made of myths, symbols, and rituals), giving the idea of the European community an awe-inspiring aura. European citizens are expected to cherish new dogmas: all need to participate in the single currency's sanctification as the holy icon of the reborn European family, and all need to internalize the myth of a new, idyllic, federal Europe. The sacred truth of the rebirth and reunification of the intimate community cannot be questioned; the spirit of the cosmogony project cannot be broken.

To help the prophets of the federalist doctrine of salvation spread the creed and enlarge their community of believers, to build brand loyalty and transform united Europe into a legend, an idol, an object of adoration, and a cult obsession, the Norwegian Nobel Committee in 2012 awarded the Nobel Peace Prize to the European Union. The EU was sanctified for its triumph in the struggle for reconciliation, democracy, and human rights, and for helping to "transform most of Europe from a continent of war to a continent of peace," thereby representing a "fraternity between nations" (Nobel Prize 2012). In his speech, Commission president José Manuel Barroso expressed pride for those "European values" that "the EU promotes in order to make the world a better place for all" and for which "people all over the world aspire," but in particular for the organization's soft power that allowed for the reunification of most parts of the European continent (Barroso 2012c). The implicit message of the celebrations was that the EU, through its transformative power, had accomplished the European dream by reunifying the members of the European family (who were feeling more and more separated as a result of a series of traumas and disillusionments). The same power eliminated the remnants of the dark era of war, destruction, poverty, and fragmentation, allowing for the metamorphosis of the continent, and again turned Europe into the paradisiacal land of Cockaigne.

The European Commission has also done its part in the intimization, emotionalization, dramatization, and sacralization of European politics. Following the nineteenth-century model of nation-state building, it set out in the 1970s to invent new symbols for family membership and homecoming. In the following decades, it revisited its symbol repertoire, reformulated the concept of citizenship, and changed its communication strategies with the hope of solving the organization's legitimacy crisis. In the mission of top-down identity manufacturing, the common currency came to play the role of the protagonist. The journey toward a federal Europe, based on a common monetary policy, became symbolic of an imminent individual and collective rebirth—Frenchmen's, Greeks', Danes', and Germans' transformation into enlightened (and enlightening) "Europeans" and the Eurozone's metamorphosis into a secure and cozy home. Yet the journey back to Europa's maternal womb turned out to be much longer than expected. In an effort to expedite the process, European commissioner for communications, Margot Wallström, decided to change course. A new strategy was proposed to make the European home more intimate and attractive. A "fundamentally new approach" was adopted to make the "inhabitants of Planet Brussels more human" and easier to love (Wallström 2007). Wallström was resolute that the superficial American method—"Make up a slogan, double the advertising budget and come up with a nice campaign"—should be abandoned as a point of reference, opting instead for "a more difficult path of actually changing structures" (2007). She recognized that the lack of a European story lies at the heart of the EU's problem of "emotional deficit." Although understanding that the previous generations' popular narrative of the peace argument was not sufficient anymore to fire Europeans' imagination, the European commissioner for communications was not poetic enough to invent a new story for the "Erasmus generation." A different route was proposed, but no compass was offered as a guide to the destination.

Europeans had to wait until Mario Draghi assumed the role of the superhero with determination to triumph where others had failed. For the celebration of the tenth anniversary of the construction of the house of the European family, he launched what he called a "new product"—the Europa series of euro banknotes—and propelled an advertising campaign to *sell* it to "Europeans." Portraying the euro through the verbal and visual metaphor of the newborn child of the European family in 2002 was meant to help citizens give meaning to something difficult to grasp and attribute affects to something difficult to love. In a similar way, decorating the new euro series with the image of the Phoenician princess (Europe's "founding mother") in 2012 was intended to provide significance, hope, and healing in a painful period. This visual metaphor was supposed to offer people a secure and intimate shelter in the chaos of the European crisis and act as a compass for their individual and collective journey.

To transform Europeans' passionless relationship with the euro into a magical love affair, the ECB president decided to blow life into a seemingly dead currency; to attribute a sense and desire to the inanimate euro; and turn it into a maiden with an irresistible seductive power and a mother that protects, nourishes, and is loved by all her children. By placing the image of "seductive Europa" on the new series of banknotes and transforming the euro into a female figure, he sought to make people accept the notion of the European family as part of their own universe and to kindle hope and faith in an imminent European transformation and rebirth. Yet citizens holding the new banknotes in their hands might decode the image in a different way. Most likely, the portrait in the hologram would remain unnoticed, and among those who would recognize the face of a female figure, only a very few would be able to link it to the Europa myth. To make sure that Europeans would get the message and make it their own, Draghi launched a new (only *seemingly* less aggressive) communication campaign. In order to convey to citizens the desired (encoded) message, to sell not just a new product but the meaning and connotations that producers attached to it, video ads were released with precise explanatory (both written and audio) texts. Following the central tenets of advertising strategy, these ads invite viewers to imagine themselves within the world of advertisement: the euro is "your money" (i.e., "seductive Europa" is also yours). They encourage citizens to "touch, feel and tilt" (i.e., to love *her*), thus experiencing, as a result of mystic reunification, the idyllic feeling of paradise and homecoming. This book seeks to unveil supranational institutions' attempts to sell infinite pleasure and to perform a traumatolytic function.

All the symbolic totems, captured so often through familial and nonfamilial metaphors and re-presented more and more frequently as images, are poetic devices that serve to reinforce the mythical dimension of the European integration project and to contribute to the sacralization of European politics. Metaphor is not a special trick used in verbal and visual communication but a natural form of expression. For the Italian political philosopher, rhetorician, historian and jurist Giambattista Vico (1668–1744) all the first tropes are corollaries of the poetic logic; in line with metaphysics, they give meaning and passion to insensate things, and each one of them could be seen as "a fable in brief" (1725/1948: 116). Additionally, the world in its infancy was composed of poetic (heroic) nations where the first poets, like children who take inanimate things in their hands and talk to them in play as if they were living persons, attributed to bodies the being of animate substances—reason and passion—and in this way made fables of them. Vico recognizes in this poetic wisdom the crude beginnings of all human activities: it is the poetic or creative metaphysics out of which morals, economics, and politics developed. For this Italian intellectual, poetic truth is metaphysical truth, and physical truth, not in conformity with it, should be considered false.

Since the verbal and pictorial metaphors used in politics activate in their audience unconscious responses and reinforce the emotional impact of the political message, they should not be viewed as stylistic ornaments of political rhetoric but rather as illustrations of fantasies, as the symbolic (figurative) expression of unconscious desires and fears. The word *metaphor* derives from the Greek *metapherein,* which means "to transfer" or "to carry" from one realm to another. Karsten Harries's *Metaphor and Transcendence* (1978) suggests that, in modern poetry, metaphors express a pursuit of unity, a yearning for a magical presence. As this philosopher and art historian underlines, metaphors imply lack; they speak of what remains absent: "God knows neither transcendence nor metaphor—nor would man, if he were truly godlike" (1978: 84). Through metaphors we express our striving for words that would be the "creative words of God" (1978: 90), which could create a poetic (sacred) world out of the fragments of the world, let us rediscover where we belong, and allow us to leave the familiar reality for the sake of a more profound transcendental vision.

Metaphors in the political discourse have a similar function. The imagery used in political speeches and in visual messages allows the storyteller to take leave of the ordinary world, to carry his or her listeners from painful reality into the realm of fantasy, from the profane to the holy. Verbal and pictorial metaphors become an additional instrument for sacralizing politics and reinforcing the emotional bonds. Today, the official discourse in supranational institutions is overwhelmed with metaphors, symbols, allegories, and analogies. By interpreting this imagery, we may gain some insight into the sealed kernel of Eurofederalists' *palingenetic* agenda, their desire to leave behind the profane (painful) reality and let a new, *sacred* community emerge. Conscious of the fact that complex or overly abstract images would not be internalized easily by European citizens, and therefore would not fulfill their political-communicative function (they would increase rather than diminish Europeans' sense of confusion and uncertainty), the architects of the European cosmogony project have opted instead for familiar representations already present in European rhetoric for several decades. By reviving the terminology of the ancient family-politic, they have further enhanced the fantasy dimension of their political narrative; the illusion of a return to the idyll of the primordial mother-child relationship and the feeling of the communal rebirth and magic recreation of the fantastic family have become even more powerful.

Convinced that familial tropes and images represent respectively the principal linguistic and visual means of our imagination, this book explores the use of these metaphors in the elite-driven project of building a new community and constructing a European identity. Since "psychoanalysis is essentially a metaphorical enterprise" (Arlow 1979: 373), I will act psychoanalytically and attempt to unearth and interpret the consciously conveyed metaphors and translate into words the unconsciously enacted ones. This publication must necessarily be divided into three parts—necessarily, because every good book is divided into three parts (Hamvas 1945/2007: 209). According to this great Hungarian metaphysical thinker, the perfect division is three: three is the manifestation of the divine, and three is the number associated with wine (which the *krater* chosen by Draghi contained in ancient times). This publication explores the sacralization of European politics through the analysis of visual communication—how the European elite have turned the political ideology of federalism into a soteriology, how they have appropriated from religion the function of myths (part 1), symbols (part 2), and rituals (part 3) and thereby sought to attribute a transcendent quality to the vision of United States of Europe. Official visual narratives claim to display the *real* image of Europe. This book shows how the illusionary character and even the logic of forgery underlying the elite-driven cosmogony project of giving birth to a new Europe is illuminatingly exposed in the currency iconography of the new series of euro banknotes and in the communication campaigns launched to raise awareness of the new sacred totem (the new euro banknotes) and of the sacred ritual (the 2014 EP elections). While trying to sell the European Union's cosmogony project, these visual tools reveal the authoritarian nature of European utopianism and the betrayal of the promise of building together with citizens a new democratic Europe.

Similar to nation-states, the European Union requires institutional narratives to create a basis for legitimate political authority and members' allegiance. In the first part, "Numinous Stories about Europe's Rebirth," I will discuss the many ways Europe's official storytellers have been narrating the paradise myth, preaching about the spiritual renewal and rebirth of Europe to convince citizens that the European integration process will conclude with the restoration of pristine unity. I will portray federalism as the European manifestation of what Roger Griffin portrayed as "*palingenetic* ultranationalism," a political religion that conducts what Slavoj Žižek defined as "politics of *jouissance*," with the fantasy of the "ever-closer union" constituting a *objet petit a.* I will explore the soteriology that conjures up a fantasy world, where all obstacles that hinder the realization of the paradise dream are disregarded and where there are no limits to what the EU can achieve. We will discover why the Europa fable is still relevant for today, how the human yearnings concealed in this story reflect the spirit of our time, and why it can be seen as a perfect visual metaphor for federalists' *palingenetic* myth of the United States of Europe. We will speculate on what drove the ECB to embellish the new banknote series with the face of Europa and discard the ambivalent figure of Dionysos. I will highlight the similarities between the two protagonists' stories, focusing in particular on their homeward voyages and on their seductive and transformative power. An iconological interpretation of the rich symbolism of the Europa myth's artistic representation on the vase will be offered.

In the second part, "The Promise of a New Symbol," Europa will be portrayed as a totem, a condensation symbol, the holy icon of the European integration process. It will attempt to explain the pictorial turn that has taken place in the EU's communication strategy and how Europa has become the visual metaphor of the euro and the protagonist of many of the official visual messages of the Commission and the ECB. The imagery of the European currency will be compared to the iconography of national currencies, with an emphasis on their function and power. The analysis of the visual communication strategy of the ECB (centered around the "sacred gaze" of Europa) will allow readers to gain a better understanding of the supranational elite's politics of transcendence and its political marketing strategy—their endeavors to *sell* Europeans a new story of abundance, fulfillment, and homecoming by creating the (illusion) of a carnivalesque atmosphere for the occasion of the euro's tenth anniversary.

The third part, "European Festival Tales," will seek new answers to the question "What the devil does a man need?" that Czesław Miłosz posed in *The Captive Mind* (1953) by further elaborating on the theme of political allegiance, in particular on citizens' *affective* attachment to the European Union. The meaning of citizenship will be redefined, relying on Arpad Szakolczai's concept of home and on psychoanalytic interpretations centered on people's longing for home. Popular attachment to the EU will be seen as a relationship that evokes the mother-child dyad in order to highlight the importance of the emotional dimension of political allegiance versus its rational, interest-based counterpart. Events, celebrations, and rituals will be analyzed as novel pillars of the EU's politics of transcendence in relation to 1) their function of provoking liminal moments: short periods of collective effervescence during which the EU may turn into a true fantastic family, a *communitas,* based on authentic interpersonal relationships; and 2) their function of evoking the atmosphere of a carnival-like performative democracy. The 2014 Eurovision Song Contest and the 2014 European Parliament elections will be analyzed as possible liminal sources of a new European democracy. The ritual of the direct election of the members of the European Parliament had been introduced in 1979 with the hope of contributing to the creation of a European demos and a European public space, thereby enhancing the organization's democratic credentials. The 2014 elections were portrayed by the prophets of the federalist soteriology not just as a tool to reinforce the affective dimension of European citizenship but also as a sacred rite of passage—an opportunity for citizens to swear allegiance to the holy mission of the United States of Europe, enact citizenship, and become actively involved in the federal project of palingenesis. I will explore the information campaign and the various video ads that aimed to awaken unenthusiastic EU citizens and carry them in a purifying carnival that would renew all. Readers will discover how these tools are revealing of the authoritarian nature of the federalist ideology and why the plan that foresees the purging of evil (the fight against "populists" and "nationalists"), the merging with mother Europa, and collective rebirth could end in a painful fiasco. Based on the belief that music, more than other tools, can enhance a sense of individual and collective purification and rebirth, the unofficial prophets of European federalism have entrusted the Eurovision Song Contest (ESC) with bringing forward the art of European unification. It is as if the organizers of the festival, the performers, and even the viewers were all invited to participate in a European carnival and make the fantastic European family resurrect and become *whole* and *home* again. I will suggest that Conchita Wurst's song "Rise Like a Phoenix," winner of the 2014 edition, embodies today's zeitgest (longing for rebirth) and the federalist ethos—"nothing is impossible." The part will bring evidence to claim that the Austrian singer's performance offers a powerful musical and visual interpretation, a suggestive ritualization of the supranational cosmogony myth, and that therefore it may be recognized as the sacred anthem that supranational policy-makers have been long searching for.

In my concluding remarks, I will invite readers to consider Eric Voegelin's political theory when reflecting on the reasons why federalists have not succeeded (and will not succeed) in persuasively playing the role of the magic bridge-builders, why their cosmogony project has failed and is still doomed to failure. I will argue that the politics of artificial intimacy, Barroso's authoritarian family model, must be transcended, and that Donald Winnicott's concept of "transitional space" should inform the European elite's parenting technique for strengthening citizens' home-feeling. The EU should not be seen as a "community of interest" or as a "community of identity" where there are no limits to what can be achieved. A playful European public space is closer to being a precondition of a democratic polity. Mario Draghi is not a superhero, but the EU needs no heroes to become a *cosmion,* or a true *communitas.* One of the greatest endowments of the Europa fable is that the story (just like the meaning of European family) can be narrated, interpreted, and re-presented in innumerable ways depending on time, space, the cultural priorities, necessities, and imaginaries of various peoples and epochs. The "destiny" of the myth can be considered analogous to the destiny of the Freudian drive (Passerini 2002b: 157) and the destiny of European identity—none of these can be determined a priori; they are elastic with respect to their scope and can assume very different and unexpected physiques. The most important legacy of the Athenian democracy (what is seen as the cradle of European democracy) is not (just) the pan-Hellenic identity construction but diversity-management, the ability to go along together (Ober 2005). In this vein, I will contend that a democratic political order must leave room for the Dionysian dimension.

PART I

Numinous Stories about Europe's Rebirth

CHAPTER 1

Need for a Paradise Dream

In his essay *Leviathan: A Myth,* Michael Oakeshott asserts that the substance of civilization itself is *myth,* a *collective dream*:

> We are apt to think of a civilization as something solid and external, but at bottom it is a collective dream. ... What a people dreams in this earthly sleep is its civilization. And the substance of this dream is a myth, an imaginative interpretation of human existence, the perception (not the solution) of the mystery of human life. (Oakeshott 1947/1975: 160–61)

Oakeshott admired poets' and writers' capacity to *dream* more profoundly—to preserve, rather than to break the dream, "to recall it, to recreate it in each generation, and even to make more articulate the dream-powers of a people" (1947/1975: 161). He believed that literature's gift consisted in offering us imagination and, as a result, the expansion of our faculty for dreaming. Seen from this light, even a book of philosophy may aspire to evoke the common dream that binds the generations together and makes the mysterious narrative more comprehensible. For Oakeshott, the myth that Thomas Hobbes inherited and that gave coherence to the collective dream was the myth of the Garden of Eden: as a result of an original sin, mankind was banished from the garden, from the ambient of peace and happiness, but, despite humans' disappointing conduct, divine grace promised an ultimate redemption, the restoration of the pristine order.

The notion of the broken unity and its renewal has been a central strand in the whole of Western thought (Berlin 1990); the return to a state likened to the golden age had already been envisaged as early as Virgil (Eclogue IV). The belief that the reign of Saturn during the early days of humanity signified a golden period of virtue and justice was a vulgate mythological notion and commonplace in ancient poetry. The association of *Saturnia tempora* with the idyllic era occurs in classic ancient mythology after which the god Saturn, probably originally the protector of the harvest, became identified with the Greek Kronos, king of Crete. Since the primary trauma, provoked by the expulsion from paradise and by the splintering of the pristine unity, man's primary desire has been to put the fragments in order, to restore serenity, so reestablishing the perfect state that had been lost. Nostalgia for paradise runs through European thought from its earliest beginnings; it underlies all the old utopias and has deeply influenced Western metaphysics and moral and political ideas (Berlin 1990: 23–24).

As Oakeshott asserts, a civilized life is created out of the desires, fears, and other inner drives intrinsic in human nature, the anxiety provoked by expulsion from the Garden of Eden and the longing for a definitive return. Many contribute to the construction of the paradise myth; theologians, poets, and artists may become the true custodians of the dream.

The fantasy of returning to the idyllic land has an immense *political* significance if we consider that every political agenda contains a reference to paradise. All political projects promise and seek to foster the illusion of the reappearance of the lost state of harmony, unity, and fullness; what differentiates them from each other is their image of the sublime Garden of Eden and how their members fantasize about bringing back the "fantastic family." The European Union is no exception; at the core of the integration process has always been a (paradise) dream. According to Joseph Weiler, for example, the legitimacy of the organization is rooted in the "politically messianic": the justification for its actions is "the vision offered, the dream dreamt"; its motivating engine derives "from the ideal pursued, the destiny to be achieved, the 'Promised Land' waiting at the end of the road" (2011: 7). European integration may be seen as a "political messianic venture par excellence," with the messianic representing a key component of its political culture, manifest both in its rhetoric and in its policy decisions. On the one hand, the ceremonial and sermonical language is rich in pathos (and in bathos); on the other, the persuasive vision that has inspired generations of European idealists of the "ever closer union among the people of Europe" as the only route back to paradise is indicative of the mythical dimension of the European art of unification (Weiler 2011: 8).

The Maastricht Treaty that sanctioned the birth of the European Union did not assign to the new community "that power of symbolic crystallization which only a political act of foundation can give" (Habermas 2001: 6). Yet the desired political goal of the reunification of the European family requires some kind of symbolic legitimation that in the national settings emerged from religious, quasi-religious, or mythopoetic factors. For Europe the only religious option, asserts Richard Roberts, is Neo-Paganism, "a paganism of the shamanic type," which would treat nature as bearer of an imminent sacred and provide people a sense of the immanent sacred (2006: 159). The supranational elite have proposed another way to reinforce the religious dimension of its legitimation. A transcendent quality has been attributed to the project of federalism and to the new euro: around the cult of the United States of Europe an official soteriology has been developed; Europa, and not Gaia, has been identified as the deity that Europeans should adore.

The transitional period of disorder and uncertainty has strengthened people's quest for transcendence. Today, more than in the past, the EU needs awe-inspiring capacity in order to shift citizens' loyalty from the states to the organization as a source of identity and existential security. As a response to the 2008 crisis and to citizens' deepening sense of alienation and quest for transformation, Eurofederalism has asserted itself as a political soteriology, appropriating from religion the function of myths, symbols, and rituals, thereby seeking to intensify the sacral aura of supranational Europe. Political religions, says Emilio Gentile, "reproduce the typical structure of traditional religions, … and propose to bring about … a 'metanoia' of human nature out of which shall come forth a regenerated 'new man', totally integrated into the community" (1993: 309). The prophets of Eurofederalism have launched new symbols and rituals, an iconography and a semiotic discourse though which they promise their community of believers an encounter with the sacred, spatial and temporal transcendence, and feelings of individual and collective rebirth. Conscious (or not) of their immense influence, federalists use myths more and more often as a political tool for constructing and strengthening a European collective identity, legitimizing the EU, creating loyalty and a sense of belonging, and for strengthening the affective dimension of Europe's "fantastic family." The crisis the EU suffers from is frightening, disorientating, paralyzing, and therefore unacceptable. But once it acquires a sacred meaning, a mythological dimension, the symbolic reintegration into the primordial chaos may also signify a chance to regain paradisiacal conditions and to discover the (European) Land of Cockaigne.

Political communities are inconceivable without myths. Myths are common and accompany normal political life; however, when they become overflourishing and overpowerful, the conditions are laid for an onset of social neurosis or psychosis. In transitional periods (as we have today), myths proliferate. In times of uncertainty and continuous flux, myths revive people's hopes—they seem to provide the possibility of eluding present difficulties, finding refuge in an imaginary glorious past or future, expecting resolution of problems from idealized leaders, fostering the illusion of creating order in the universe, and returning to paradise by putting together the fragmented pieces of the broken whole. Some of the paradise myths are explicit, others implicit; some are evident, others veiled; some are generated consciously, others unconsciously.

The European Union, similarly to nation-states, requires narratives to create a basis for legitimate political authority, to foster an intimate community feeling, and to strengthen members' allegiance. Yet in Europe, shared memories are missing, and therefore the affective element, the feeling of belonging to a European family, is absent or weak. There is no passionate identification by individual citizens with the EU, only feeble allegiance based on economic and political calculations. It is because nations have navels, genuine or fabricated (Gellner 1997), and these navels and the myths and symbols, memories, and traditions they represent have such a strong value for the people that so far we haven't seen the shift of allegiance from nation-states to supranational Europe. Federalists believe that to transcend European citizens' attachment to the nation-family, to create and reinforce identification with the European Union, an umbilical cord has to be invented linking Europeans to the polity. Similarly to attempts seeking to tell the story of the nation, the narratives of Europe hark back to a golden age (ancient Greece, the Renaissance, or the era of Enlightenment), to traumas suffered (World War I, World War II, or communism), and to exceptionalism and a civilizing mission—a sui generis organization, a model for others to emulate (della Sala 2010: 6). The vision of the United States of Europe, the *New Narrative for Europe: The Mind and the Body of Europe* (a manifesto written in 2014 as a response to European Commission president José Manuel Barroso's call), with the symbolic representation of Europe as an epic phoenix, and the story of mythological princess Europa (narrated by the European Central Bank) are different versions of the same ancient paradise myth. The custodians of these collective dreams are national and supranational policy-makers, intellectuals, artists, and (some) citizens.

While myths perform several functions, this part of the book chapter explores the role they play in provoking moments of transcendence, the perception of a return to the pristine idyll. Suzette Heald and Ariane Deluz, in a collection of essays, explore the interface between the psychoanalysis and anthropology through the interpretation of culture with a particular emphasis on the symbolic process and the nature of subjectivity (1999). Insights from psychoanalysis and anthropology will offer us the opportunity to give more depth to explanations of the proliferation and the growing role of myths in Europe and to reveal people's intrinsic quest for paradise and the political elite's endeavors to sacralize politics.

Psychoanalysts understand paradise as representing the happy period of our life when we could enjoy ourselves without anxiety or compulsion: the idyllic infanthood, the era of omnipotence, the joyful period previous to the trauma, the ontogenetic and phylogenetic paradise of the primal sea-mother Thalassa (Ferenczi), the pre-oedipal, pre-symbolic imaginary realm (Lacan), the period when mother and infant constituted a unit (Winnicott). Longing for the golden era previous to the expulsion from the Garden of Eden is part of the universal quest for happiness. Adults, as well as children, need to experience those special moments of perfect harmony, wholeness, and pleasure. As Géza Róheim points out:

> In growing up we substitute active for passive object love. We find substitutes for the love objects of infancy, but under the veneer of giving love we always retain the desire to receive love, and the loves and triumphs of adult life are really 'Paradise Regained', the refolding of the infancy situation on another level. (1942: 164)

For Christopher Bollas, a renowned writer and member of the British Psychoanalytical Society, throughout the whole of life there is a search for "transformational objects," which provoke the metamorphosis of the self and the conversion of emptiness, agony, and rage into fullness and contentedness. Transformational object-seeking in adulthood is an endless memorial pursuit of transcendental experiences. The object is sought not because of its characteristics but for the magic experience it may deliver. What Bollas calls "aesthetic moments" are liminal moments that provoke the metamorphosis of the self, something that can allow for the reexperiencing of the golden era of early infanthood when, feeling protected and loved by the mother, the infant was filled with a sense of joy. This British psychoanalyst asserts that moments provoked by the encounter with "transformational objects" constitute an intimate relationship between subject and object and provide the person with a generative illusion of fitting with an object, evoking an existential memory: "the aesthetic induces an existential recollection of the time when communicating took place solely through the illusion of deep rapport of subject and object" (1978: 386).

Bollas's thoughts have great relevance for political and social studies. Often we assign to the political elite the ability (and/or the duty) to transform our total environment and to (re)establish today those paradisiacal conditions that characterized our (real or imaginary) infanthood. Time and again we yearn for a strong and intimate relationship with an object that could provoke the experience of metamorphosis. Though neither culture nor politics can possibly fulfill our needs and desires as our (imaginary) mother did, they may occasionally offer moments for recollections of intense ego memories and for self-transformation.

Lacan is pessimistic about man's longing for reencountering the mother of idyllic infanthood. He used the term "imaginary solutions" to describe people's attempts to replace unmanageable reality with wish-fulfilling fantasy by constructing all kinds of self-defeating solutions. His thinking again recalls Freud, who in "Totem and Taboo" defined fantasy as "tak[ing] flight from an unsatisfying reality," which implies also one's withdrawal from the community of man (Freud 1913: 74). Immersion in fantasy represents for Lacan not the denial of difficult inner and outer realities, but perhaps the only way to accept them and find a symbolic resolution. The fact that nothing in the Symbolic can fulfill our desire to transform our division into completeness drives us to bring something in from another realm—the quasi-imaginary *objet petit a,* from the field of fantasy, in the hope of being able to leave behind our frustrating state.

Lacan argues that a residue of the "primal union" with the maternal body survives the infant's entry into the symbolic order. After its ban by the Symbolic, the "fundamental phantasy" is attached to the remnant of the Real in the form of the little nugget of originary enjoyment, which Lacan called the *objet petit a.* He used the term *jouissance* to capture the satisfaction provoked by the use of the desired object. The subject's only object of complete satisfaction, the mother, is forbidden; the subject will search for substitutes, but these desire-provoking objects will never fulfill the dream of complete joy. *Jouissance* is something total but impossible; it is what desire can never reach, the void that can never be filled. *Jouissance* is an excessive pleasure and pain, something extra that turns pleasure into a fascinating, even unbearable intensity; it represents the "excess beyond the given, measurable, rational, and useful … for the stake of which we do what might otherwise seem irrational, counterproductive, or even wrong" (Dean 2006: 4). Unlike the pleasure principle, *jouissance* provokes a rise (rather than a drop) in tension.

One consequence of the subject's dependence on ego-gratifying fantasies is that they mislead him to seek self-fulfillment through the *objet petit a*—the objectified cause of desire that the subject believes will return to him the precious sense of wholeness that has been lost. The *objet petit a* represents the desired integrity or wholeness; it does not refer to a specific need, but to the wish to become complete again, to be fully loved by the other, which is both impossible (since the self, created only after the separation, has no access to the primal union) and prohibited (through the action of language and Law). The *object petit a* is a compelling marker that pushes the subject toward substitutes that hold the potential illusion of fulfilling the constitutive lack, only to be reminded again and again that this lack is not fulfilled. It makes all substitute objects inadequate, deferring and differing pleasure, always in search of something else or more or elsewhere. This *objet petit a* is the inner secret or the kernel of the subject, creating a ceaseless and descriptive pressure to return to the "primal union," which at the same time gives rise to an awesome, obscene enjoyment. As the Slovenian philosopher and psychoanalyst Slavoj Žižek asserts, the *objet petit a* is "a gap in the centre of the symbolic order—the lack, the void of the Real setting in motion the symbolic movement of interpretation, a pure semblance of the Mystery to be explained, interpreted" (1992: 8). Phantasy is a construction that stimulates desire exactly because it promises to cover over the lack in the Other, the lack created by the loss of *jouissance*:

> It is because reality is articulated at the symbolic level and the symbolic is lacking, that reality can only acquire a certain coherence and become desirable as an object of identification, by resorting to fantasy; the illusory nature of fantasy functions as a support for the desire to identify. (Stavrakakis 1999: 46)

In a nutshell, fantasy is a longing for reconciliation and fullness, an attempt to compensate lack, to heal the wound caused by the primary trauma. The *objet petit a* and the "transformational object" do not refer to a specific need but to the wish to become again complete, to be fully loved by the other, in a way that would fill the lack. They both function as metaphors for the lost paradise: a paradise where we can enter for a limited period of time (Bollas), a paradise that will remain for us forever unreachable (Lacan).

Fantasy is not a strictly individual entity. From Freud's standpoint, fantasy has always been present at the societal level in all civilizations in the form of legends, fairy-tales, and myths. Lacanian thinkers also believe that fantasy belongs to the social world because it is a construction whose primary function is to cover over the lack in the Other.

People's shared dreams manifest themselves in myths. Myths constitute the common illusory experience that holds communities together. On the one hand they express populations' striving for a return to idyllic infanthood and for ideal parental figures; on the other, they mirror politicians' attempts to create the illusion of a pristine family and of regained order, harmony, stability, and happiness. Like dreams, myths surface as expressions of the mental state of societies. They disclose people's shared needs, desires, fears, and traumas suffered. The tendency to explore wish fulfillment rules not only nocturnal dreams but daydreams as well, not only individual but also collective fancies. Myths are like the concealed fulfillment of a repressed wish. Societies in their fancies attain just that which is painfully missing; they may escape from a real or imagined danger or obtain the extinction of real or imagined enemies. Myths reflect man's longing to attain rebirth through a return to the womb, a yearning that received various symbolic representation.

According to Jung, in ancient times man expressed his creativity by narrating and re-narrating myths; the realm of myths was the "world of fantasies," the result of the activity of a highly artistic mind, where rather than seeking to gain an objective understanding of the real world, the goal was to adapt it aesthetically to collective fantasies and expectations (1979: 20–21). In this sense, the world represented in ancient myths had little to do with the external reality and reflected instead man's inner reality. The Swiss psychoanalyst compared this psychic reality to children's way of thinking. Just like imaginative children who attribute to their dolls and toys the qualities of animate things, ancient Greeks with their myths created and became inhabitants of a world of marvels. An expression of the indissoluble link that binds us to the men of antiquity is "fantasy-thinking," which corresponds to the archaic ways of thinking and feeling and which "re-echo the dim bygone in dreams and fantasies" (Jung 1979: 28).

Myth for Lacan is a mixture of the Imaginary and the Symbolic; its main functions consist in "papering over the impossible, real kernel" around which the myth is constructed and for which it was originally formulated (Grigg 2006: 55). Žižek's extensive study of the role of fantasy and myths in contemporary social and political life finds that ideology is an imaginary domain that is reproduced though the fantasy identifications of human subjects. In line with Lacan, he argues that the purpose of ideology is to fill in or cover over the lack caused by the loss of *jouissance.* Its function is "not to offer us a point of escape from our reality but to offer us the special reality itself as an escape from some traumatic, real kernel" (1989: 45). The French-Greek psychoanalyst and philosopher Cornelius Castoriadis, inspired by Freud, arrived at a similar conclusion. According to Castoriadis, people have difficulties in accepting the chaos, the abyss, and the groundlessness from which humanity has emerged. Many refuse to recognize the death dwelling within every life; thus, "myth is essentially a way for society to vest with meaning both the world and its own life within the world—a world and a life that, otherwise, are obviously meaningless" (1997a: 11). Myths, which are expressions of the negation of the chaos, allow for circumscribing the abyss, for covering over the groundlessness.

Žižek contends that politics has become the "politics of *jouissance,*" concerned with "ways of soliciting or controlling and regulating jouissance" (2006: 307): "all politics relies upon, and even manipulates, a certain economy of enjoyment" (Žižek & Daly 2004: 114). A nation exists "only as long as its specific enjoyment continues to be materialized in a set of social practices and transmitted through national myths or fantasies that secure these practices" (1993: 202), and a community may fall into pieces if the belief in a shared enjoyment, connected to an idealized past or future, evaporated. What really binds a community together, argues Žižek, is not their knowing what laws to follow "but rather identification with a specific form of transgression of the Law, of the Law's suspension" (1994: 55). Myths unveil that the enjoyment of the in-group members is jeopardized by the out-group members who are determined to steal it or to devastate the community by infecting it with its own (obscene) *jouissance*. For these reasons, in order to understand the real nature of political forces, one has to confront their underlying phantasy, "the nonrational nugget, the fantastic stand-in for enjoyment, that can be what we desire but can never achieve" (Dean 2006: 47).

According to Bernhard Giesen the "return of religion" is a fundamental trait of the project of modernity: political ideologies and social movements have emerged as secularized versions of the religious revival where a religious devotion is justified by reasons and convictions (2009). Harald Wydra believes that transcendence can also be a political force: individuals' attachment to a political community may derive not from rational principles but from structures of thought "derived from religious practice, such as conversion experiences, rituals, cults of hero worship, and messianic expectations" (2011b: 266). The sacred, he asserts, has shifted from the symbolism of the king's two bodies to social forces, cultural practices, and ethical imperatives (2015a). The "politics of enchantment" implies the nonrational and the sacred, which have become "pillars for the reconstitution of legitimacy in the reordering of people's entire meaningful worlds" (Verdery 1999: 25). Sacralization of politics is often a symptom of disenchantment and crisis. Today's transitional period provides a fruitful ground for exploring people's overwhelming desire to reexperience the paradisiacal conditions of the golden age and the elite's response—the endeavor to attribute sacred and mystical elements to secular institutions. According to Harald Wydra, sacred spaces and practices often originate in violence and death, in times of extraordinary politics, "in feeble moments of the social and political flux, when people's yearning for ontological security becomes stronger and stronger" (2015b: 2, 3). Relying on Alessandro Pizzorno's notion of absolute politics (1987) and Eric Voegelin's political anthropology, he claims that in liminal situations the dissolutions of order and the disillusionment with traditional models entail a void of markers of certainty that may give orientation and meaning to the collective community, a void that may be filled with emotional excitement, crowd action, and collective ecstasy (Wydra 2011b: 268).

In the transitional era provoked by the trauma of the euro crisis, feelings of uncertainty, anxiety, and alienation seem to prevail. The drama of 2008 has created an out-of-the-ordinary, incomprehensive, incommunicable situation where political reality has been shattered and markers of certainty have evaporated. The roots of the collective trauma lie in the loss of an illusion, the broken promise of the EU as the Land of Cockaigne. The profane circumstances felt to be unbearable have triggered in people a longing for the transcendental feelings of unity, order, and completeness. Perhaps, more than in the past, people require a sacred compass in order to orient themselves and overcome uncertainty. A quest for the transformative power of the Sacred, promising to compensate for feelings of fragility and existential insecurity, has resulted in the supranational elite's attempt to make redress for the disenchantment. This recompense comes in the form of what is commonly perceived as a bureaucratic and technocratic organization, the application of eschatological visions to politics, the linking of transcendental symbols to the questions of power and legitimacy, and the binding of citizens to the Sacred. The hope is to shift allegiance from nation-states to Europe through the ritualistic form of equating federal Europe with salvation, thereby providing through the transcendental an extra sense of legitimation to the EU.

The federalist notion of the United States of Europe (USE) represents the contemporary manifestation of the ancient paradise myth. This political utopia has acquired a sacred dimension and is presented as the holy canopy, the only compass that can redeem the community. The supranational elite perform on the stage of European politics as authentic masters of ceremonies, whose goal is to give an end to our turbulent era and inaugurate the return of the golden age. The utopia of the United States of Europe is not only meant to fire Europeans' imaginations and kindle their fantasies, but also to enchant them with a sense of completeness, homecoming, and rebirth. Similar to nineteenth-century intellectuals who called for some type of humanistic "civil religion," a new "spiritual power," a "religion of humanity" to foster human progress and to counteract the power of egoism and greed (Nussbaum 2011: 7), supranational policy-makers seem to draw on Auguste Comte to articulate their vision of the European Union and of the new civil religion. According to Comte, the new civil religion, like traditional religion, must have an object of worship and it must include a multitude of carefully planned ceremonies, rituals, and festivals that give meaning to time (1865/1957). The 2008 crisis prompted supranational policy-makers to recognize the central role civic emotions play in politics and turn Eurofederalism into a political religion. Today they are convinced that their sacred mission consists of giving birth to a new (idyllic) Europe by combating tendencies toward the pursuit of national interests, putting "European values" on the altar, strengthening citizens' awareness of their "shared past" and "common destiny," and encouraging them to extend sympathy and love to the whole European community. Supranational policy-makers see themselves as those who possess the right (the only) answer for today's crisis, as the only ones legitimized to play the role Comte assigned to the council of philosophers—a new spiritual authority. In the European soteriology, the object of devotion is the "ever-closer Europe," which, to be imagined and addressed as a deity, has received a singular name: the United States of Europe. Central in the EU's communication strategy is the image of a united Europe threatened by the destabilizing forces of populist, nationalist, and Euroskeptic movements. Another fundamental feature of Comte's religion, the spirit of control and homogeneity, also seems to resurface in the EU; to turn the dream of the USE into reality, supranational policy-makers demand a submissive reverence to their authority and offer no (or very restricted) room for opposing views.

The dreams of today's federalists may also recall Julien Benda's vision of Europe sketched in *An Address to the European Nation* in 1933. The Europe this French thinker envisaged was spiritual, moral, and intellectual. He encouraged intellectuals to follow clerkly values (i.e., dedicate their lives to the pursuit of universal truths) and to save people from power-driven passions for race, nation, or class. Return to paradise (i.e., to pristine universalism) could be achieved by giving birth to a new, spiritual Europe where the passion of reason would reign (1933/1993). According to Benda, endeavors to create a united Europe had ended with fiasco because Europeans did not want to be unified. He believed that to convince people about the need to transcend the existence of nation-states and create a *new* Europe, to make them *love* the idea of Europe, steps had to be taken to shift people's political passions from the nation-states to the "European nation." To realize this project of *rebirth,* intellectuals, once they converted to true intellectuals, were entrusted with the task of fostering people's moral and spiritual metamorphosis by making *new gods,* inventing a new religion. Today's Eurobureaucrats champion themselves as an enlightened order of priests possessing spiritual power and representing the real source of moral authority in Europe. They seem ready to accomplish the task Benda attributed to *clercs*: vanquish nationalist passion with another passion, replace old idols with new idols, old myths with new myths, old mystique with new mystique.

Roger Griffin's concept of "palingenetic ultranationalism" (1996) may help us better understand the underlying fantasy of the European federalist agenda. *Palingenetic* refers to the myth of regeneration; it is driven by the vision of the triumph of a new life over decadence and decay, by the expectation of an imminent rebirth following literal or figurative death, by the desire to leave behind what is perceived as an intolerable present to be born anew. Eurofederalism seems to be dominated by Euronationalistic connotations in which the problems of the old European nationalisms reverberate on a new level. Applying Griffin's theory we could portray "*palingenetic* ultra-Europeanism" as an ideology driven by the mythical force of a regenerated European Union that emerges when ultrafederalism combines with the myth of a radical crusade against populism and nationalism and considers the utopian project of the United States of Europe as its symbolic manifestation par excellence. For the prophets of this soteriology, the realization of Europe's mystic rebirth is hindered by the invasive presence of the nation-state. According to this view, the European Union requires not simply the erosion of national barriers to facilitate the free circulation of trade, capital, and persons, but the complete elimination of all state borders, seen as rocks in the sea journey toward federal Europe. Thus, collective renewal, the construction of a new Europe (the USE), must be preceded by the dismantling of the nation-state and its associated ideologies of nationalism.

Similar to "*palingenetic* ultra-nationalism," the federalist soteriology is born of a human need for a sense of transcendence. It offers to its followers the prospect of returning to the golden age; it resorts to the sacralization and dramatization of discourse as a means to conjure up a spiritual and mythical atmosphere that may facilitate the emergence of new order, a new faith, a new transcendental community. Through the persistent use of myths, symbols, and rituals, it seeks to convince citizens that they belong to a supranatural reality, to replace the primacy of affective attachment to the nation. "*Palingenetic* myth" itself is the belief in the imminent transformation of the old world into a new one. As in rites of passage, the new status ("European citizens") represents a new beginning, the possibility of entering a new, more mature phase of life. In this sense, the progress toward the United States of Europe becomes the journey toward a *rebirth* and the dawn of a *new era*.

The federalist discourse portrays the robust reaction against the "populist," "nationalist," and "Euroskeptic forces" as a soul-saving crusade against the evil, as an intent to destroy those who threaten the paradise dream from coming true. It aims to purify from the community of "true

Europeans" any "anti-European" myths and influences, to destroy the virulent social disease menacing European democracy, and to restore and disseminate the cult of federal Europe. The European federalist agenda has strong Romantic components; its vision is inherently unattainable. Just like romantic nationalism, it is a kind of chiliastic doctrine seeking perfection on earth. It preaches an ethic of brotherly love, the purification of the elect, the destruction of barriers, and the abolition of this corrupt world for a new dispensation of absolute love and justice on earth. The federalist agenda doesn't take into account the real world of the European Union in which there is imperfect organization and dividing lines among members are growing in number and becoming deeper, all the while the willingness to unite weakens more and more.

According to Stefan Auer, like the Great Gatsby of F. Scott Fitzgerald's novel, the European Union is "never satisfied, always wanting more; insanely rich, yet unable to pay their bills" (2013). Like Gatsby, Europeans grew accustomed to living in a fantasy world in which everything must be possible. The European elite became so infatuated with the vision of "an ever-closer union" that they chose to disregard real-life obstacles to their plan (Auer 2013: 2). To reinvent himself, Gatsby is ready to remake not only his own history but also Daisy's past (to wipe out her husband forever, she must deny that she ever loved him). In a similar vein, the supranational elite, in order to reinvent themselves and their object of love (Europe), are not just ready to recreate through new narratives Europe's past, but they seem to be committed to deny unacceptable factors (present and past moments and periods of distrust and conflicts between nations). All those who embrace the religion of European federalism need act as if cleavages did not exist, as if unconditional love characterized the relationship among the members of the European family.

Federalists perform on the stage Žižek's "politics of *jouissance.*" The fantasy that supports their political agenda and what is supposed to bind together the members of the European family is the shared enjoyment of the mother imago. Identity entrepreneurs appear on the political stage resolute (and desperate) in their willingness to liberate European citizens from the suffocating feeling of castration, to create a new order free from the burden of the Law of the Father. This particular *jouissance* is transmitted though verbal and visual (mythical) discourses and reinforced by rituals. The revival of the fantasy of the USE exemplifies the willingness to deny the loss and to celebrate the everlasting mother-child union. For the new European family to resurrect, the phantoms of the past need to be entombed. The construction of a new European order cannot be accomplished without seizing the "cathartic moments" of the fiscal and debt crisis as they allow for purification, for experiencing a miracle, for transformation.

Perhaps supranational architects' plans for a federal Europe and the populist movements' (Syriza in Greece, Podemos in Spain, Five Star MoVement in Italy, and so on) projects of direct democracy and "liquid politics" in reality represent different versions of the same phantastic object, different versions of the same paradise dream. Palingenetic ultra-Europeanism and "populist movements" (re)appeared on the political scene for the same purpose—to interrupt the painful reality of chaos provoked by the economic (and identity) crisis with a utopian *topos* of sacred serenity. Both supranational identity entrepreneurs and Euroskeptic populists are driven by the (omnipotent) fantasy of constructing an idyllic community. Both models have mythical connotations: they are disguised cosmogony projects in which the goal is to initiate a *new era* in European politics. Alexis Tsipras, Beppe Grillo, Pablo Iglesias Turrión, and Nigel Farage on the one hand and José Manuel Barroso, Herman von Rompuy, Vivian Reding and Mario Draghi on the other present their own plans as the *last* occasion, the last opportunity of a Greece/Italy/Spain/Great Britain and Europe dangerously sliding toward the edge of the abyss. Their catastrophic discourse exemplifies a black-and-white thinking. In case regeneration does not happen, the phantoms of the past will return: skies will collapse on us, the crisis, the enemies (both inner and external) will destroy our lives, deprive us of our pleasures, and prevent us from recovering for a long time to come. However, if we are successful in our struggle, then we can again be the first. Failure of the mission would entail the demise of Europe, while victory would allow her to become an archetype, a model to emulate.

While both supranational architects and populist leaders seem to be active in *building* a new democratic European *home* with a new European *demos,* they both conduct utopian, antidemocratic politics. They function according to an exclusionary logic. In their utopian politics they need an anti-figure, a stigmatized scapegoat, an archenemy. While constructing the fantasy of an idyllic community they produce its reverse and call for its elimination. Supporters of a united Europe and "populists" have become each other's archenemy: each group is present in the other's fantasies as the evil that threatens the accomplishment of the in-group members' dream. Both perceive themselves as the moderate defenders of democracy and the other as representing irrational, radical forces. Both construct a Manichean view of society, leaving no place for authentic playful discussion and for the emergence of divergent positions. Both seek to create a civil religion and release "collective effervescence."

CHAPTER 2

Manifestations of Eurofederalists' Paradise Dream

According to George Soros, the European Union was, in its boom phase, what the psychoanalyst David Tuckett calls a "fantastic object"—unreal but immensely attractive, a desirable goal firing people's imagination, invested with extraordinary powers and vested with emotions (2011). The boom phase according to many did not last long. Agnes Heller, back in 1988, claimed that the time had come for the funeral oration of the European dream. Among the symptoms of Europe's deadly illness, she mentioned that the promised land had already ceased to exist as a museum, as a leader, and as a powerful source of inspiration for the rest of the world and that it lacked a creative future-oriented social phantasy. She pointed to the possibility of Europe becoming again "the initiator of a new imaginary institution of signification," a completely new discourse, as highly unlikely (Heller 1988: 158). At the same time, she also contended that no prologue could be written to a dream and that something that had never lived could not die. There is no corpse to be buried because there is no "natural" European identity; the European project is rootless because it lacks a history; European culture does not exist, either, because there are no European stories and legends about gods, demigods, and heroes transmitted from one generation to the next. She did not omit to remind us that what had never existed could still one day come to life. Those sharing the "European dream" certainly cannot write an epilogue; for them the dream still might come true (Heller 1988: 159).

As the treaty establishing the European Economic Community declares, the aim of the European integration process is "to lay the foundations of an ever closer union among the peoples of Europe" (1957). Notwithstanding the official denominations such as "common market," "internal market," association of sovereign states, etc., the mission of Europe's "founding fathers" has always been to create a deep political union, an intimate "European family." Ingrid Kylstad correctly argues that "The idea of Europe shares with Christianity the idea of a redemptive end, an end characterized by unity" (2010: 5).

The flourishing of the myth of a federal, united (and idyllic) Europe can be traced back to the post-1918 period. For the Austro-Hungarian intellectual Richard von Coudenhove-Kalergi, with the end of the First World War, the moment had come to finally give birth to the centuries-old "object of longing" (Villanueva: 2005). He urged the creation of a peaceful, united, and prosperous Europe in the form of a pan-European union of free nations, based on the Constitution of the United States of Europe, following the pattern of the United States of America (1926). His (anticommunist) Europe was to be bound together by Christian religion, European science, art, and culture. In 1929 Aristide Briand, French prime minister and honorary president of the Pan-Europa Movement (founded by Coudenhove-Kalergi), delivered a speech before the Assembly of the League of Nations proposing the idea of a federation of European nations; in 1931 French politician Édouard Herriot published *The United States of Europe*; and in 1933 Julien Benda penned *An Address to the European Nation.* In the 1930s and during the Second World War, several Italian anti-Fascist thinkers dreamed about a constitutional federation of Europe (Delzell 1960). Luigi Einaudi, Carlo Sforza, Carlo Rosselli, Altiero Spinelli, Ernesto Rossi, and Eugenio Colorni were among those who talked and wrote about the necessity to create a United States of Europe and launched concrete initiatives such as the European Federal Movement (Movimento Federalista Europeo). Others believed that only after the end of World War II was the moment ripe to accomplish the dream. Speaking on 19 September 1946 "about the tragedy of Europe," Winston Churchill warned Europeans about the possible reappearance of the phantoms of the past—the dark ages "in all their cruelty and squalor ... may still return"—but he also believed that there was a remedy that "would as if by a miracle transform the whole scene, and ... make all Europe, or the greater part of it, as free and as happy as Switzerland" (1946). His *pharmakon* consisted in the re-creation of the European Family, in the construction of "a kind of United States of Europe," a new home where reborn Europeans could dwell.

Despite the several cleavages dividing federalists, most were united by the core fantasy, inspired by the same paradise myth—the vision of a new mythical European community modeled on the famous American archetype. Soon, already in the 1950s and 1960s, however, the more modest model of functionalism began to replace the grand narrative of the federalist imaginary. Return to paradise still remained the final goal, but the journey was imagined as long and gradual (albeit still one-directional and teleological in nature). There was a widespread belief that integration in one area would provoke spillover effects and lead to integration in other areas, forming a chain of transformations at the end of which a political federal model would automatically emerge. The initial intergovernmental cooperation would yield to supranational cooperation, national identities would cease to evoke strong attachments, a strong (both cultural and civic) European identity would prevail, the EU would again become not just a legitimate organization but also an intimate community for members and an object of desire for potential members.

Starting from the 1970s, European cultural policy (officially the respect for cultural and linguistic diversity and promotion of a common cultural heritage) came to be seen as one of the key pieces missing in the puzzle, one of the last trials before completing the project of *palingenesis* through which the European family (with new Europeans) was to be born. Since then, transnational institutions have been active in developing the various dimensions of a "European cultural policy," hoping to boost people's awareness, facilitate the internalization of a "European cultural identity," and ensure that Europe occupies its desired place in Europeans' hearts, minds, and fantasies. According to Patrizia Isabelle Nanz, what prompted the EU to face its legitimacy through identity politics was the incapability of solving the problem of its "democratic deficit" through encouraging political participation in its institutions by means of institutional changes (2010: 286). For Stråth, in a period when the legitimacy of the European integration project was widely questioned, "identity replaced integration as the buzzword for the European unification project" (2010b: 385–86).

It was back in 1973 when the member states of the European Communities decided to pen a document on European identity. For them, what makes "the European Identity" original is

> the diversity of cultures within the framework of a common European civilization, the attachment to common values and principles, the increasing convergence of attitudes to life, the awareness of having specific interests in common and the determination to take part in the construction of a United Europe. (European Council 1973)

The European identity was portrayed as a necessary element in the "dynamic construction of a United Europe," in particular in the framing of a "genuinely European foreign policy." The purpose of the Tindemans Report (published two years later, in 1975) was more general; it proposed measures aimed at transforming the "technocrats' Europe" into a "People's Europe" by bringing Europe close to its citizens and kindling the imagination of its disenchanted populations. Cultural policy received an official recognition at the Stuttgart European Council meeting: there was a call for a "closer co-operation on cultural matters, in order to affirm the awareness of a common cultural heritage as an element in the European identity" and improve upon "the level of … information on Europe's history and culture so as to promote a European awareness" (European Council 1983: 25, 28).

The "Adonnino Report," launched in 1985, aimed to adopt measures to strengthen and promote the European Community's identity and its image both for its citizens and for the rest of the world, thus contributing to the "realization of an ever closer union among the peoples of Europe." It therefore proposed: the foundation of a European Academy of Science, Technology and Art, an institution with international influence able "to highlight the achievements of European science and the originality of European civilization in all its wealth and diversity"; the creation of community symbols such as a flag and an anthem; the formation of European sports teams; the confirmation of 9 May as Europe Day; the use of European stamps; the minting of a European coinage (the ECU); the launching of a Euro-lottery, "to make Europe come alive for the Europeans"; and the setting-up of a center displaying European achievements and the common heritage, backed up by a collection of documents and works relating thereto (Adonnino 1985: 22, 24). The publication of the "Adonnino Report" was the first explicit step toward *selling* the Community. As a result, the marketing of Europe as a kind of "brand product" became the key strategy through which the Community sought to tackle its problem of image and communication. These initiatives contradicted the official rhetoric that portrayed European integration as a "natural process." Furthermore, the artificial creation and promotion of European symbols, starting in the mid-1980s, as part of the so-called "A People's Europe" project is justly portrayed by Chris Shore as a form of (illegitimate) ideological indoctrination by European institutions (2000, 2001).

Pascal Fontaine's *A Citizen's Europe* (1991) expressed conviction about the irreversibility of the process of European unification and its metamorphosis from a purely technocratic process into a "profoundly humanistic enterprise":

> The goals of "A people's Europe" have been achieved. Who would fail to recognize the European flag symbolizing European unification? Who would not feel moved when listening to Beethoven's Ninth Symphony, the future anthem of a united Europe? Who does not enjoy following the "European Community" sign in airport arrival halls and possessing a uniform passport, and of course, "What European would not feel at

home visiting Europe's high spots of culture and savoir-vivre?" (Fontaine 1991: 44)

These and other symbolic measures are not purely decorative according the document. They fire most Europeans' imaginations; they are similar to national symbols that represent state sovereignty and "testify to the substantial progress made by an idea which has now been transformed from myth into reality" (Fontaine 1991: 7). What proves the triumph of the EC's cultural policy, asserts the author, is the emergence of *Homo europeus*. To increase the number of "new Europeans," citizens must be enlightened through public information and consciousness-raising programs; they all need to gain awareness of the positive aspects of European integration and then be ready to "push ahead," to leave behind the "hamstrung and impotent" community and create a new powerful one, based on a single currency, "the most visible sign of the unity and power of Europe" (22). Bearing in mind Jacques Delors's comment—"nobody falls in love with a growth rate" or a single market—the document calls for the need to make sure that a "people's Europe" exists in Europeans' hearts (23, 40). To this end, it demands more investment in the use of the magic instruments of television, cinema, and videos that transmit culture through images capable of shaping citizens' mindset day by day.

A year later, in 1992, the Maastricht Treaty conferred to the European Community prerogatives in the realm of cultural policy. According to Article 128, "The Community shall contribute to the flowering of the cultures of the member states, while respecting their national and regional diversity and at the same time bringing the common cultural heritage to the fore" (Council & Commission of the European Communities 1992: 48). The Treaty formally enabled the organization to intervene and propose measures in the fields of education, youth, and culture. As a result, in order to promote awareness of the European integration project, education and training programs (Erasmus, Leonardo, Tempus, and Socrates) were launched to reinforce the "European dimension" in educational discourse.

The document most revealing of the fantasies underlying European federalists' *palingenetic* agenda is entitled *Reflection on Information and Communication Policy of the European Community* (De Clercq 1993). Officially, it was conceived as a contribution to the debate on the present and future of Europe in the period of the adoption of the Maastricht Treaty and as a response to citizens' growing perplexity about the image of the European community. From this document's diagnosis the reader can learn that the community is sick because its members are questioning the worthiness of the "good project" (i.e., European construction and integration), because there is little feeling of belonging to Europe. The causes of the illness are to be found in the EC's failure to communicate to the citizens the "good project" in a relevant and persuasive way (so that everyone can understand and appreciate the benefits of a united Europe). The attempt to "sell the 'wrong product'" (i.e., the Maastricht Treaty), the lack of clarity about what must be communicated to whom and why, the absence of a clear and plain message with precise stimuli able to guarantee the desired reactions, and the failure to make a long story short are listed as factors contributing to the fiasco of trying to engrain European identity in peoples' minds.

To build public awareness and approval of the European Union and to help win back credibility and trust in European institutions, a new communication and information strategy was proposed that would take into account citizens' needs, hopes, and preoccupations. Bearing in mind that perhaps the deepest hope is return to maternal womb—the most heartfelt desire, especially in times of crisis and flux, relates to the prospect of enjoying again the idyll of primordial paradise—the De Clercq-led expert group came to the conclusion that European institutions "must be brought close to the people, implicitly evoking the maternal, nurturing care of 'Europa' for all her children" (De Clercq 1993: 9). Rather than offering *more* information, fewer *electrifying* and *warm* messages are needed to excite, motivate, move, and change the attitude of people (10). The Commission can launch these warm messages only if it possesses a "human face" and turns into a sympathetic, warm, and caring maternal figure that can guarantee the (physical and psychological) well-being of the citizens of Europe (15). While in the 1970s and 1980s, the goal was to bring European institutions *closer* to citizens, with De Clerq the mission was more ambitious—they had to exist *together*; they needed to form one inseparable dyad, reestablishing the perfect primordial unity:

> Inherent in the notion of Union are the concepts of solidarity, harmony, common action. In human and personal terms, these can be expressed in the single concept "Together". This is not just an adverb defining the relationship necessary for achieving objectives; it is also an imperative, a rallying call for action: "Together!" (De Clercq 1993: 14)

"Togetherness" became the new symbolic dogma, the inspirational credo that was supposed to appeal to the emotions, the common sense, to the hearts and minds of European citizens, and "involve us all in the great enterprise of building Europe" (22). "Mother Europe must protect her children"—narrates the document—so that the "European way of life," the European heritage based on human rights, tolerance, democracy, and savoir-vivre, and the European culture "make us the envy of the world" (24). The star that was meant to show direction during Europeans' journey back to the maternal womb is a "billboard" fabricated by experts of American marketing strategy. It suggests the promotion of the European Union as a "good product" (13), the *positioning* of the "good product" in the minds of the people as "the largest democratic, socio-economic, and political entity in the world," and the *selling* of the European Union to *target audiences.* The document emphasizes the need to call on board PR experts to launch "total and continuous" programs covering television, radio, and press relations, editorial support, advertising, public relations, direct marketing, public speaking, interviews, visits by special-interest groups, special-issue EC postage stamps, the publication of specific-interest pamphlets, etc., in order to explain European citizenship in "acceptable, motivating terms" (awarding personalized certificates to all newly born babies attesting their birth as citizens of the European Union is mentioned as an example) (De Clercq 1993: 13, 14, 31). The (road)map that identity entrepreneurs were supposed to keep in their hands was the "Europe 99" program, seen as the best means to exploit all the excitement and expectations inherent in the arrival of a new millennium.

De Clercq's authoritarian approach is evident in his recommendations to accompany every decision taken by the Commission with a *binding agreement* about the message to communicate and the means for its communication (the theme and scheme of each of the Commission's programs must obtain the prior approval of the central office of communications). He pinpointed the necessity to start a continuous process of education about Europe at secondary-school stage, including the review of school books and the introduction of a "European dimension" in the study of the past; found a "European house" comprising a library, a museum, and various operational offices to disseminate information; promote European events in the fields of leisure, sports, culture, academia, and food; organize "European weeks" on issues of common concern; award European prizes particularly in areas relating to youth; persuade targeted newscasters and reporters to become "enthusiastic supporters of the cause"; and adopt the "utmost rigour" in formulating the questionnaires when testing citizens' "European identity" "to ensure that emotional feelings as well as cerebral attitudes are accurately probed"—all of this in order to make Europe "the envied focus of culture, civilization, intellectual life and savoir-vivre in the world" (De Clercq 1993: 27, 35, 37, 33).

The "communication gap" between the European Union and its citizens, which dates back to at least the discussions that had taken place before the referenda about the Maastricht Treaty, has deepened since the rejection of the Constitutional Treaty in 2005. The Action Plan to Improve Communicating Europe (2005a) and the Plan D for Democracy, Dialogue and Debate (2005b) were launched by the European Commission to improve the image of EU institutions and restore public confidence in the European project, as well as to help the emergence of a "European public sphere." The "White Paper on a European Communication Policy," published one year later, departed from the belief that there is a sense of alienation from Brussels. The limited, one-sided communication on the part of the Commission had not kept pace with the transformations taking place in the European Union, and as a result prevented citizens both from knowing what was going on and from participating fully in the decision-making process, something "essential to a healthy democracy" (European Commission 2006: 2, 7). The expected overall result of a new communication policy was the enhancement of the public debate in Europe to accelerate the formation of a pan-European political culture with pan-European political groups and foundations. The new approach foresaw the attempt to leave behind the one-way institution-centered communication and opt for a "reinforced" citizen-centered dialogue, moving from a centralized to a more decentralized approach. The new "human-centered" attitude came to the foreground through proposals to give Europe a "human face." The idea was to put political information in a "human interest" frame to make sure that citizens understand that it is relevant to them personally, and to give a "human face" to the information provided by EU institutions, making sure that the European Union, instead of being *faceless,* possesses a clear public identity (European Commission 2006: 9).

Today federalists have no doubts—we need to reenact the heroic deeds of Europe's founding fathers, pass all the necessary trials, and complete the original project of cosmogony by giving birth to the United States of Europe. "We need to breathe new life into the sails of the Greater Europe envisaged by its founding fathers. … We also need to dream about this Greater Europe," said former European Commission president Jacques Delors (2013). José Manuel Durão Barroso, president of the European Commission between 2004 and 2014, presented his plan for *palingenesis* in his 2012 State of the Union Address (2012b). He put on the mask of the mythical hero and revealed the details of his (impossible) mission called the "Decisive Deal for Europe." This decisive deal, which was supposed to transform the long-cherished dream into reality, required the creation of a democratic federation of nation-states—the completion of a deep and genuine economic and union, the development of a European public space, and the reconstruction of the European Parliament as the "house of European democracy." Barroso used the metaphors of the European family to portray the Eurozone, suggesting that integration into the Eurozone accounts for entering the house (whose construction has not been completed) and becoming a member of the intimate European family. He resounded the idea that the accomplishment of the European dream is threatened by the rise and strengthening of nationalist and populist forces ready to destroy what has been built so far, and he set a "with-or-against" battle line for the dream of the United States of Europe with a (feeble) call to action: "We must not allow the populists and the nationalists to set a negative agenda. … I expect all those who call themselves Europeans to stand up and to take the initiative in the debate" (Barroso 2012b). It is not the USE, which is not real, but rather today's painful reality "that is not realistic" that cannot continue. The European Commission president portrayed his era gloomily in the interest of suggesting that in order to avoid the final doom, a new beginning is necessary; a new community must emerge on the ruins of the old. He implicitly referenced Europe's founding fathers and the responsibility of their sons and daughters to reenact the moment of creation: "Previous generations have overcome bigger challenges. Now it is for this generation to show they are up to the task" (Barroso 2012b). Barroso's moralizing, almost religious tone is even more evident when he introduced the metaphor that "we are all in the same boat." To stress that the sacred cause of federalism demands not just a feeling of togetherness but also unconditional devotion, he reverberated: "When you are on a boat in the middle of the storm, absolute loyalty is the minimum you demand from your fellow crew members." He made no secret about the authoritarian nature of his salvation doctrine: in the moral community of true Europeans there is no room for nonbelievers; those who are not ready to internalize the sacred dogmas of *palingenetic* ultra-Europeanism are excluded from the possibility of redemption.

A month later, Viviane Reding, vice-president of the European Commission, further elaborated on Barroso's heroic plan. Keen to sweep away all doubts, she dedicated a long speech on "Why We Need a United States of Europe Now" (2012). She prompted her audience (students, often portrayed as "young Europeans," belonging to the "Erasmus generation") to embark on a collective journey that would (surely) lead them to salvation, the magic land of the United States of Europe. She encouraged them to join the army of European federalists and be ready to wage a war against those who threaten the realization of (true) Europeans' paradise dream—"populists" and "nationalists." In an oratory style reminiscent of marketing experts, she seems to have set as her goal the enlightening of her audience about the qualities of her product. She set out to explicate the meaning and origins of the notion of the United States of Europe and to reveal why politicians betrayed the courage of the founding fathers by abandoning the concept for more than two decades, as well as to explain the reasons behind the recent return of United States of Europe to the political agenda.

What was imagined as a moment of redemption (creation of the European Union through the Maastricht Treaty) turned out to be a moment of disillusionment. While the common currency was conceived, no decisions were taken to proceed toward political and fiscal union; an independent European Central Bank was created, but it was not supported by a European economic government and a common budget. As a result of the trauma suffered, the notion of the United States of Europe ceased to be a "symbolic taboo." Instead of recognizing the need to come to terms with the loss of the loved object, Reding believes that it is time to revive the vision of a United States of Europe and bring it back to the EU agenda. As a key prophet of "*palingenetic* ultra-Europeanism," she sticks to its core doctrines: the creation of a new, federal Europe is the only way to avoid impending catastrophe, to opt for life in this critical period of flux. Like Churchill, Reding asserts that if Europe is to be saved from infinite misery, and indeed from ultimate doom, there must be an act of faith on the part of the European family and an act of oblivion against the painful (and shameful) past. The mistake made at Maastricht must be corrected. The love object cannot be renounced; there is a need to demonstrate that nothing is impossible. The EU can have a banking union, a fiscal union, an economic union, and a political union; it can even turn democratic.

In the voyage toward the European Country of Cockaigne, Victor Hugo's ideal of the United States of Europe should remain Europeans' compass. Viviane Reding quotes the words of the "democratic pacifist," saying: "A day will come when … all you nations of the continent will merge, without losing your distinct qualities and your glorious individuality, in a close and higher unity to form a European brotherhood" (2012). She omits to mention, however, that besides couching his vision of a United States of Europe—"Let us be the same Republic, let us be the United States of Europe, let us be the continental federation, let us be European liberty, let us be universal peace!"—Hugo also expressed his belief in an exceptional Europe. As he emphasized, "the torch of Europe, that is to say of civilization, was first borne by Greece, who passed it on to Italy, who handed it on to France" (Hugo 1862/2007: 100). Greece, Italy, and France are portrayed as "divine, illuminating nations of scouts" that have to hand on the torch of life to Europe: "Books must cease to be exclusively French, Italian, German, Spanish, or English, and become European, I say more, human, if they are to correspond to the enlargement of civilization" (Hugo 1862/2007: 364).

For the prophets of *palingenetic* ultra-Europeanism, Hugo's quest for European regeneration will be fulfilled by the Erasmus generation. The former vice-president of the European Commission harbors hopes that these students will see the emergence of the United States of Europe; they, as true (i.e., reborn) Europeans, will gain the right to enter the land of Canaan. At the same time, those who refuse to embark on the journey that leads to federal Europe, those who are not courageous enough to face the challenges and participate actively in the project of sacred metamorphosis, according to Reding, behave like "the devil at the sight of holy water" (2012). Ornamenting her discourse with this metaphor serves to add a spiritual dimension to her political agenda. In her imagination, the USE is the totem that sanctifies all those who come into contact with it; citizens who reject its blessing, refuse to take part in the rite of passage, to undergo through a transcendental metamorphosis a spiritual cleansing, a collective rebirth, and resurrection as true Europeans are necessarily those who made a pact with the devil. Implicit in the use of this image is the perceived superiority of federalists in respect to "others"—the holy water's power overrides the strength of the devil. The USE possesses a sacred dimension: it helps people pass the threshold between profane and holy; it protects citizens against evil and allows for their adhesion to the community of faith. It is as if she asked her audience to make a signal of faith, to dip their fingers in the holy water and make the sign of the cross to indicate their membership in the community of believers, their adherence to the political religion of European federalism. It is as if she asked the Erasmus generation (which symbolizes, for the supranational elite, the "new Europeans") to confirm their true European identity in a daily plebiscite, to be ready to renew their baptism and feel as though they are reborn Europeans day by day.

The belief that the United States of Europe represents the right dream to fire Europeans' imagination, the right political religion to believe in, and that this political soteriology should be spread by leaders using a more poetic (heroic) language was confirmed by Italian prime minister Matteo Renzi. Speaking at the State of the Union in Florence, he launched a call to convince European leaders to abandon "the cold language of technocracy" and explain to people that a stronger and more cohesive Europe is the only solution to solve the problems of our time (Schianchi 2014). "For my children's future," he said, "I dream, think and work for the United States of Europe." Renzi appealed to Europe's "courageous leaders" to work toward transforming this dream into reality and to defeat those who threaten or fight against this heroic mission. He warned against the phantom of the past: if the enemies of the USE prevail, what has been built by the European family could be destroyed. The only solution, from his perspective, is to acknowledge that the EU is "an attractive adventure" and that it has "not only a common past but a common destiny, to which it is impossible to escape" (Schianchi 2014).

While the Treaty of Lisbon (approved in 2007 and implemented in 2009) consecrated the EU's active role in the realm of culture, "drawing inspiration from the cultural, religious and humanist inheritance of Europe" and promising to "respect its rich cultural and linguistic diversity," "ensure that Europe's cultural heritage is safeguarded and enhanced," and "promote culture and heritage conservation" (European Council 2007), "communicating Europe to people" has nonetheless remained an unsolved problem. European federalists' enhanced efforts have been unsuccessful. Far from being powerful storytellers, they have failed to make the myth of a new Europe relevant, to make citizens internalize the sacred dogma of the United States of Europe as the promised land waiting at the end of the (linear) process of European integration. Barroso recognized that the myths, if left only to institutional actors to tell, would further alienate citizens, and on 23 April 2013 he made a call to artists, scientists, and intellectuals to write a "new narrative for Europe." Aware of the fact that the old dogma of peace, prosperity, and unity no longer provoked in EU citizens a sacred gaze, he made an appeal to European intellectuals to write a new "book" narrating in a different way Europe's present, past, and future. His nondeclared hope was that a new story of European *palingenesis* would enroll citizens (in particular the new generations) in the holy mission against populists, nationalists, and even Euroskeptics, who with their "pessimistic and destructive agenda" "threaten to destroy the dream made real." He prompted them to endorse the federalist soteriology by putting an end to the "aberration of dealing with European issues at the national level" (Barroso 2013).

To make sure that the new storytellers would triumph in selling the federalist paradise dream, in enlarging the community of believers of the new doctrine of salvation, Barroso reverberates in his call the idea that culture represents the missing link in the realization of the cosmogony project. From his perspective, culture is supposed to make Europe's founding fathers' dream come true by giving birth to "a human enterprise which will promote peace and mark a major step forward for civilization." To make the EU easier to imagine and to love, he discards the idea of Europe being technocratic or bureaucratic and instead attributes to it human characteristics: "Europe has a soul, and that soul is its civilization." In his appeal, Barroso seems to demand that the new narrative be ceremonial and romanticized enough to raise awareness of the glorious nature of the EU, to "ensure that our citizens are inspired by the great achievements of European culture" (Barroso 2013).

The instructions were far too detailed and the encoded message was far too explicit for a true authentic debate (which in theory he was meant to encourage) to take place. "A New Narrative for Europe: The Mind and Body of Europe," a manifesto written by a group of artists, writers, and scientists, seems to represent an enthusiastic endorsement of Barroso's call (Cultural Committee 2014). Supranational policy-makers endorsed enthusiastically the new tale and, driven by their well-known frenzy, transformed the catchy four-page essay into an illegible 249-page book (European Commission 2015a). The plot of the story is the same offered by the institutional narrative—Europe's rebirth. "A New Narrative for Europe: The Mind and Body of Europe" is also informed by a mythical understanding of the European Union and inspired by a cosmogony myth, but it is written in a different (more effective) style. The content of the European narrative has remained substantially the same; it still emphasizes the magic ability of Europe to transform chaos into order. The difference lies in its form (and arguably in its impact on people): while the old myth emphasizes more the traditional, the political, and the economic benefits Europeans can gain from the integration process, the new story has at its core the cultural and spiritual dimension; it makes the implicit mythological nature of the supranational project explicit.

Unlike Barroso, Europe's new storytellers have pathos, logos, and ethos. To appeal to (young) Europeans' hearts, thoughts, and fantasies, and to transport their readers in a new and special world, they use several (ancient) tools of persuasion—personification, a different punctuation of time, and rhetorical devices such as metaphors and tropes. In line with Barroso's thinking, the European Union is represented with human attributes: it is endowed with a mind and a body; it can suffer, die, and even resurrect. As the narrative goes, in 1914 "Europe lost its soul"; in the era of Fascism and Nazism "it damned itself"; and after World War II, thanks to European values, ideals, and modus operandi, it gained "redemption"; "Europe's soul was restored" (Cultural Committee 2014). The metaphor of the body politic is perhaps used as a means to prompt citizens to sacrifice their body and soul for the cause of the new political religion.

The European integration project, as the authors reveal, "was born like a phoenix out of the ashes of World War I and World War II" (Cultural Committee 2014). In 2014, a hundred years after the primal trauma, what Europe needs in order to leave behind the painful consequences of the shock (2008 crisis) is "nothing short of a 'New Renaissance.'" As in bureaucrats' rhetoric, the frequent use of religious and mythological idioms serves to add a mystic, spiritual dimension to the political projects. To similar ends, the authors sacralise time by restructuring the official EU calendar. Until recently, European history has always been told by the European elite in a teleological fashion as the story of the European family's linear march, starting in 1950 and advancing gradually but without interruptions toward complete union. Today, however, Europe's (chosen) intellectuals give a cyclic vision of time; they describe the story of Europe following the mythic structure of trauma and triumph, death and rebirth. Portrayed as the mythological phoenix, the European community is cherished for its ability to resurrect time and time again and arise from the ashes of its predecessor to return to the mythical age.

In both narratives crisis appears as something not just natural, frequent in the history of European integration, but also as something necessary—as a "great regenerating experience." In both cases the sacralization of politics suggests that in order to resurrect one has to die; for Europe to restore its golden age, it must first undergo the painful destruction of the crisis. The symbolism of death and resurrection, the commitment to Europe, the mysticism of trauma and triumph, blood and sacrifice, the cult of Europe's heroes and martyrs, the "communion" of citizens are all meant to contribute to the spreading of the myth of *palingenesis,* to the reinforcing of the belief that membership in a new united Europe would renew all forms of existence.

CHAPTER 3

The Tale of Seductive Europa

As the "White Paper on a European Communication Policy" demands, European institutions all need to have a "human face," not just to demonstrate that they possess a "clear public identity" but also to strike a chord with citizens and to make sure that they are perceived as personally relevant. In 2012 Europa became the "new face of the euro." The portrait of the mythological princess was incorporated into some of the security features of the new series of euro banknotes, a series that, not surprisingly, was baptized as the "Europa series." At first sight this choice could appear to be a response to the Commission's continuously repeated call that invited every EU institution to cease to be faceless. But is that all? Is it just one of the profane political measures serving simple "community goals?"

The ECB seems ready to attribute the characteristics of an animate being to an inanimate object, to personify the euro, to symbolize it, to make sure that the currency has both a public and a private function. Personification is part of the rich legacy of ancient Greece—a "strange disposition of Greek thought to turn concepts into gods and gods into concepts" (Gombrich 1971: 248). According to Gombrich we are perfectly accustomed to and even renounce asking questions about the

> extraordinary predominantly feminine population which greets us from the porches of cathedrals, crowds around our public monuments, marks our coins and our banknotes, and turns up in our cartoons and our posters. (1971: 247)

Yet for us it is worth reflecting on the considerations and fantasies underlying the decision to ornament the new euro series with the portrait of Europa. Could we see in it an attempt to transform once and for all the euro's humble story into a *numinous* tale? The image of the Phoenician princess has been traveling for various centuries through different territories, adorning everyday objects such as plates, medals, mirrors, stamps, and coins. Could it be that her voyage, ensured by the circulation of the European common currency, has several mysterious elements, conundrums difficult to decipher?

As Roland Barthes points out, myths represent a "type of speech," a system of communication, a message that includes not just written but also visual discourse, not just modes of writing or of representations but also photography, cinema, reporting, sport, shows, and publicity (1972: 109, 110). While EU officials have offered several different verbal narratives about the origins and the rebirth of the "European family," the ECB president chose the Europa myth and provided a visual (and partly verbal) and somewhat artistic representation of the paradise dream.

Before becoming a geographical expression, a political concept, a cultural identity, an economic fortress, a paradise dream, or a *sui generis* organization, Europe was a beautiful Phoenician princess, the daughter of king Agenor and the sister of Cadmos, whose story, in Moschus's interpretation (1912), starts with a dream. Numerous versions of Europa's story exist; the one written by this Alexandrian bucolic poet in the second century BC is interesting for at least two reasons. In recent studies the prevalent idea is that the name of the Phoenician princess and that of the continent were independent in origin. Moschus, however, is one of the few who identified Europa both with the maiden and with the continent. Furthermore, he opened his tale with a dream-image, which may remind us that at the core of the European civilization lies a myth, a collective dream.

Europa on the eve of her rapture dreamed that two lands, in the form of two women, were fighting for her possession. One looked familiar, the other, a stranger. Although the former (the native Asia) claimed that she was her nursing and nourishing mother, the maiden felt more attracted by the foreigner and more willing to submit to her violent advances. Once awake, the vision remained in her imagination. Feeling frightened by the obscurity of the dream, she wished to know which god had sent her forth such phantoms, what the meaning of the dream was, and, in particular, who the unknown woman represented: "how did desire possess my heart for her, and how gladly likewise did she take me to her arms and look upon me as I had been her child!" (Moschus 1912: [1]). In Moschus's story we then see Europa gathering wildflowers in a seaside meadow with her companions. All of a sudden, she catches sight of a beautiful, unusually gentle white bull—Zeus in disguise—whose fragrance is more pleasurable than that of the flowers. It is worth quoting how the strong sensuality of the magic encounter is described (the image chosen by Draghi seems to capture exactly these moments of seduction):

> There went he then and stood afore the spotless may Europa, and for to cast his spell upon her began to lick her pretty neck. Whereat she fell to touching and toying, and did wipe gently away the foam that was thick

> upon his mouth, till at last there went a kiss from a maid unto a bull. Then he lowed, and so moving-softly you would deem it was the sweet cry of the flute of Mygdony, and kneeling at Europa's feet, turned about his head and beckoned her with a look to his great wide back. (Moschus 1912: [89])

Attracted irresistibly by the bull, the Phoenician princess climbs upon its back. At that moment, the bull jumps into the sea, determined to carry the maiden across the sea from Tyre to the island of Crete. During the journey, nereids rise from the water and become her companions while Tritons with their long taper shells sound the marriage-music. Once she is far from the land of her fathers and cannot see any more the shore, but only the endless sky and sea, she starts to feel that her sea voyage is being guided by a divinity. The bull reveals to her that in Crete she will celebrate her wedding with Zeus and give birth to famous children who shall all be kings. When they arrive at their destination the animal unveils his true identity, and "upon a bed made him of the Seasons [unloosens] her maiden girdle" and transforms the virgin into his bride, and the mother of his children.

Concerned about Europa's disappearance, Agenor sends his sons Cadmus, Cilix, and Phoenix to find their sister and bring her back home. Cadmus decides to follow an Oracle of Delphi who orders him to embark on a different journey: to follow the cow that he meets on his voyage and found a city upon the spot where it lies down. Instead of finding his sister he creates the Greek city of Thebes and becomes its first king. Europa gives birth to Minos, Rhadamanthys, and Sarpedon; she becomes the first queen of Crete by marrying Asterion, who rears her children. Minos marries Pasiphae and receives a bull from Poseidon for sacrifice. Enchanted by the bull's beauty, he decides to keep it and sacrifice another. As a redress for Minos's betrayal, the god of the sea makes Pasiphae fall in love with the bull, have sexual intercourse with it, and bear the monstrous Minotauros (a man with a bull's head). Minotauros lives in the Labyrinthos and is fed on human flesh. After the conquest of Athens by Minos the Athenians are compelled to send their children to feed the monster until Theseus comes with them, and with the help of Ariadne, kills it and escapes.

The myth of Europa evokes the stories of figures of the female Greek pantheon who abandon their virginal state by leaving their own land, and through the humiliation of abduction become wives and mothers. Unlike many other women who had had the misfortune of meeting Zeus, Europa's case is special: while Medea and Elena accept the journey for love of a man consciously, she seems to follow her deep (unconscious) inner impulses. Furthermore, in acquiring regal power and dignity, even the love of a god, not only will she not be killed like many of Zeus's other lovers, but she will continue to live happily with a regal husband. The story of the Phoenician princess and Zeus represents a foundation myth par excellence—it narrates the foundation of the Cretan dynasty by Minos, the creation of the city of Thebes in Boeotia by Cadmus, the foundation of Phoenicia by Phoenix, and, in Asia Minor, the naming of the land where Cilix settled after the unsuccessful search for Europa, Cilicia. It is a cosmogony myth that unites land, sea, sky, continents, and people and comprises the human, the vegetable, the animal, the male and the female, the conscious and the unconscious (Passerini 2002a: 20).

The story of Europa has had an immense impact on the history of the idea of Europe, becoming "one of the most perennially popular illustrated tales of all time" (Wintle 2004: 13). Since ancient times the Europa myth has been widely represented in fine and applied art. Though it was pushed to the background in the Middle Ages, it regained its popularity during the Renaissance and has maintained its attractive power ever since. The myth has always been used to provide artistic expressions of passion, eroticism, and rivalry (between the Greeks and Persians, between true Europe and Nazi regimes, etc.), but also to define and raise awareness of the qualities and characteristics that have been imputed to the continent of Europe. For Wintle, the reasons why artists throughout centuries have appreciated and used the story lie in the following: its potential for humor; its "suitability" as a subject for decorative purposes; its potential for portraying aesthetic beauty, nobility, and queenliness; its dramatic qualities and sense of kinetic energy, rapid speed, and energetic travel that Europeans could and can enjoy; its treatment of romance and sensuality; its role as a symbol of power (2004: 12, 22, 28).

The tale became a highly charged political symbol for the European Community as well. In the post–World War II period the Phoenician heroine reappeared as the symbolic icon of the noble, united, reinvigorated part of the continent. In political discourse she became the allegory of soft power while the bull more often than not assumed the sinister connotations of the enemy that jeopardized Europe's future peace, prosperity, and unity. Sometimes inclusionist, sometimes exclusionist interpretations came to the fore: the myth was used to acknowledge Europe's wider, non-European roots (the Phoenician princess herself is from Asia Minor and is only carried to Europe by the bull), to argue that European citizens were not necessarily European, or to recognize the dark side of European civilization (in the myth Europa is a progenitor of the minotaur, just like European history produced its own monstrosities). When a more rigid interpretation prevailed, queenliness and uniqueness were emphasized; the phantoms of the past and the present were eliminated.

According to Ian Manners (2010) there are at least three different ways of representing this myth in terms of global Europa: the "rape of Europa," the "seduction of Europa," and the "transition of Europa." The version of the "rape of Europa," in which the bull symbolizes violence, oppression, and the destructive forces of nationalism and Nazism, provides a foundational story of how European integration contributed to defeat extremism, nationalism, and authoritarianism. In the story of the "seduction of Europa" the role of the bull is played by the United States of America, representing the liberator and the savior, the mythical hero who, as a result of his legendary accomplishments, conquers the heart of the princess and marries her. This is the foundational story of a special relationship, the matrimony of a couple where America helped his spouse overcome trauma in order to forget the devastating past and move toward a bright future. Manners interprets the myth of the "transition of Europa" following Judith Barringer (1991), who depicts Europa's journey as a metaphorical passage, a "critical life transition" both from maiden to woman and from life to death to rebirth (Barringer, 1991: 662, 666). In this sense, Europe's journey in the 1930s and 1940s could be read in relation to the metamorphosis of the Phoenician princess and seen as a transitional period in which the Europe of nationalism dies and a postnational Europe that is ready to face the challenges of the twenty-first century is reborn (Manners 2010: 69–70).

Every artistic representation of the myth of Europa is unique in terms of time, space, artist, audience, and the spirit of the era. Europa results as an interpreter of a series of affections that vary from surprise to trepidation, fear to sensual abandon. The fact that privileged moments from the mythological narrative vary in accentuation and interpretation as well is not surprising if one considers the communicative effectiveness of the syntactic structure (Cerulo 1993). Syntactic structure that orders and organizes, combines or repeats the various elements of a symbolic construction (in our case the different components of the Europa myth) may emphasize one element over another. While retaining the elements, it can change the symbol's message, effectiveness, and emotional appeal. To sketch the allegory for a project of peace, prosperity, and unity, EU institutions have frequently revisited the myth's syntactic structure. The decision to choose an ancient Greek portrayal out of the several artistic representations of the tale to ornament the new euro banknotes reveals what the privileged moments of the story are for the European Central Bank and anticipates how it will seek to use *this* artistic representation of the myth for its political agenda.

A glance at the new euro banknotes brings us back to antiquity and reinforces the narrative, according to which an umbilical cord links the European Union to ancient Greece. Mario Draghi perhaps shares Husserl's view that

> spiritually Europe has a birthplace. By this I do not mean a geographical place, in some one land, though this too is true. I refer, rather, to a spiritual birthplace in a nation or in certain men or groups of men belonging to this nation. It is the ancient Greek nation in the seventh and sixth centuries B.C. In it there grows up a new kind of attitude of individuals toward their environing world. ... In the emergence of philosophy in this sense, a sense, that is, which includes all sciences, I see—no matter how paradoxical this may seem—the original phenomenon of spiritual Europe. (Husserl 1965: 158–59)

He might agree with Vaclav Havel, for whom the large set of values at the bases of the European Union has a clear moral foundation and obvious metaphysical roots in antiquity (1994). This choice, this "preference for the primitive," may have something to do with what the art historian Ernst Gombrich called "Cicero's Law":

> How much more brilliant, as a rule, in beauty and variety of colouring are new pictures compared to the old ones. But though they captivate us at first sight the pleasure does not last, while the very roughness and crudity of old paintings maintains their hold on us. (Cicero, Dc Oratore III. xxv. 98; cited by Gombrich 2002: 7)

The prophets of *palingenetic* ultra-Europeanism (quite similar to premodern communities) believe that the power of their community lies in its (imagined) origins. The origin myth, the Europa narrative of the foundation of the Cretan civilization, this image of primordial paradise, assumes outmost importance and *regressus ad originem,* the restoration of the period of pristine harmony, becomes a key concern for European myth entrepreneurs advocating "rebirth" and "new beginning." The European Central Bank arrived at the conclusion that it was not enough to bring Europe back to the post–World War II period, when Europe's "founding fathers" laid down the foundations of today's European Union; a return to the sacred origins was needed in order to transform the Eurozone into a sacred space, an absolute fixed point in the global chaos, the point of departure for constructing a new *cosmion.*

Antiquity "imparts dignity"; old words and images give our discourse "an air of sanctity and majesty" (Quintilian VIII, iii, 24; cited by Gombrich 1966: 35); they can project us into another (sacred) world. If, as Anthony Cohen asserts, "mythological distance lends enchantment to an otherwise murky contemporary view" (1985: 99), the Europa myth may be seen as a tool to inject sanctity into a profane political project.

According to Antony Smith, there are three vital elements that determine how collective memory shapes national identity (2004). The first component, the drive for regeneration, is based on the memories of a golden age: the age of great splendor, power, and glory, the golden epoch of saints, sages, and heroes that serves as a model for successive generations to emulate. A second element has to do with a sense of collective mission and national destiny, inspired by the collective memory of the past and by the vision of a common journey that people feel they have to undertake together. The third component relates to a sense of national authenticity, what makes the members perceive their community as unique. Smith points out the importance of the ancestral territory—the place where, in the shared memories of its inhabitants, the great events occurred, where saints, sages, and heroes lived and worked and where the ancestors are buried (Smith 2004: 75). Besides lending an aura of mystery to the EU and its history, the memories of the golden age establish a sense of *continuity* between the generations. Through the fantasy of ancient Greece the ECB president sanctions the notion of connections between glorious past periods and the present and confers a sense of dignity and authenticity on European citizens. In Eurofederalists' vision, all Europeans should perceive the EU as an outgrowth of Greek democracy and share not just awareness but pride for Europe's past greatness and the mission that comes with this magnificent legacy. The memories of a golden age remind Europeans of the glorious *destiny* that awaits them if they are ready to continue their forefathers' mission and follow the path set out for them.

To understand more about the aesthetic underpinnings of ECB's decision and to unveil the fantasies underlying its *palingenetic* agenda, we need to ask questions about the decorations of the Greek *krater,* provide an iconographical interpretation of the images, and speculate about the possible meanings of its symbols and representations, the emotions they evoke, and the messages they convey. Before undertaking a journey in the realm of imagination, let's listen to the story as narrated by Mario Draghi:

> Portraits have traditionally been used on banknotes all over the world. Research has shown that people tend to recognize faces easily. The portrait of Europa was chosen to feature in the new euro banknotes because it has an obvious link to the continent of Europe and also adds a human touch to the banknotes. This particular image was taken from a vase in the Louvre in Paris. Why was the figure on the vase chosen to become a European symbol? First of all, because of the innovative iconography which transforms the love story between Zeus and Europa. The painter did not focus, as so many before him, on the abduction of Europa by Zeus, in the form of a bull, but on the seduction scene which precedes the

> abduction. Aphrodite, the goddess of love, and her son Eros place this episode in the repertoire of gallant mythology. Evident too is the coquetry of Europa, richly adorned and mirrored in the water of the nearby pond, and the gesture of reverence by the magnificent bull in brilliant white, of which the poets speak. This is a seductive Europa.
>
> In addition, the complex history of the vase perfectly reflects the exchanges underlying the construction of a European identity. The vase was made in the second quarter of the fourth century BC in a mixed cultural environment in the Taranto area, southern Italy, where Greeks were living alongside the natives of that region. Its Greek origins emphasize the importance of antiquity in the formation of a common culture. (Official website of the new euro banknotes)

The video "Europa, the New Face of the Euro" (ECB 2012a) gives some further clues on the origins of the choice. As Anne Coulié, the curator of Greek ceramics in the Museum of the Louvre explains in the video:

> This vase is a *krater* that was used for mixing wine and water. The two protagonists are at the center of the image and in the foreground. On the left is this young woman, with curly hair, adorned with jewels: a necklace, bracelets, wearing a finely pleated dress. And in front of her is a bull, in brilliant white, the literature tells us, which seems to be bowing down to her in a gesture of reverence. It is indeed Europa and Zeus, transformed into a bull.

Henri Loyrette, president-director of the same museum, adds: "That the Louvre contributes a little, I would say, with its works of art, to the construction of Europe it is obviously something that goes straight to the heart." While Ton Roos, director of banknotes of the European Central Bank, highlights the practical reasons, pointing to the banknote's enhanced security features, Mario Draghi concludes with a rhetorical question: "We chose Europa because these are euro banknotes after all. So is there any figure better than Europa to serve as the new face of the euro?"

With this chronicle, Draghi provides an enthusiastic response to the Commission's call for arms and an unconditional endorsement of European federalists' identity politics and cosmogony project. The ECB president points out the need for the euro to catch up with the great majority of the banknotes of the world that include a portrait. This recommendation is based on the belief that currencies' imagery contributes to the creation of a community: portraits more easily than abstract forms can add a "human touch" to the euro, go straight to the heart, allow for immediate recognition, and evoke memories of the golden age, thus reinforcing people's ties to the polity (see chapter 5). Furthermore, as a powerful cultural and civic symbol, the circulation of a currency ornamented by the face of Europa may contribute to the creation of a more European and more intimate public sphere. Mario Draghi (in line with Moschus) suggests that the Phoenician princess can be associated both with the myth and with the continent, and therefore can easily lend herself for the foundational myth that the European Union has been lacking and whose re-evocation and reenactment is necessary in order to accomplish the *palingenetic* project, the elimination of the old and the re-creation of a new mystic community. His preference for the Greek vase is explained in reference to how the *krater*'s story mirrors Europe's dynamic multicultural roots and the way the artistic heritage treasured in the Louvre can contribute to the construction of European identity by appealing to citizens' hearts and emotions. Draghi thus adheres to the idea that Europe's roots lie in antiquity, with ancient Greece representing the cradle of European cultural heritage and the *illud tempus* when the Sacred first appeared. He uses the tale as a communication tool to make a statement of continuity: the new monetary union is still the old spiritual Europe. It is Europa's beauty that allows for the community's transcendental metamorphosis.

The vase was chosen because it *transforms* the story of the abduction of Europa by Zeus into a story of seduction of Zeus by Europa. It captures the preliminary playful moments of philandering preceding the voyage and the amorous union. It is ornamented by a "seductive Europa" whose *transformational power,* resulting from her splendor and irresistible charm, queenliness, and superiority (even in respect to the king of the gods of Mount Olympus), is perhaps what convinced Draghi about the story's usefulness as symbol of the EU's rite of passage. At first sight it seems that in Draghi's syntactic structure the moments of seduction of Zeus by Europa are put to the fore (in respect to the elements of abduction and maternity). The message that is apparently emphasized is that Europa is the personification of soft power; her seductive and transformational command will consummate turning the euro into an "object of desire," thereby conquering the hearts and the minds of citizens and, as a result of frequent and intimate encounters, allowing for their metamorphosis into newborn Europeans.

Most, if not all, images have a meaning that is preferred by their producers. Not just artists and filmmakers but policy-makers as well seek to prompt us to see and interpret the images they produce (and/or spread) in a specific way. Already during the initiation ritual (i.e., at the unveiling ceremony of the first €5 banknote of the new series), Draghi tells a story presenting "seductive Europa" as personification of the new totem. His words direct our eyes to particular aspects of the image;

he tells us what to see in the picture. With his detailed explanation, the ECB president imposes the meaning of the image; he induces us to look at the euro in a certain way and teaches us how to decode the meaning of the image, what iconological interpretation to give.

The image of the maiden flirting with Zeus may evoke in many of us Jan Van der Straet's drawing *Vespucci Discovering America* (ca. 1587–89). For the explorers, possessing the land paralleled the carnal possession of a woman; for Eurofederalists, possessing the new euro is associated with the possibility of a return to the primordial idyll. While both Europa and America represent the "object of desire," Draghi's allegorical personification of the Eurozone as a feminized land is different from Jan Van der Straet's representation of America. America's naked body, evoking barbarity and primordial nature, contrasts with the pathos of Europa's flowing clothing; the European land is perceived as noble, not savage. Both are depicted as sexually available, but while America is just about to be subdued by the invader, the Phoenician princess is perfectly in control of the situation. Her look and pose reveal her enjoyment and spirit of initiative rather than compliance. She is not a rape victim, not a vulnerable maiden, or a mother in need of protection, but a queen-like figure that rules and exerts influence over others. She is able to impose her will even on the "father of gods and men." The attributes chosen by Draghi, such as the clothing, jewels, river, flowers, and necklace of pearl, which complement the classical elements such as the damsel and the bull, serve to enable Europa's metamorphosis from noble rape victim to triumphant heroine. These elements add dignity, uniqueness, and superiority to the Eurozone and emphasize Europe's (perceived) queenliness.

To reveal more about Draghi's choice we could now attempt to provide one possible iconological interpretation of the extraordinary imagery that ornaments the Greek *krater.*

One basic premise we need to consider is that the figures on Attic vases mirror the *mental* rather than the "real" world of the ancient Greeks and that they were addressed to the users of the object on which the scenes are depicted. As Cornelia Isler-Kerényi shows, in the figurative art of Greek vases, there is no hierarchy between tangible and imaginary elements. The images are allusive rather than descriptive: they are not "scenes" that can be turned completely into words or translated into a narrative but combinations of figures and signs intended to evoke specific facts and situations (2007: 3). In Isler-Kerényi's hypothesis, the combinations of subjects on the same vase, the bodily forms, the gestures, and the attributes were used by the painters to evoke specific liminal moments in a man's life and to provide psychological support to the individual who was mentally and physically undergoing that metamorphosis. Since the symposium was one of the privileged settings for ritualized transitions of this type, the imagery on vases created for the symposium is of special interest to us. Both wedding and sympothic vases performed a private and a public function. The images on wedding vases were meant to reinforce social expectations and advertise virtues that would create a happy marriage (Peitho, Harmonia, and Eukleia) and promise the benefits (prosperity, health, and childrearing) that might result from adherence to these values (Smith 2005). Similarly, the figures decorating the symphotic vases could also be seen as personifications or anthropomorphic representations of things, ideas, and fantasies.

Might the lovely Greek (symphotic) *krater* chosen by Draghi contain various political messages to our contemporary Europe as well? Does it represent a special *pharmakon* not just to the people that used it on occasions of the symposium but also to its contemporary audience? In particular to the community of the Eurozone that is undergoing a metamorphosis in a transitional era characterized by flux, uncertainty, and anxiety? What narratives does Draghi try to transmit? What feelings does he wish to evoke? What political concepts, values, and fantasies can we associate to Europa, Zeus, and Dionysus? What do the protagonists of the images personify? How can we tell how these anthropomorphic representations were intended by the creator of the vase and by Draghi, and how were/are they experienced by ancient Greek and contemporary European users/audience?

In the second half of the fifth century and all of the fourth century BC the depictions of the myth appeared in great numbers in Attic ceramics and in the vases produced in the workshops of southern Italy. On the one chosen by Draghi, Europa appears at the center of the scene. Unlike in most artistic representations in which she is portrayed on the back of the bull in the moment of undertaking her sea voyage or already in the sea turning toward the shore where her desperate companions chase and call after her, in this version the damsel is seated on a rock next to a source of water, perhaps the shore of the sea or a river. She is richly dressed and adorned with jewels; with the right hand she keeps the veil above her head and regal hairstyle. The cloaked woman on the right holds an amphora. To the left of Europa, a forwardly outstretched bull is depicted. In the upper register, to the left, two young damsels converse, while on the right, a *putto* entertains a young woman. The *krater* captures the moment of the myth when the virginal activity (she is collecting flowers with the damsels of Tyre) is interrupted by the appearance of Zeus, disguised as a white bull. The damsel is portrayed enjoying the magic playfulness of preliminary seduction; the bull is captured in a pose of veneration, completely conquered by and devoted to the virgin, masking, to a certain extent, his sexual excitement. The other side of the *krater* is decorated with a procession of Dionysus. The Dionysia (or Bacchanalia) festivals saw the participation of women who entered a trance, danced to the beat of drums, and waved thyrsi (symbols of fertility, reproduction, and intoxication). During their frenzy, maenads (the female followers of Dionysus) gained supernatural powers (the ability to tear apart animals and humans).

The landscape in the myth plays the essential role of establishing the atmosphere of idyll, cosmic peacefulness, and joy. Damsel and landscape are linked together in a mystic and intimate relationship and become the allegory of the pristine paradise. The creatures are irresistibly drawn to one another, blended together in a perfect unity, attributing to the whole image the primordial quality of the golden age. The bucolic idyll enjoyed by Europa and her companions may serve as a reminder of the pleasure and peacefulness enjoyed by Europeans in *illud tempus.* The presence of Eros and Cupid (the most evident personifications of love and sexuality) is a clear indication of the amorous nature attributed to the myth. The seductive power of Europa is portrayed through her beauty and pose. Her hair is one of the (veiled) symbols of irresistible charm. Women's hair, particularly when it is golden but not only then, endowed with both magical and symbolic powers, has always played a key role in Western civilization. It became associated with wealth and female sexuality apt to attract fascination both with money and with female sexual power. No matter whether women have used their hair to shelter their lovers or to strangle them, women's hair has always been a source of magic, the symbol of something precious, powerful and sacred, and a totem to adore. Folk, literary, and psychoanalytic traditions, but also anthropological literature, link the qualities of hair to the vigor of sexuality, drawing a link between the sacrifice of the hair and sexual surrender on the one hand and the abundance and beauty of the hair and sexuality and fertility on the other. Perhaps for these reasons the popular imagination could transform hair into valued currency. Attitudes toward the power and value of both money and women have always been ambivalent—they could be synonymous with something precious and divine but also with something filthy and evil. Draghi's princess is no longer only an innocent heroine but also a woman at the apex of her femininity. She is a "seductive Europe," a delightful goddess of love and fertility at the maximum of her soft power. Europa sitting on the rocks and displaying her perfectly combed beautiful hair constitutes a sexual exhibition. Her hair is seducing and reassuring rather than threatening. Her coiffure has a noble style, like a nest, warm and sheltering, and perfectly able to convey the idea that the euro is a benign source of prosperity; it has been purified and redeemed by the virtuous European values, its power is true and lasting, and its commercial use has a purely noble function. Europa's seductive role as the personification of both personal and civic material prosperity is clearly expressed; she becomes a perfect anthropomorphic representation of seduction and soft power, of a flourishing Eurozone.

Mother Europa, or at least the heartfelt longing for the mother, the desire to reenter her womb in order to be reborn through her, is also present in a much more concealed form on the image in the symbolism of the pearls and the sea/river.

If the hair is an emblem of sexuality, necklaces of marine shells are symbols of fecundity, marriage, and birth. Similar to women's hair, they have a magical value and a cosmological function: they are meant to protect us from enemies and bestow long life and prosperity. Pearls played a central role in many cultures, including Western civilization. Among the Greeks the pearl was the emblem of love, marriage, and birth; since pre-Hellenic times, shellfish have been closely connected with the Great Goddesses. As Mircea Eliade explains, the resemblance of the marine shell to the female genital organ was doubtlessly known to the Greeks: the oyster is like a woman carrying the fetus in her womb, "gravid with the pearl," "the womb of the pearl"; "as the marine animal comes out of its shell, so is a man born from the womb of his mother" (1991: 131, 133). The myth of Aphrodite's birth from a marine conch was widespread in the Mediterranean world; it represented an illustration of the mystical symbolism of perpetual renewal and regeneration and inspired, through its creative power, the ritual function of shells in initiation ceremonies.

Due to their magico-religious virtues, shells in ancient Chinese society and in traditional societies perform a function in the administration of justice. As an emblem that exemplifies a cosmic principle, it is expected to guarantee the just application of the law (Eliade 1991: 134). In the imaginations of many, necklaces of shells defend women, children, and cattle against misfortunes, illnesses, and sterility and are expected to play a similar role in a wider sense as well: imposing norms and promoting order and a state of well-being both in the social realm and in the cosmic world (Eliade 1991: 135). In Gnostic and Christian theology, the pearl acquired new valences. In "The Act of Thomas" it signified the mystery of the transcendent revealed to the senses, the manifestation of god in the Cosmos. The lust for the pearl symbolized the spiritual drama of the fall of man and his salvation; it represented both the fallen man and the savior (Eliade 1991: 149).

Since the sacred virtue of shells extends to *images* of them, one might harbor hope that the euro, with Europa's necklace, may function as a talisman, putting Europeans into communication with the cosmic forces that rule life, fertility, birth, and prosperity. Or, it may serve as a *pharmakon,* able to cure with generative powers an ailing community, to heal through its tonic and aphrodisiac power Europeans' melancholia, frustration, anger, and pessimism. In the fantasies of many it may also function as a sacred object that purifies and facilitates salvation; in other words, it may be a talisman of physical, psychic, and spiritual regeneration and complete rebirth.

Yearning for regeneration and rebirth is captured also through the symbolism of the water. Just like the pearl, many associate to water a healing function; it is said to represent a sacred *pharmakon* (that can cure physical and psychic illnesses), a source of youth and fertility, and a magic force that binds all living beings together. In both anthropological and psychoanalytical literature immersion in the water (pearls' original habitat) suggests a return to the maternal womb, a regression into the sacred realm of primordial unity. All civilizations developed along the banks of rivers, making the river, in a metaphorical sense, the mother of the civilized world as we know it. The maternal significance of water is evident in the whole field of mythology. Homer saw the "genesis of all" in the river Oceanus, which has been closely associated with the goddess Tethys, the mother of rivers and oceans. Water was seen in ancient Greece as the primary substance from which all things developed and upon which the earth rested; the sea became the symbol of generation. In literature, mythology, and fairy tales, rivers and streams are often portrayed as beautiful. Poets tell us that "the lure of the mysterious and unknown, of the 'dark' and the 'deep' and the sea, are basically the same—the perennial longing for the mother as well as the perils connected with it" (Niederland 1956: 501).

European culture dates back to the Danube Valley civilization. József Attila in his poem "By the Danube" (trans. by Zs. Ozsváth & F. Turner) gives a sublime representation of the river as symbol of mother. The presence of Zeus in the myth and on the *krater* could also be seen as a reference to the primordial (sacred) origins. Just like Europa, who transforms from maiden to the mother of European civilization, Zeus could also be seen as a "cultural hero," a founding father (with trickster characteristics) that assigns a divine dimension to the queenly continent.

In mythologies, tricksters play tricks on both humans and gods. Nearly all mythologies in the world have trickster characters whose nature and actions are complex, ambivalent, and difficult to decipher (Radin 1956). For Lewis Hyde, "Trickster is the mythic embodiment of ambiguity and ambivalence, doubleness and duplicity, contradiction and paradox" (1998: 7); for Jung "he is metallic yet liquid, matter yet spirit, cold yet fiery, poison yet healing draught—a symbol uniting all opposites" (1979: 295). The trickster is a liminal figure: he is a fervent boundary crosser, a mediator between the human and divine worlds, the forerunner of the savior, and, like him, god, man, and animal at once, "both subhuman and superhuman, a bestial and divine being" (Jung 1979: 263). All mythical figures correspond to inner psychic experiences. What is quite unique of the trickster is his tendency to act out those (extreme) human urges and desires that people living in communities learn to control to maintain social order. His "most alarming characteristic is his unconsciousness. … He is so unconscious of himself that his body is not a unity, and his two hands fight each other" (2014a: 263).

The trickster may destroy as well as create worlds. According to Radin, for example:

> Trickster is at one and the same time creator and destroyer, giver and negator. … He possesses no values, moral or social, is at the mercy of his passions and appetites, yet through his actions all values come into being. (1956: ix)

The trickster never accepts reality as a given; he is always ready to break the rules of society and create an alternative social reality that reflects and responds to his fantasies and dreams. Hermes is seen as the par excellence example for the trickster figure. We could note that, similar to the actions of the god of thieves, Zeus steals what he regards as most precious and, through the abduction of Europa, creates a new reality. With his playful but also shameful action (he appears disguised as a bull and with his charm seduces the innocent maiden) he accomplishes an anarchic assault on the status quo—he destroys the idyll of Anthologia, giving an end to the paradisiac conditions of virginity, provoking chaos, confusion, and bewilderment among the damsels—and, after his voyage and marriage to the princess, he becomes a culture hero giving birth to the Cretan civilization.

The trickster merges in himself two independent personalities, the "selfish buffoon" and the culture-hero (Carroll 1981). He is a "selfish buffoon" because he is obsessed with sexuality, and to fulfill his almost perpetual and seemingly uncontainable sexual drives he is ready to resort to any means necessary. But, he may also appear as a hero, associated with the origins of culture, who, with his transformational power, creates a new world for humans by eliminating the monsters and providing all the necessary preconditions for building a new and more human community. But how can "uninhibited sexuality" be reconciled with "the origin of culture?" If we endorse Freud's theory of civilization elucidated in particular in *Civilization and Its Discontents* (1975 [1930]), we may argue that the maintenance of civilization requires the renunciation to fulfill all our pleasure and aggressive drives. As Michael Carroll points out, whereas from Freud's point of view, in real life, uncontrolled sexuality would lead to the destruction of culture, in the trickster myths "uncontrolled sexuality" (which includes both an obsession with eating and an obsession with sexual intercourse) comes to be associated with the origin of culture (1981: 305–6).

Is thus the world portrayed in the Europa myth, with Zeus's almost immediate gratification of his sexual desires, a complete inversion of the world on which Western civilization (at least in a Freudian sense) is based on? Tricksters have always been closely associated with carnival and other rituals that turn reality upside down. Can Zeus too be seen as a carnival figure (similar to Pulcinella and the clown)? Can he thus be forgiven for his trickery and praised instead for his transformational power through which he can manage to get rid of an unacceptable reality and found a magic (and imaginary) realm of existence? Shall we, as a result of his contribution, consider the Europa tale the foundational myth of the European Land of Cockaigne, the joyful place of the European carnival where every day is holiday?

If we rely on Horvath's and Thomassen's interpretation of the trickster we get closer to Draghi's possible response to these questions. The editors of the *International Political Anthropology Journal* depict the trickster as an outsider, as an "eternal migrant and wanderer" devoid of a home, of deeply felt human relations, and of existential commitments. The trickster feels at home in liminality; his real interest lies in making liminality permanent rather than solving the liminal crisis (Horvath & Thomassen 2008: 14). In this sense we could perhaps view our trickster Zeus as a symbol of homelessness rather than homecoming, whose nature does not fit in Draghi's project, which foresees the transcendence of the transitional period of confusion, flux, uncertainty, and turbulence from which Europeans find it so difficult to liberate themselves. Rather than letting the trickster gain control and escalate chaos, the ECB president prefers to play the role of the "master of ceremonies"—the "charismatic hero" who, once the stabilities of everyday life are dissolved, intervenes to reestablish order, to make sure that the carnival ends and Europeans find their new home in the reborn European family.

Could it be that Dionysus—associated (erroneously) by many only to transgression, orgy, and immorality, another eternal nomad—was purged from the official narrative for similar reasons?

Initially the thesis that juxtaposed Dionysus to Apollo and saw him as alien to the polis prevailed among classicists; while the latter became associated with the Enlightenment, ascetic Protestantism, and then Rationalism, Dionysus's connotations became synonymous with chaos, subversiveness, immorality, and irrationality. In reality, however, Dionysus is much more than the god of wine, and wine is much more than an intoxicating drink. Beyond being the symbol of drunkenness, madness, unrestrained sexuality, and regression to the wild state, his nature included a productive, integrative, and even resurrective side. Under the Dionysian tendency

> ... at the evangel of cosmic harmony, each one feels himself not only united, reconciled, blended with his neighbour, but as one with him, as if the veil of Maya had been torn and were now merely fluttering in tatters before the mysterious Primordial Unity. (Nietzsche 1995: 2)

As Isler-Kerényi shows, Dionysus, being the god of wine, is a civilizing god. Wine is a "symbol and at the same time a means of civilized interaction" (to perform its functions it has to be consumed in the correct manner and in the right amount), a "way of being moved transitorily to a level above daily life: to see and also reveal reality beyond appearances" (Isler-Kerényi 2007: 233). It is also a symbol of existential metamorphosis; "like the whole cosmos, and like the citizen who has attained his akmè, it is the result of a long process": the introduction of the cultivation of the vine and the art of wine-making are important events in the metamorphosis of the world from a primordial and uncultivated to a civilized one (Isler-Kerényi 2007: 233, 155).

Béla Hamvas believes that wine, being one of the manifestations of the divine, is sacred (1945/2007). For this Hungarian metaphysical thinker, man believes either in god or in surrogates of some kind (principles, ideologies, dictators, etc.). His book *The Philosophy of Wine* is a "praying book for atheists," based on the belief that to live fully one must drink wine, that bibulousness is a much higher level of state than ordinary rationality—it is the beginning of wakefulness. From wine we can learn what illuminated life truly means; only by drinking wine can we reach authentic sobriety; to be truly sober means to be elated (Hamvas 1945/2007: 278). For Hamvas, the history of wine has three phases. The metaphysical part refers to the prediluvium epoch when humanity did not know wine but dreamed of it. The second phase began when Noah started cultivating vine, and the third started with the transformation of water into wine (and we live in this era). Human history is supposed to end when wine comes out of springs and wells and rains down from the clouds and the lakes and sea turn into wine (Hamvas

1945/2007: 210–11). The day of the wine is Saturday; its number is three; its planet is Saturn—the symbol of the sacred, the golden age. Wine is a spiritual drink that lifts man and takes him from the addled world to the realm of the great primordial paradise. In every wine, argues Hamvas, there dwells a tiny angel that does not die when the wine is consumed but joins instead those innumerable angels and pixies that live inside man. When we drink, those present welcome the coming genius with singing and flower-rain. The elf is enchanted and about to be set on fire (Hamvas 1945/2007: 233). There are peoples of wine and peoples of grappa. The former group is genial; the latter is made up of atheists, or those who tend to lean toward idolatry. Peoples of wine live in the tradition of the golden age—their land, thanks to the sublime nectar contained in vine, is idyllic (Hamvas 1945/2007: 238).

Another characteristic of Dionysus is revealing about the special role he could play in the European narrative of *palingenesis*—besides being the god of wine, he is also the god of rebirth. He is seen as a symbol of death and resurrection (and not just because crops die in winter and return in spring). In most myths, Dionysus appears as the son of Zeus and the daughter of the founder of Thebes, Semele. Semele dies, struck by the jealousy of Zeus's wife Hera, but Zeus pulls Dionysus out of her womb and places the unborn child inside his thigh. Opening up his thigh a few months later, he gives birth to Dionysus and entrusts him to Semele's sister, Ino. Hera drives Ino and her husband (and in some versions of the myth Dionysus as well) insane. Dionysus becomes a rambler; he wanders around the world moving with his teacher, Silenus, and with a procession of male and female followers—bands of satyrs and maenads (who join in the hope of better performing their female responsibilities such as childbearing and harvesting), grotesque dancers, nymphs, matronly brides, and riders on mules. Another myth about Dionysus's birth states that he is the son of Zeus and Demeter, the goddess of crops and vegetation. The Titans are commissioned by the jealous Hera to tear the body of Dionysus to pieces, but his heart is rescued by Athena and is given first to Zeus, then to Semele, who eats it and gives birth to Dionysus again. As we can see, in both stories Dionysus is born twice. He is also the god of homecoming—he returns to Greece, to Thebe, his motherland. On his way back he meets with his grandmother, the earth goddess Cybele, who cures him of his madness and reveals to him the mysteries of life and resurrection. The French analyst and philosopher Luce Irigaray describes Dionysus as the child-god. "The child-god," she writes, "seeks again and again the way back to before the division and always comes to grief against the contradictions already in place. They tear him apart, and he carries and receives life and death at the same time" (1991: 131).

On the new euro banknotes, the god of wine, rebirth, homecoming, excess, and primordial paradise does not appear; Draghi seeks to bind our gaze to the image of "seductive Europa." In the promotion ad of the new currency, while Anne Coulié is telling us the story, the camera zooms in on one particular section of the *krater*—an enchanted Zeus bowing down to Europa in a gesture of reverence. Draghi's "seductive Europa" is a dream that evokes Europa's dream in Moschus's sensual poem. If it is tempting to interpret the dream as a projection of Europa's feelings and desires, the tension of feeling attached to her family (mother) and at the same time her desire to leave home for a new love, it is tempting to look at Draghi's dream as one representing Eurofederalist fantasies, the desire of seducing citizens and prompting them to abandon their motherland, to play an active role in building a love story with EU institutions, and to establish their new home all because they are fired by a new passion for (federal) Europe. Unlike most of Zeus's (passive) lovers that are *touched,* Europa is active: she *touches,* and her touch is magic, transformational. With her touch the Phoenician princess calms the bull's madness (she caresses him and wipes the foam from his lips). Federalists' hope is that with their gentle touch they can conquer the hearts of ordinary citizens (still too attached to their original homelands) and even transform furious and "crazy" populists and nationalists into docile and mild creatures.

In Moschus's poem, once the nuptial bed is prepared by the Hours, Europa quickly turns into a bride, gives birth, and becomes a mother. The thoroughly unclassical heroine—who once felt free to externalize and even to fulfill her sexual drives—abruptly reverts to the traditional passive role (Schmiel 1981). From the new euro banknotes Europa is looking back at us with her *maternal* eyes; seductive Europa plays a role only in the *first* scenes of the *palingenetic* drama. Her role consists of seducing citizens, helping them externalize their deeply felt nostalgia for paradise and conjuring up in them a passionate attraction for a new home (and willingness to abandon the old fatherland). Once people feel liberated in their new passion for the European Union, once they experience the magic feeling (the illusion) of being reborn as enlightened Europeans, fully incorporated in a (fantastic) European family that seems to evoke pristine idyll, the same touch that empowered them will turn them into docile bulls. They will be prompted to assume a passive role (which will manifest in religious reverence), join the community of believers, and show unconditional loyalty to the new political religion and its prophets.

Before leaving Europa, Zeus gave her three presents: Talosa, who would be the guard of Crete; Laelaps, a hunting dog that always caught its prey; and a magic javelin that could always hit the focused target. Laelaps reappears in Greek mythology, entrusted with the (impossible) mission of hunting down the Teumessian fox, a fearsome animal designed by the gods never to be caught. It is as if supranational policymakers were still safeguarding these divine gifts—symbols of their Gatsby-style "politics of *jouissance*."

PART II

The Promise of a New Symbol

CHAPTER 4

Welcome to the Center of the European Mandala!

Since 2013 the European Union has had a new symbol. In the imagination of its creators, the new Europa series of the euro banknotes, ornamented by the portrait of the Phoenician princess, has all the requisites to challenge the supremacy of the flag as the most powerful emblem of European integration. What kind of visual signifier, aesthetic artifact, do the new banknotes represent? "Who" is looking back at us? What does the uncanny image of Europa evoke? What are the primal fantasies mobilized by this portrait? What is the promise sealed in *her* gaze? Is there a risk that supranational policy-makers' eschatological expectations may remain unfulfilled and lead to citizens' disenchantment with, rather than idyllic attachment to, the European Union?

There is extensive literature on the role of symbols in political communities and on the symbolic repertoire of the European community. My goal is to complement these studies with an analysis of some of the most recent visual symbolic tools used by the European Central Bank in order to highlight the transcendental function of the new currency iconography. By reflecting on the banknotes' imagery and on official videos, we will unveil the ECB's attempt to transport people in a special world, to engrave in their fantasies the vision of the Eurozone as an idyllic land of paradise, conveying the message that the European cosmogony plan can be accomplished; the advent of the new golden age is imminent.

The European elite have launched a new version of intimacy politics. In today's "apocalyptic era," the prophets of *palingenetic* ultra-Europeanism seek not only to bring Europe closer to the people but also to project the idea of a *new* emerging community, the *rebirth* of Europe's "fantastic family," open to embrace all those who are ready to undergo a collective transformation and become "true Europeans." Instead of fostering a "banal sense" of Europeanism, they demand an unconditional belief in and the enthusiastic endorsement of the dogma of the United States of Europe, adherence to the community of believers, and passionate participation in the fight for the sacred cause of ever-closer union. The recent injection of European federalism into the EU's official (albeit undeclared) soteriology calls for a deeper analysis of the metaphysical functions of its symbolic tools.

A religion "tunes human actions to an envisaged cosmic order and projects images of cosmic order onto the plane of human experience" (Geertz 1973: 90). In this part of the book we'll explore those symbolic undertakings through which the European Central Bank has tried to project images of a miraculous transformation: the visual tools that are meant to invoke the transformation of chaos (linked by many to the 2008 financial crisis) into cosmos and the rituals through which people are encouraged to reenact yearly, weekly, daily, or hourly the magic moments of Europe's creation.

In the previous part we looked at Europa as the protagonist of the EU's new foundation myth. Now it is time to study the uses that her *image* has been put to, its role in official (verbal and visual) narratives, and its place in ritual practices. According to many, images are not effective in and of themselves; it is the relationship established between the image and the viewer that will make the image more or less powerful. In this sense, the power of images does not derive from their inherent qualities and characteristics; it depends on how they are displayed, how they are used, and what impact they exert on those who use/perform them. Horst Bredekamp with his *Theorie des Bildakts* ("Theory of the Image-Act") enriches and complements this literature by unveiling the active nature, the sovereign agency, and the intrinsic potency of images, those self-sufficient forces that are distinct from how these images are used (2015). He differentiates between the "schematic," the "substitutive," and the "intrinsic" "image-acts" and illustrates how inanimate matters start to *live,* how they acquire an independent life force—the capacity to *see, move,* and *speak*—when they assume the form of an image. While emphasizing the importance of image agency, Bredekamp also puts to the fore the powerful effect images exercise on society; how they shape human reactions, emotions, perceptions, and fantasies; how they hold a community together; and how they construct human reality (2015: 157).

Whether or not the portrait of Europa can become a powerful symbol of the ECB's cosmogony plan will depend not just on the elite's ability to construct a myth about Europe (about the Eurozone and Europeanness) but also on their ability to prompt citizens to endorse the encoded meanings of their core symbol. In order to succeed, the European Central Bank realized the need to engage in visual communication and compete in the arena of political contest for EU citizens' hearts and fantasies. To win the battle for Europeans' allegiance, it enlivened a lifeless Eurozone by transforming it into images, using the *face* and the *gaze* of Europa as key communication tools. Horst Bredekamp's thoughts will help us unveil more about the supranational elite's endeavors to make the new banknotes custodians of the "intrinsic iconic act." By exploring the role of Europa as the protagonist of the various visual narratives of the ECB and the European Commission, I intend to underscore the importance of what Nicholas of Cusa described as the "all-seeing eye" (1453/1988) and what David Morgan called the "sacred gaze" (1997) in the supranational construction of the European land of paradise and in the federalist mission of achieving (the illusion of) EU citizens' theurgic union with the gods, their primal union with the mother.

For most, knowledge of Europa's image on the Greek *krater* is not firsthand but comes through the ECB's reproduction of the image on the euro banknotes and her performances in campaign videos. The original image has been modified, computerized, and reproduced; its meanings and its effect on viewers have also changed with its different uses. The prophets of federalist soteriology felt puzzled: How to make Europa (omnipresent in campaign videos, stamps, official documents etc.) appear as magical as she seems on the vase? How to make her become the emblem of seduction, the European representation of the universal concepts of love and transformation (with seduction being ubiquitous in European thinking, art, music, and literature)? How to turn her image icon, something culturally valuable but powerful also as a political statement, into the sacred symbol of a new Europe coming to life? What if the original goal, reinforcing the mythical dimension of the ECB, backfires, resulting in the demystification of a (mythical) piece of art?

In 2012, the European Commission launched (and then recalled) a video publicizing the European Union and celebrating its enlargements. The protagonist of the video, a modern-day woman (plain personification of Europe) is attacked by armed warriors, possibly representing Europe's inner or external, real or imaginary threats (European Commission 2012). The video apotheosizes Europe's heroes and diabolizes its enemies. Europa's queenliness, her calm, cool, and collected attitude, contrasts with the male aggressors' uniformly irate, seemingly barbaric, uncivilized, and irrational nature. The East Asian character is introduced with very stereotypical string music and onomatopoetic "kung-fu" utterances. The (possibly) Indian character appears on the scene with an oriental(ist) musical piece and an obsolete scimitar. Then follows a dreadlocked, half-nude, black man whose entrance incorporates the destruction of a door, a suggestion of the rabid and barbaric nature of Africa. As a response to the threat posed by the "others," Europa closes her eyes and miraculously reproduces herself in twelve perfectly identical copies to form a circle around the men. The warriors surrender, and they all sit down in a yoga position. They then disappear and the twelve Europas transmute into the twelve stars of the European flag.

This *ad* video represents a miserable performance of orientalism. It encodes the *product* (larger and larger Europe) with the aura of transcendence. It *sells* membership, and at the same time it *sells* difference. The viewer is interpellated (invited to be part of the ad) as a white person who can enlighten dark ones. S/he is promised an authentic experience of transformation. The video stresses the importance of belonging to Europe while establishing codes of difference. The distinction between the unmarked category (i.e., the unquestioned norm) and the marked category (the one that is seen as different or other) could not be more evident. Europa, the white model, is the unmarked normative category (we will not even register the fact that she is white); the non-white models, on the other hand, are marked by race.

The personification of Europe, its portrayal as a woman, and her representation as culturally superior to other continents is not new. But why is she dressed like Uma Thurman in Quentin Tarantino's film *Kill Bill*? Why has the oriental art of yoga been chosen as the magic solution that will offer resolution and a happy ending to a "European story"?

As Michael Wintle shows in *The Image of Europe: Visualizing Europe in Cartography and Iconography throughout the Ages*, geographers had adopted as early as the Renaissance the technique of personification in order to promote the status of Europe (2009). Europe and other continents were represented as people, usually as women, and the perception of Europe as superior was captured though various visual strategies. By the end of the sixteenth century, artists and craftsmen used "Queen Europe" as an iconographic representation, and by the mid-seventeenth century, Europe became embedded also in the popular imagination as the continent with superior attributes. Several Enlightenment thinkers used the concepts of "civilization" and "Europe" interchangeably and viewed non-Europeans as innocent primitives. In the iconography of the period, Europe's alleged dominance over other continents and colonized territories was also portrayed in relation to race, religion, and gender. The Eurocentrism of the Renaissance not only endured but also spread and deepened. For Wintle, Eurocentrism reached its peak in the nineteenth century and in the years leading to the First World War with "Eurocentric arrogance and imperialism in the geographical imagery of European visual arts, especially in the portrayal of the continents" (2009: 349).

European superiority was a feature of national imagery in the period of nineteenth-century nation-state building, and it seems to be present in the fantasies underlying today's doctrine of European federalism. The video publicizing the enlargement of the European Union is one of those visual representations of the European meganarrative that portrays the EU as a continuation of the Enlightenment project—the virtuous heir of the ideals of reason, progress, and civilization, whose mission consists of sacralizing profane spaces through the spread of sacrosanct "European ideals." We are observing the emergence (return?) of a new political soteriology that must extend its community of believers and weaken its enemies, hence their kitschy, caricature-like representation.

Yet what the video alludes to, in a sexist and imperialist manner, is not just Europe's (presumed) general superiority over the entire globe but also her mystic (cosmic) strength. It conveys the fantasy that the European Union is an inhabited microcosm surrounded by turbulent regions representing chaos. In advertising, race has traditionally been associated both with exoticism and foreignness. In this video, exoticism has meaning only in reference to Europa; the nonwhite others have one clear connotation—they are threatening. The scene with the male warriors getting closer and closer to Europa warns us about the danger of the return of the dark ages. The viewer is immediately assured by her reaction and message of hope: the abolition of order and reemersion in a state of anarchy can be avoided; the members of the EU can form a perfect community (a circle around a center), undergo a magic transformation through a rite of passage, be born again, and reenter paradise.

As Eliade explains, every microcosm has a "Centre," a holy place where the sacred manifests itself in the form of elementary hierophanies, the point from which all that is noble can expand outward (1991: 39). In the imagination of European federalists, the European mandala is a series of concentric circles at the center of which we find the Eurozone (with countries that have reached the deepest level of integration). This center is the holy place of European integration. The video portrays EU enlargement as a way to cosmosize chaos, sacralize space, and extend the sacred from the core toward the periphery of Europe. It suggests that full integration into the EU (penetration into the mandala) stands for an initiation ritual: a metamorphosis into "true Europeans." Entering the circle is a return to paradise; the neophytes (new Europeans) will be protected against every harmful force and will discover the mandala (Europeanness) in their own bodies, manifesting a desire to identify themselves with the mythical European microcosm. Since every human being tends, unconsciously, toward the Centre, where s/he can find integrity and sacredness, it is no wonder that in the video all non-Europeans are oriented toward the EU (represented by Europa) to fulfill their nostalgia for paradise. The video shows Europa's mystical journey to the Centre, candidates' death and resurrection, descent into hell, the fight against evil forces, and ascension into heaven. Sitting in a circle is part of the transitional phase, the bridge passage from one mode of being (profane non-Europeans) to another (celestial Europeans). The moment when all sit in a circle in a motionless yoga position, allowing for a communication between heaven, earth, and hell, represents the attainment of the cosmological point. Europa transforms herself into a star to reach, together with the other members of the European family, the celestial world. With the guidance of Europa, all participants may reach the zenith. In the mystic moment of reaching the center, time and participants remain motionless; their spiritual enlightenment and bodily transformation is captured through the lightning of the stars. The flash signifies the realization of Brahman: the discovery of one's *true* self (one's European core), the transcendence of time and space, and the reaching of stasis. The happy ending of this video is guaranteed by the visual and musical representation of the "favorable moment" of enlightenment, the comprehension of reality—Europe is the solution. The stars and the light capture the sudden revelation occurring through the magic mediation of Europa. The viewer should have no doubts that this magic moment (rebirth as Europeans) will be followed by a prolonged period of mystical peacefulness and harmony.

The search for symbols is a search for images through which the EU may express the following: its voyage toward rebirth; the passage from ignorance to enlightenment, from death to life, from being non-European to being European, from chaos to cosmos; and the return to paradise. Because the prophets of *palingenetic* ultra-Europeanism lack the imagination to portray "European normative values" in a "more European" way and are perhaps sensitive to Europeans' renewed fascination with the Orient and the widespread belief that Buddhism may represent the highest level of religious spirituality, they resorted to the use of yoga to provide an alternative way to express citizens' longing for harmony. Through yoga, the profane man, weak, distracted, enslaved by his body and his psycho-mental life, may turn into a glorious man and gradually transform the chaos into cosmos (Eliade 1991: 85–86). Driven by a similar intent, the EU promises order and mystic metamorphosis for the candidates, a place in the secure and sublime European *cosmion*. New member states' conduct (symbolized by the yogis' rhythmic breathing) will become perfectly integrated with the rhythm of European integration (cosmic Great Time). Membership means not just rebirth as enlightened Europeans but also the possibility of reexperiencing paradisiac conditions. As a result of this passage, the past is abolished, sins are collectively purged, and a pure existence starts through the restoration of the perfect form of Europe, as symbolized by the "peace, stability and prosperity" mantra.

In the video Europa is wearing a yellow jumpsuit and is reminiscent of the character "The Bride" played by Uma Thurman in Quentin Tarantino's *Kill Bill*. The film tells the story of a woman who fights to be reunited with her child. The visual narrative of the European Commission and Tarantino's film are both hero stories, and they are both female stories in which the protagonists must pass a series of trials in order to reestablish an intimate mother-child bond. Neither brides are victims; rather, they are portrayed as equally powerful or even dominant over the "others." Both could be seen as symbols of Mother Earth, but while *Kill Bill* provides a convincing representation of Great Mother's ambivalent (both destructive and creative) nature, the EU video depicting Europa as a pacifist goddess reflects federalists' wishful thinking. In Tarantino's film the women fight as brutally as any male characters, using a variety of tools in their arsenal. Unlike The Bride, the EU damsel does not need a sword to triumph over her aggressors and become a dominant figure. Through the video, the Commission seeks to debunk the idea that the EU is a phallocentric community in which men's power is dominant. Instead, it seeks to establish it as an organization that triumphs thanks to her mind, allowing her to achieve her ultimate goal and find peace through spiritual strength and soft (i.e., transformative) power.

From Xavier Morales's standpoint, Tarantino presents violence as a form of expressive art by transforming an object of moral outrage into one of aesthetic beauty (2003). The EU video too has the pretension of offering an aesthetic experience to its viewers. Rather than elegantly blurring the distinction between beauty and violence (as the film does) it conveys the message that Europe's soft power consists (also) in her (magic) ability to turn violence and conflict into peace and beauty.

But then which space represents the magic center of the European microcosm? Where is the home of the Great Goddess? Which object is to become the new hierophany of the European Union?

Since political reality is symbolically constructed (Cassirer 1955, Cohen 1974, Turner 1975, Lukes 1975, Kertzer 1988), and all versions of soteriologies deal in symbols and myths (Eliade 1991: 10), European federalism—a doctrine of salvation that calls for the transformation of the

EU into the United States of Europe and portrays it as the future land of paradise, the only option for Europeans to leave behind the painful reality caused by the crisis—is unimaginable without symbols.

Symbols have a multiplicity of different meanings; they evoke different sentiments and unconscious responses and perform various functions. Symbols' importance consist in their capacity to a) justify the existing social or political order or to legitimize a new one; b) convey ideas, norms, and values; c) stir emotions, foster identification with the community, and rally popular support for particular political goals; d) reaffirm (or reinvent) collective identity, strengthening a we-feeling and drawing boundaries between ingroup and outgroup; f) transmit promises; g) appeal to people's sense of beauty by presenting values, projects, and promises in a ceremonial form; and, finally and most importantly, h) respond to people's yearning for transcendence, their nostalgia for paradise through the sacralization of the political realm.

Already in 1951 the memorandum from the secretariat general of the Council of Europe on the European flag stated, "There are no ideals, however exalted in nature, which can afford to do without a symbol" (Council of Europe 1951). Most of the European symbols were launched through a top-down approach in the last four decades: the flag and the anthem in the 1970s; the European passport; the Day of Europe in the 1980s; the European currency and the position of the High Representative for Common Foreign and Security Policy in the 1990s; the Charter of Fundamental Rights; the Constitutional Treaty (rejected at the Dutch and French referenda in 2005); the positions of the High Representative of the Union for Foreign Affairs and Security Policy; Permanent President of the European Council in the early twenty-first century; and many others. After more than forty years of symbol construction, many contended that the time had come to revisit the symbolic dimension of European transnational politics to propose and use efficiently "new unifying symbols," improving the EU's "plethora of old tools, some blunt or rusty, and a few new tools, which have not yet been honed into efficient service" (Wallace 2009: 20, 21).

Many harbored hope that the European symbols would justify and legitimize an ever-closer union, that they would convey European values, evoke enthusiasm, and rally popular support for the deepening of the integration process and the enlargement of the community. There was faith that they could construct and reinforce collective European identity, forge at least a "banal sense" of Europeanism, transmit promises about the prosperous, peaceful future of Europe and about a European Union with a "human face," perfectly able to speak with one voice. The desire was to appeal to people's sense of beauty using the imagery on the euro banknotes, the symbolism of the flag, the melody of the anthem, etc. With the rejection of the Constitutional Treaty, the five symbols listed in Article I-8 (the flag, the anthem, the euro currency, the European motto, and the Europe day) were ultimately purged. In an attempt to (partially) compensate for this fiasco, the Lisbon Treaty included as a supplement a solemn declaration in which sixteen EU member states confirmed that, for them, the same symbols would continue "to express the sense of community of the people in the European Union and their allegiance to it" (European Council 2007: 257).

The meaning and the efficiency of these symbols have been object of an ample debate. The anthem is "Ode to Joy" from Beethoven's Ninth Symphony (music to Friedrich von Schiller's lyrical verse "Ode to Joy"). Officially, it symbolizes an open European continent in a broader sense; it is meant to convey without words through the universal language of music the European ideals of freedom, peace, and solidarity. Europe Day ("celebrated" on May 9) commemorates the day when, in 1950, the Schuman Declaration (which served as a basis for the treaty establishing the Coal and Steal Community) was signed. The hope was to give Europeans the possibility of reenacting every year on one particular day the heroic acts of their ancestors, to return to the sacred moment of creation. The motto "united in diversity," calling for collective efforts to achieve peace and prosperity and celebrating the continent's many different cultures, traditions, and languages, was to become the official inspirational credo of the European family.

Most EU citizens do not identify themselves with the European Union; many are unaware of the existence of these symbols and when they happen to associate them to the EU, they hardly invest them with emotions; only a few would be ready to venerate them. For Slavoj Žižek, the "Ode to Joy" represents an "empty signifier," a symbol that can stand for anything and be meaningful and evocative for any political entity from Nazi Germany, Maoist China, Saddam Hussein's Iraq, to George W. Bush's America (2007).The rituals of the anthem and Europe Day cannot induce strong emotional responses either. They cannot even be performed actively; Europeans can only listen to but cannot sing "Ode to Joy," and they are given no holiday to celebrate Europe Day.

While the anthem, the motto, and Europe Day are seen as "unrecognizable totems for most EU citizens and non-citizens" (Manners 2006), a much wider resonance, even some mystic power, is attributed to the flag and the currency. Why these two symbols? The reason lies perhaps not (just) in their omnipresence, frequent use, and therefore easy identification but also in their evident aspiration to play religious symbols' key role of responding to people's yearning for paradise, promising a return to sacred times, and fostering feelings of collective transformation and rebirth.

Emile Benveniste (1969) asserts that ancient Romans used the Latin term *religio,* while among Greeks the concept of *threskeia* (referring to the performance of rituals) was more common (Fabietti 2015: 22). For Cicero, *religio* derives from *lègere* (meaning "reunite"); for the first Christian authors like Lactantius and Tertullian, the term comes from *ligàre* (meaning to bind). In the first case, the idea was to reunite people, in the second case, to bind human beings to a divinity (Fabietti 2015: 25). The term "symbol" comes from the Greek verb *sun-ballo,* meaning to bring together, to put together the two sides of a broken object or place, re-forming a whole, reachieving a complete reunion. In Neoplatonism, divine symbols had a transformative and elevating power; they were directly attached and unified to the gods and became an immanent receptacle of the transcendent principles. Their mysterious power consisted in reestablishing the theurgic union with the gods.

Mircea Eliade deems symbolic thinking consubstantial with human existence; the symbol, the myth, and the image are of the very substance of spiritual life that may become concealed, denied, or marginalized, but may never disappear (1991). Symbols unveil the deepest aspects of reality. Far from being irresponsible creations of the psyche, images, symbols, and myths respond to deeply felt human needs and fulfill precise functions by bringing to light the most hidden modalities of being (Eliade 1991: 12). Through the study of symbols, images, and myths, we can gain a better understanding of man and man's deepest yearning—nostalgia for paradise. Rather than representing an external truth, symbols are "psychologically true" (Jung 1979: 231). What drives the production of symbols, says Jung, is the need to transform libido: symbols serve as an outlet for pleasure drives; they allow for the transformation of libido and for its conversion from a "lower" into a "higher" form (Jung 1979: 228–29, 232). Symbols often mirror the yearning to experience rebirth and convey the promise of a return to the mother. By means of (powerful) images and symbols, we may reenter the idyllic realm of primordial paradise, experience rebirth, and recover the magic feeling of a lost omnipotence.

If we identify symbols' primary function in their role to provide a representation of and a response to the primal fantasy (i.e., our quest to return to paradise), we may consider the symbol politics of supranational institutions as an attempt to *lègere, ligàre,* and *integer*—to *reunite* Europeans, to *bind* them to the transcendental myth of the United States of Europe and to its prophets, to elevate them to the realm of the sacred, and to *remake* the fantastic European family as a whole, providing a new home for reborn Europeans and fostering their sense of *pristine* wholeness and harmony.

The European flag (adopted by the Council of Europe in 1955 and taken up by the Community in 1986) has rightly been celebrated as the most powerful symbol of the EU—a sacred totem of the European art of unification. Its symbolic description states that "against the background of blue sky, twelve golden stars form a circle representing the union of the peoples of Europe. The number of stars is fixed, twelve being the symbol of perfection and unity." The flag fulfills all the requirements of an ideal emblem: it can be recognized by Europeans and non-Europeans easily, it has a simple and easily interpretable symbolism, and it satisfies sacred symbols' primary function—providing a visual promise of a return to paradisiacal idyll, pristine harmony, and abundance. The circle, the stars, the colors, and the numbers all suggest the possibility of regaining paradise lost. Symbolically, the EU is not just an open community (the stars do not touch) but also an entity with magic power able to guarantee a cosmic relationship between man (the five-pointed star is also the symbol of man as an individual possessing five fingers and toes, five senses, and five limbs) and nature (stars and sky) (Centre Virtuel de la Connaissance sur l'Europe 2012). The stars are symbols of the cosmic order. The fact that (the twelve) "European stars" are five-pointed stars and thus can be drawn with a single, unbroken closed line further reinforces its mystical meaning of perfection. Twelve is a number representing cosmic harmony and completeness; twelve are the signs of the zodiac, the months of the year, the hours of the day and the night, the tribes of Israel, the gates of the New Jerusalem, the explorers sent by Moses to the lands of Canaan, and the apostles. Twelve is the symbol of the union between the divine and the terrestrial world, which, together with the crown of stars, reflects the vision of the Virgin Mary in the Book of Revelation (12:1) and is the symbol par excellence of popular Marian iconography with an anagogic effect similar to that of the halo of a saint. The flag is blue, the color of the sky and the universe, the European continent, and also the color of the Virgin Mary. On the blue background the twelve stars form a perfect homogeneous circle; the circle is another symbol of unity, wholeness, and perfection. The flag design may have been inspired by both a late eighteenth-century version of the US flag (the so-called Betsy Ross flag, where the stars formed a circle) and numerous images of Christian saints with a halo of stars above their heads (Fornäs 2012). In short, the European flag is a perfect symbol, because with all its elements, its colors, and its syntactic structure, it provides a powerful visual representation (and promise) of transcendental idyll. It promises to lift Europe up to an almost divine superiority and to offer for Europeans a ladder for ascent to the holy.

When the new European currency was introduced, many attributed sacred qualities to it and hoped that it would perform similar metaphysical functions. The euro became associated with the Virgilian *puer,* the harbinger of a new advent of the golden age, while the Eurozone came to be seen as the realization of the long-cherished dream of a European land of paradise. Between 2002 and 2008, however, the advocates and the followers of the *palingenetic* myth decreased in number and the goals driving the euro as the engine of integration became much less ambitious. The EU's symbol politics, with the common currency playing the role of the protagonist, served to transform the EU into what Benedict Anderson (1991) described as an "imagined community"; the desire to enhance its metamorphosis into a "sacred" community was repressed. Identity entrepreneurs did not put the euro in charge of fostering passionate, religious feelings toward an EU imbued with mystic connotations. Its role instead was generating a "banal sense" of Europeanism, i.e., building "European identity" based on what Michael Billig described as "banal nationalism" (2005) where people's we-feeling is fostered by everyday representations of the community.

Anderson suggests that every nation is an "imagined community" that exists in the minds of its members as an internal and not external reality (1991). Imagined communities are inevitably unstable, indefinite, and contingent human constructs rather than objective, definite, and permanent entities. They are supported by a horizontal political communion where members have a shared conception of an embodied political space and feel connected to each other: "in the minds of each lives the image of their communion," and this bond will form the basis for nationalism (Anderson 1991: 6–7). Based on the conviction that the feeling of belonging to a distinct sovereign nation of people is a "cultural artifact," one created, not organic or primordial, Anderson explains how political actors within the nation-state invented a series of symbolic technologies in order to create and strengthen "deep, horizontal" ties of comradeship and a "profound emotional legitimacy" (1991: 4, 7). He is right in suggesting that "communities should be distinguished, not by their falsity/genuineness, but by the style in which they are imagined" (Anderson 1991: 6).

European identity entrepreneurs took the nineteenth-century process of nation-state creation as a model to emulate and identified in the euro one of the most suitable (if not the most suitable) tool to transform the EU into an imagined community. Throughout history, currencies have been introduced and used by policy-makers as a means to provoke the transformation of collective identities: colonizers sought to transform the identities of colonized people, liberal nationalists to strengthen people's allegiance to the new polity, and advocates of common monetary systems to foster cosmopolitan sentiments transcending patriotic feelings (Helleiner 2003). In particular, the project of nation-building was intimately linked to the introduction and use of territorial currencies. Eric Helleiner regards this bond as established through the imagery and the naming of the currencies, the formation of a medium of national communication, the forging of a "spiritual unity" of the nation based on the association between money and trust, and the definition of national sovereignty. In a communicational environment characterized by widespread illiteracy and lack of infrastructure, money came to be seen as the most effective way to convey symbolic messages to a vast number of citizens. It used a language that could be spoken by all members of the community and was a powerful instrument of "banal nationalism" (Billig 1995: 41–42) and an object to be shown in the daily referendum on the nation. New money had to symbolize the birth (and the stability) of the new nation-state, create trust in the new order, elicit pride for the common cause, and strengthen allegiances to the community.

Since the early phase, the European integration has been an elite-driven project. In the spirit of the functionalist logic, European monetary unification could not but represent the logical outcome of the single-market project, the predictable coronation of progress in European integration. Inspired by the model of nation-state building, European identity entrepreneurs believed that the circulation of the common currency (starting in 2002) would have contributed to the creation of an imagined community in Europe. They aspired to shape people's mindset and psychic apparatus, to foster a sense of Europeanness and we-feeling in a *human* community. There was a shared conviction that through the possession and the use of the euro, people would pay a daily (hourly) homage to the community, giving a ritualistic expression of their trust in the Eurozone. Identification, feelings of oneness with the EU, came to be seen as a natural consequence. While Europe Day, the European anthem, and the flag were not intended to replace their national counterparts, the euro was introduced after the purging of the previous national currencies, making this symbol's legitimacy more contentious and also lending the common currency an exceptional status among other symbols. To help Europeans mourn the loss of an often deeply cherished national currency, it was necessary to make citizens believe (and feel) that the euro belonged to them—that it was, as the official narrative emphasized, "your money."

Until recently, the forging of a bloodless and lukewarm emotional attachment characterized the European project of identity (and community) creation. This trend changed with the 2008 crisis. Gradually, the myth of the United States of Europe returned to fire the fantasies of the supranational elite as the core imaginary construct; Eurofederalism reentered the scene of European politics as the only official soteriology for citizens to *believe* in and sustain.

In 2013 at the Frankfurt Chamber of Commerce, Mario Draghi unveiled the true (and only possible) destination of Europe's journey. During his speech he explained that in 2012 the ECB responded to the appeal made by *The Economist* magazine at the end of 2011 to establish new supranational institutions—a "European mini-IMF with enough funds to assist troubled countries" and a "pan-European banking regulator and a bail-out fund"—to create, in a nutshell, "a blueprint for the United States of Europe" (Draghi 2013b). Unlike the magazine, which considered the EU's voyage toward this magic land "utterly beyond reach," Draghi quoted Walter Hallstein, the first president of the European Commission, to remind his audience that "anyone who does not believe in miracles in European matters is not a realist." Not only did he portray the plan to give birth to the USE desirable, he also expressed his convictions that the true mission of European leaders was heroic—to believe in miracles and have the ability to transform dreams into reality. In her Mackenzie Stuart Lecture in Cambridge in 2014, Vice-President of the European Commission and EU Justice Commissioner Viviane Reding made a plea to gain support for the same mission: "There is a strong case for a true fiscal and ultimately political union ... the Eurozone should become a kind of 'United States of Europe'" (Reding 2014).

In recent years, *palingenetic* ultra-Europeanism, based on the core myth of giving birth to a new, fully and perfectly integrated, union, has turned into the official doctrine of salvation. The United States of Europe has become the primal dream to guide Europe's new visionary leaders in their heroic trials toward paradise and to assist citizens in leaving behind today's overwhelming conditions. If Europe is to avoid collapse and triumph over those forces that seek to bring back the past, says the new mantra, it has no choice but to continue on the path of "ever-closer union." In federalists' soteriology, the center of the European microcosm where the sacred will manifest is the Eurozone. According to this doctrine, the transformation of chaos into cosmos and the resurrection of the European family must be accomplished from its central point, from the navel of the Eurozone (i.e., at the ECB) and occur through the enlargement of the center (i.e., through the revision of external borders and adoption of the common currency by other member states). In ultra-Europeanists' fantasies the ECB is a *temenos,* an area removed from the space of men and consecrated to the gods, an object of veneration, separated from profane daily living.

In 2013, in an era of social distress, flux, and uncertainty, the European Central Bank launched a new series of euro banknotes to gradually substitute the old series introduced on 1 January 2002. According to the institutional narrative, the euro banknotes have become not *just* "the most visible symbol" (ECB 2013a) but also "the most tangible symbol of European integration" that "touch the lives of every one of us" (Draghi 2015b). We can see and touch the common currency, and, vice versa, the inanimate euro can *see* and *touch* us. Through its magic attributes the euro is meant "to reflect the unity and diversity of our continent" (ECB 2013a), "bring us all closer together," and strengthen and maintain people's trust in the euro (Draghi 2015b). Another expected outcome of the introduction of the new banknotes is the creation of a European collective memory. The ECB celebrates (and seeks to make citizens remember) 1 January 2002 as "one of the milestones laid down by the founding fathers," the day when the euro finally became "real" (ECB 2013a). The sacred roots of this magic process (and of the European family in general) are to be found in ancient times: "the inclusion of the mythological figure Europa, who gave her name to our continent, shows how Europe draws on its shared history" (Draghi 2015b).

Imagery is explicitly used as a tool "to symbolize how the currency brings people together" (ECB 2014a, ECB 2015a:3) and to create a new community based on a shared collective memory. Besides the € sign, the name of the new "Europa" series conveys the idea of classical Athens as the cradle of European democracy and intellectual life, and thus as the location of sacred beginnings. The use of the Greek mythical universe helps to foreground the fantasy of the euro crisis as a milestone in the process of Europe's cosmic cyclic renewal. The fact that Greece (i.e., where the Sacred first appeared) turned out to be the most vulnerable country lends to its symbolic dimension. The withdrawal (or removal) of Greece from the Eurozone would threaten the promise of a new era. It comes as no surprise then that by invoking the "whatever it takes" credo, pronounced in 2012, Draghi reiterated that the Eurozone project was "irreversible" and that "to speculate on a potential exit from the monetary union doesn't make any sense" (2015a).

The new series of currency serves to make the European public space intimate and to reinforce the mythical dimension of EU politics. The Europa series was ideated and today is proposed to citizens as the harbinger of a new era; the herald of a new Europe resurrecting from the ashes of the crisis; an agent of the return of the golden age, which comes at the end of a succession of periods marked by impiety, ready to suffocate populists' and Euroskeptics' strong voice of pessimism. The progressive introduction of the new banknotes (the €5 euro in 2013, the €10 in 2014, the €20 in 2015, the €50 in 2016) suggests that the European art of unification as performed by the ECB is a linear, awe-inspiring process that leads toward rebirth and return to paradise. The new Europa series is meant to nurture an adherence to the *palingenetic* ultra-Europeanism, a widespread acceptance of the idea of the USE as the only salvation. In this reasoning, a passionate attachment to the European family should replace a weak identification with the EU. The new euro should not be a banal emblem that "may even pass unwaved, unsaluted, unnoticed" (Billig 1995: 46); it should be recognized and adored as a sacred totem. Europeans' passive reinforcement of a shared consciousness should become active; the love for Europe should be performed. The use of the new series of banknotes is supposed to provide a daily reenactment of the foundational moment and provoke moments of ecstasy. Encounters with the hierophany should prompt Europeans to perform the ritual of "feel, look and tilt." The slogan "feel, look and tilt" was introduced in 2002 with the declared purpose of educating the public on the banknote security features of "our money." The idea was to give Europeans a vested interest in monitoring its authenticity and trusting its value. In the federalist soteriology this ritual refers to a sacred rite of passage. Touching the euro, holding it to the light, encountering the gaze of Europa, experiencing the magic she emanates, and, as a consequence, feeling a visual piety toward what she represents are presented as steps of a sacred ritual. Magic moments of the cosmic triumph are offered in return for the ritualistic handling of the new euro banknote: citizens are promised to discover the "vera icona," feel transformed, and experience a sense of wholeness and pristine idyll.

For European federalists, the new banknote should become a modern totem (in the Durkheimian sense): an object perceived as sacred, whose worship would create social cohesion and a sense of identity. It should perform the function of what Victor Turner (1967) described as "condensation symbols": through the use and circulation of the common currency, "European norms and values" should be recognized and saturated with emotion. In a transitional period of intensive social change, the new a symbol should become mythically infused with timelessness. It should succeed in reasserting the (fantasized) integrity of the EU in the face of the subversive forces of the crisis, express symbolically the mythic circle of death and rebirth, make Europeans personally invest in this highly symbolized Eurozone, and recognize in it the most efficient tool for the expression of their yearning for paradise.

How can the new banknote best communicate federalists' promise of the return of the golden age? To turn the euro into the "holy icon" of Europe's new political soteriology, the ECB renewed the currency's iconography. To better symbolize cosmic resurrection, to endow the new currency with a numinous existence, to turn it into an elixir that people will constantly carry with them to reexperience the magic moments of pristine wholeness, the Eurozone was converted into an image and represented as a human figure. It received nothing less than the face (and, as we'll see as we discuss the videos, the *gaze*) of the mythological princess, Europa.

CHAPTER 5

Europa's Sacred Gaze

Since ancient times, those who govern have publicized their power and authority by ornamenting the money they issue with their portraits. Currency, one of the most successful institutions of ancient societies, represented a valuable economic agent of public power and an indispensable support of an iconography with a strong political coloring. Augustus made majestic use of money as an instrument not only to pay the armies but, in particular, to represent his power and provoke a widespread adhesion to his political project. A new figurative language made of complex iconographic procedures, a wide range of decorative motifs, and mythological references served to make the rebirth of the empire visually explicit and to construct the image of the emperor as a hero with divine attributes, the harbinger of new advent of the golden age. His decision to use his zodiac sign, Capricorn, as a monetary form was dictated by his wish to link his reign to the return of the Reign of Saturn, the antique golden age (La Rocca 2013). Divine and heroic images of Augustus spread through personal objects and luxuries such as gems and cameos in which he was portrayed as divinities such as Apollo, Jupiter, *Sol,* Neptune, and Mercury. The circulation of these objects contributed to transforming the public sphere and spreading a religious atmosphere.

Most rulers following Augustus recognized the link between power and the circulation of money. The carefully constructed images of emperors and monarchs served to both guarantee the value of the money and also to foster their authority. The ritual gesture of the *sparsio,* i.e., the launching of coins with the effigy of the sovereign on it in a pile on particular occasions such as enthronements, weddings, and triumphs, represented a powerful method to expose and spread (in a symbolic way) what Ernst Kantorowitcz (1957) called rulers' "spiritual body." The pervasive circulation of money amplified this effect: the profiles of Roman emperors arrived where they had never set foot; people living in remote places would recognize (and adore) the face of the ruler without ever having seen him.

The aesthetics of money served yet another function: often seen as a symbol of evil, it has constantly been in need of pardon. Money is not without negative connotations. In the Middle Ages (and not only), money was associated with the excrement of Satan, and lust for money with sin. The banknote, devoid of any intrinsic value, has demanded an absolution of guilt even more. An attempt to offer redemption has been made through the use of aesthetics. Beauty has offered atonement; currency iconography (just like the attractive look of warlords' and samurais' swords) represented a possible penitence.

An era when the iconography of currency returned to live its golden age was the period of eighteenth- and nineteenth-century nation-state building. Imagery has always played a central role in politics, but the epoch of nationalism is one that cannot be fully appreciated without an analysis of all those carefully sketched visual representations aimed at offering an irresistible image of the community that was being created, and thereby fostering national consciousness. Nationalists, argues Smith, "have always pictured their chosen nation in florid, even glowing images, waxing lyrical over the beauties of the national countryside and the exploits of national heroes" (2004: 82). To foster citizens' we-feeling and their attachment to the emerging nation-state, these images celebrated the community's (fantasied) glorious past, its heroes, and its (supposedly) unique culture.

In this period, currency became the "most universal form of public imagery" regularly used by the elite to invent state traditions (Hobsbawm 1983: 281) in order to enhance their own legitimacy. Gilbert (1998, 1999), Pointon (1998), and Helleiner (1997, 2003) explored how banknote iconography contributed to the process of nation-state building through the visual construction, reproduction, and bolstering of national narratives and national identities. In the nineteenth and twentieth centuries, policy-makers, inspired by nationalist thinking, exploited the possibilities offered by flourishing printing technology to provide powerful imagery of their vision of the nation on their coins and banknotes (Gilbert and Helleiner 1999: 8). When exploring the imagery of banknotes, one may be inclined to endorse Pointon's thesis—"the aggressive visualization of the nation-state through its individualistically perceived cultural history is so widespread as to be virtually universal" (1998: 229). Banknotes, thanks to their articulate iconography, belong to those aesthetic artifacts that participate in the creation of a nation by enabling the circulation of various affects, generating in people an emotional experience that gives rise to public culture. The nation is comprised of a *demos* imbued with affect in response to various aesthetic objects.

Currency iconography played a key role in the construction of imagined communities, representing one of the (many) aesthetic resources that made the emergence of a national imaginary possible. To be imagined, the nation had to be personified (hence the figure of the French Marianne or the British John Bull), symbolized, materialized, and performed through various aesthetic artifacts like national anthems, flags, memorials, museums, visual art, literature, songs, dance, poetry, films, landscapes, etc. The availability and the circulation of these verbal, visual, and acoustic aesthetic tools served to legitimize the nation-state, to educate and indoctrinate its people, and/or to convey the spirit of times. Furthermore, since they embodied moralizing, introspective, and cathartic possibilities, these (often sensual) aesthetic artifacts generated and circulated those various affects through which the public and the nation were being created.

When designing the first series of euro banknotes, the European Central Bank made no secret of the importance it attributed to the role of currency imagery in turning the EU into an imagined community and in inventing a shared collective memory, thereby producing artificially its navel. Europe came to be portrayed as a direct heir to glorious ancient Greece. The symbol €

> was inspired by the Greek letter epsilon, reflecting the cradle of European civilisation. E is of course the first letter of the word Europe. The two strong parallel horizontal lines are intended to symbolise the stability of the currency. (ECB 2007: 11)

The euro coins feature a national symbol on one side and European symbols on the other. To offer a visual representation of European integration as a linear process, a journey toward an "ever-closer union," while the 10-, 20-, and 50-cent coins portray Europe as a group of individual nations, a united Europe without frontiers is represented on the 1- and 2-euro coins. Unlike the coins, the banknotes offer no room for national symbols; on both sides we find European symbols (such as the flag and a map of Europe) and "European themes."

The winner of the design competition, Robert Kalina, used computer graphics in order to create imaginary places, making sure that no single EU member would monopolize Europe's new symbolic space. The 5-euro note depicts a classical Roman arch and aqueduct; the 10-euro note features a Romanesque church door and bridge; on the 20-euro bill we find a Gothic church window and bridge; the architectural style ornamenting the 50-euro bill is the Renaissance; Baroque and Rococo on the 100-euro bill; iron and glass architecture on the 200-euro bill; and, finally, modern twentieth-century architecture on the 500-euro bill. Then president of the ECB Wim Duisenberg offered a clear definition of the function that the banknote iconography was expected to perform: "If we are successful, we significantly will help to convince Europeans that Europe is not some abstract or vague idea, but something real, something living" (Schmid 2001). Kalina harbored hope that no one would recognize the real places:

> The idea was to create a feeling of commonality, of belonging. I worked hard so that either an Italian or a Frenchman could look at the Gothic windows on the 20 and say, 'That could be here in France,' or 'That could be here in Italy.' It was very difficult to make each universal. (Schmid 2001)

In the institutional narrative, the windows and the gateways ornamenting the banknotes symbolize "the European spirit of openness and co-operation." The twelve stars represent "the dynamism and harmony between European nations," and the bridges "the close co-operation and communication between Europe and the rest of the world" (European Commission 2015b). Jacques Hymans applauds Kalina's skills in producing a postmodern currency iconography by emphasizing the values of openness, cooperation, and communication through the main design elements of the windows, doorways, and bridges, and by depicting Europe not as *given* but as in the process of a collective making of a space that is both ubiquitous and innominate (2004). Hymans contends that, while maintaining the goal of producing legitimacy for the EU, the European currency abandoned the "celebratory" tone of nineteenth-century national currencies and proposed a democratic vision of a community brought forward both by the elite and the citizens. In his interpretation, despite the absence of landscapes or abstract shapes, and despite the hierarchical structure of human constructions, the bills reveal their postmodern nature through the "highly egalitarian idea that 'Europe' is all around us—but is nowhere in particular" (Hymans 2004: 22). Hymans praises the fact that there are no human figures staring back, that the scenes are literally uninhabited. The euro banknotes, he argues, "invite 'habitation'"; they intend to "draw us into the image and, symbolically, into Europe" (ibid.).

In reality, the EU did not move away from national currencies' celebratory tone but internalized it, albeit in a more subtle way. The imagery of the first (and the second) series of euro banknotes celebrates "European culture" and depicts European integration as a linear process of magnificent accomplishments. The historical narrative offered by banknote iconography associates the sacred beginnings of the European community with Roman (and not with Greek) antiquity. The rationale behind this could be the attempt to counteract "the potentially decentering effect of Athens, with its strong Oriental links" and situated in the cradle of Europe, by moving more centrally on the continent's landmass (Fornäs 2012). The chronological, hierarchical use of architectural themes seeks to establish links to a "common European tradition," to construct a "common European historical memory." It is revealing in regards to ideas about Europe and European monetary integration and can be seen as a fitting metaphor for the project of "building" Europe—a linear project of constructing a community, a success story (Kaelberer 2004). Similarly to most national banknotes, euro imagery romanticizes history; it celebrates triumphs and discards traumas; it alludes to a (supposedly) sacred, uninterrupted continuity leading from antiquity through the Renaissance, the Enlightenment, the technological and industrial revolution to contemporary Europe while it overlooks the painful chapters of European history. Perhaps similar to the *biblia pauperum* of the Middle Ages, through which the Church presented paintings, frescos, and icons in a chronological series to illustrate with successive episodes the story of Jesus, Mary, or a saint, the iconographic apparatus of the ECB, the euro banknotes, provides a visual narrative of the successive periods and accomplishments of European culture. According to Chris Shore, the prevalence of banknote motifs depicting architectural or technological infrastructures rather than human beings or natural phenomena suggests that the "building" of the EU results from a planned construction and not from an organic growth (2000: 112). The euro banknotes tell a "money story" of a continent that, through two millennia of steady progress, has combined aesthetics and technology to draw and transgress borders (Fornäs 2012).

The iconography received some criticism too. Fareed Zakaria contended that it was as if the currency had been "designed for a Star Trek episode about some culturally denuded land on Mars—not for the home of Socrates, Charlemagne, Martin Luther, Notre Dame, the Uffizi, Bach, Beethoven, and Mozart" (1999). Guido Crapanzano, former numismatic consultant of the Italian Central Bank and member of the independent jury on the euro banknotes, lamented the fact that, at the end of the discussions, Mozart, Leonardo da Vinci, and Marco Polo were all considered "unworthy of representing Europe" (accused of having Freemasonry links, anti-Semitic sentiments, or breaching the European moral code in some way) and that for some time the euro was running the risk of assuming the form of a cow that, in the era of mad cow disease, would have been almost surreal (Vigna 1996).

As Lina Zigelyte points out, the notes that display no people but are richly ornamented with windows, gateways, and bridges unfold a

> transitional universe that renders it spatiality anonymous, similar to Marc Augé's "non-places": identity, history and the relations between them are erased in order to construct the constant state of passage that is supposed to epitomize one's condition in contemporary Europe. (Zigelyte 2012: 10)

In fact, Kalina's computer-generated places do not invite habitation. What is presented as a postmodern iconographic element is a composite simulation of monuments. These spaces cannot even be considered "non-places," because one of the paradoxes of non-places is that "a foreigner lost in a country he does not know (a 'passing stranger') can feel at home there only in the anonymity of motorways, service stations, big stores or hotel chains" (Augé 1995: 106). Citizens feeling homeless in the European Union see no reassuring landmarks, no familiar artifacts on the banknotes. With its currency iconography, the ECB betrayed its promise of providing citizens a feeling of homecoming.

Recognizing these failures and being aware of the importance of the year 2012, the supranational elite decided to come out with a new product of exceptional beauty. The tenth anniversary of the moment when the euro turned from a virtual currency into a reality and started circulating was an occasion for issuing a new series of banknotes to rectify the Eurozone legitimacy crisis. It *had* to be more beautiful than the previous series. The euro, considered in the imaginations of many as the evil cause of economic recession and associated with the negative social effects of the crisis, had to be pardoned and receive redemption. New decorative and aesthetic features were needed in order to convey, perhaps in a style reminiscent of the era of Augustus, the promise of a new beginning, the return of the golden age.

The elite developed a consensus to consider Europa as the "new face of the euro" by putting the portrait of the Phoenician princess on the hologram and naming the new series after her. In the period before 1920, mythical female figures and classical gods in flowing robes, such as Britannia, Svea, Germania, Italia, and Minerva-Athena, ornamented banknotes in Great Britain, Sweden, Germany, Italy, and Greece. According to Jacques Hymans, from the 1920s onward, mythological figures (reflecting traditionalist goals) were gradually replaced by historical images (representing materialist goals); the use of cultural images conveying "post-materialist goals" became predominant in the 1950s and is prevalent even today (2004: 13). From his perspective, euro notes would feature mythological women if the cultural norms of the 1910s were still dominant. There is no need to explain the extent to which the early twenty-first century defers from the early twentieth century. The reasons why the Phoenician damsel from Greek mythology is looking back at us from the new euro banknotes, with her seductive gaze, are to be sought elsewhere.

The official explanation for the choice of the Phoenician damsel from Greek mythology is (unsurprisingly) clear. Ton Roos, director of banknotes at the European Central Bank, repeated in an interview the mantra provided by Mario Draghi (see chapter 3), stating that the old series "simply didn't have enough of a 'human touch'" and that the Eurosystem decided to continue with the traditional banknote iconography but chose to put a portrait of Europa in both the watermark and the hologram of the new series of euro banknotes because "people tend to recognize faces intuitively," and because Europa "has a clear association with the continent of Europe, the name of our currency, and also adds a human touch to the banknotes" (Alexander 2013). This dry rhetoric further fuels the suspicion about supranational policy-makers' awareness that Kalina's mechanical, computer-generated, "post-modern iconography" has failed to circulate the sentiments that are necessary for creating an imagined community and fostering in Europeans an attachment to the EU. Evidently, there is more lurking behind this institutional narrative.

As previously discussed, currency, and in particular banknote iconography, has been used by the European elite as a way to legitimize the polity and create community and collective identity. European identity entrepreneurs have not hesitated to imitate the nineteenth-century model of nation-state building. Their politics of seduction still reflects pre-1920-era nationalist agendas in which patria was represented by mythological female imagery; the homeland was feminized and portrayed as either an irresistible femme fatale to possess or a nurturing mother that loves and offers a home, but that requires protection and passionate attachment.

Since it is the United States of America that fires the imagination of supranational policy-makers in the federalist soteriology, it makes sense to compare through a few examples how America and Europe have been turned into images representing human beings, how they have acquired, as a consequence, the power to *see, talk,* and *feel.* The figure of Europa flirting with Zeus might recall Jan Van der Straet's drawing *Vespucci Discovering America* (see chapter 3); "the new face of the euro" may call into mind "the new face of America"; the gaze of Mother Europa might evoke the gaze of Uncle Sam. James Montgomery Flagg's poster design of "Uncle Sam" (1917) includes a text that explicates the implicit message of the figure's expression: "I want YOU for U.S. army." For William Mitchell, the picture is effective because it achieves the "Medusa effect": it "'hails' the viewer verbally and tries to transfix him with the directness of its gaze and … foreshortened pointing finger that singles out the viewer, accusing, designating, and commanding him" (2005: 37). The figures of Uncle Sam and Europa serve to awaken desire respectively in Americans and Europeans in the way holy images do. Their inhuman eyes and facial expressions may not reveal this goal, but through the verbalized messages "America wants you," "This is a seductive Europa," "Feel look and tilt [the euro]!" it becomes clear that we are asked to desire, adore, and emotionally depend on America and Europe. Citizens are requested to perform their religious duty as citizens, swear unconditional loyalty to the nation's/Europe's political religion, and participate in its holy mission.

To find another, more recent, example for the visual representation of the United States and the "desiring gaze," readers may take a glance at a special issue by the weekly magazine, *Time,* which features a computer-generated image of a woman portraying the "New Face of America" (1993a). The legend on the front cover reads:

> Take a good look at this woman. She was created by a computer from a mix of several races. What you see is a remarkable preview of … THE NEW FACE OF AMERICA: How Immigrants Are Shaping the World's First Multicultural Society (*Time* 1993a)

The "person" representing new America as a melting pot is explicitly female. It comes as no surprise that the "new woman" is named Eve. One of the articles included in the special issue expounds upon her seductive power, citing the fact that the male computer programmers who created her ended up falling in love with her (*Time* 1993b). The female figure on the cover of *Time* becomes an object of desire; American citizens are invited not just to look at her, but also to embrace their scopophilia. "The new face of the euro" and "the new face of America" are fine examples that show the role of phantasy in the construction of ideas about Europe and the United States. The American SimEve (Streeter 2003) and her European counterpart smile out to the viewers enigmatically; they are available for men to ogle, for women to identify with, for all to invest with love. "The new face of America" can be seen as a contemporary version of the myth of Pygmalion and Galatea, the sculptor who fell in love with the statue he had carved. She may be seen as an angel generated by technology promising virtual love (without the voice of Scarlett Johansson in the movie *Her*). Europa, too, seems to foreground the promise of truly divine Eros.

All religions necessitate images in order to represent ideas, concepts, and the divine figures that are part of the realm of thoughts and ritual practice (Fabietti 2015: 219). Images in religions play a crucial role in creating the experience of the sacred (Burke 2001: 46). The federalist soteriology that promises the reestablishment of paradise on earth (at least in Europe) through the transformation of the EU into the United States of Europe cannot be effective without images able to engender moments of transcendence.

When Benjamin Franklin developed an anticounterfeit technique called "nature printing" that was based on the reproduction of plant leaves on the banknotes, he guaranteed not *just* the safe circulation of banknotes and a financial system based on relatively stable trust, but he also turned the banknotes into an elementary form of the "iconic act," creating a monetary version of the "vera icona" (Bredekamp 2015: 145–46). The "vera icona" (true image) refers to the Veil of Veronica, a Christian relic of a piece of linen that, according to legend, bears not a hand-painted image but the true face of Jesus Christ. According to Horst Bredekamp, Franklin's method with the fusion of leaf and fabric followed the model of the "true image." At least on a metaphorical level, he says, these banknotes derived their authoritativeness from the "vera icona": from the moment these "true images" were marked on the paper, they became tactile and optic vehicles (transmitters) of an authentic, sacred value.

The new series of euro banknotes, which was introduced for the same reasons—to deter counterfeiters, build trust among citizens, and become the symbol of a new community—may also be seen as a monetary version of the "vera icona." Just like the leaves that turned into images and were mass-produced to facilitate their circulation and acceptance as the "true images" of a new America coming to life, Europa's portrait is entrusted to become the "true image" of a new Europe coming to life. While people may (rightly) attribute only a material value to the old series (devoid of a "vera icona"), the new series has acquired a spiritual value and seems to have all the requisites to become the perfect symbol of the EU's (messianic) legitimacy.

The new banknotes, *infused* with Europa's portrait, are meant to provoke in EU citizens a "visual piety." "Visual piety" is the feeling that a believer experiences in the moment of contemplation of the sacred appearing in the form of an image (Fabietti 2015: 210). David Morgan contends that the act of looking itself contributes to religious formation and represents a powerful practice of belief; a "sacred gaze" is "the manner in which a way of seeing invests an image, a view, or an act of viewing with spiritual significance" (1997: 2–3). "Visual piety" can take many forms, depending on the characteristics of the religion, the attributes and the various ritual uses of the image, the historical contexts, and the social and cultural conditions of the period (Morgan 1997: 4).

In all cases, however, the power of the "sacred gaze" depends on who does the looking and the predisposition of the onlooker to invest emotionally in what s/he sees. Sacred images thank their existence to the gaze that asks viewers to engage in a dialogue with them. It is the act of looking on a sacred image that may transport the observer (if a believer) to another world, to the holy realm of his/her religion.

The European Central Bank sought to intensify the *visual* impact of the new banknotes, and for this reason it enlarged and gave greater definition to the images, opted for stronger colors, and added depth to the image of the bridge when it issued the new 10-euro banknotes (ECB 2014a). With the new 20-euro banknotes, it made additional efforts to reinforce the effect of Europa's "sacred gaze," to provoke in more citizens "visual piety." The so-called "portrait window" in the hologram is celebrated as "a real innovation in banknote technology" (Draghi 2015b). "Europa: the princess in the window" (as it is called in ECB's information campaign) is a visual trick that makes visible the invisible: when the banknote is held against the light, "the window becomes transparent and reveals a portrait of Europa … on both sides of the note" (ECB 2015a: 2).

Nicholas of Cusa, theoretician of the "intrinsic image act" (Bredekamp 2015), illustrates in his treatise *De Visione Dei* (1453/1988) that the tool that can help pass the threshold between one form of "seeing" (observation) to the other form of seeing (intuition) is the mirror (De Certeau 1987: 8). The function of the mirror is to illuminate the observer by unveiling the invisible element, the inner sacred truth. "The princess in the window" seems to perform just this way; located on the new 20-euro banknotes, as a sort of monstrance, it anticipates the appearance of another (paradisiacal) world. It makes visible for initiates (who have performed the sacred ritual of "look, feel and touch") a new, special dimension that normally cannot be seen (even though it is always there). The window is the revealing agent of the *palingenetic* myth that becomes visible and accessible only to those "enlightened" by the sacred gaze of Europa. Her gaze, fixed on "true Europeans," recalls the miracle of the Golden Legend. Similar perhaps to the Golden Legend in which the gaze is the reward granted by heaven to a young secretary who resisted the devil using the sign of the cross, "seeing" the *vera icona* is a privilege reserved for those who resist the devil (populism, nationalism, or Euroskepticism) using the holy flag of the United States of Europe. Only "true Europeans" who believe in the federalist soteriology will be able to glimpse in the euro a splendor that the eye normally cannot see. After performing the ritual and experiencing internal transformation, the reward is to encounter the sacred gaze of Europa, to *see* (Europe and the world) in another way. The rainbow-colored lines around the value numeral on the front and rainbow-colored value numerals on the back that appear when one performs the sacred ritual "feel, look and tilt," serve to strengthen the magic moments of visual piety.

From Christopher Bollas's viewpoint, the mother from whose body we arrive may be regarded as "the God who delivers us into our being" (2000: 38). Europa's portrait in the window is the Cusan mirror in which the holy appears, but at the same time it is also a Winnicottian mirror in which we see the mother's face. Both psychoanalytic and anthropological literature suggest that on a primitive perceptual level the face may be associated to the breasts, the eyes to the nipples. According to Almansi, the etymology of the term *pupilla* confirms this correlation:

> The Latin word "*pupilla*" is the diminutive of "*pupa*" or "*puppa*," which means "girl" or "damsel." "*Puppa*" was also used in vulgar Latin to indicate the nipple. ... The modern Italian "*puppa*" or "*poppa*," a vulgar word for the female breasts, is derived from the same Latin word, as is the common verb "*poppare*" or "*puppare*," which means "to suckle." ... In one of the Malay dialects, the nipple is called "*mata susu*," literally the "eye of the breast." (Almansi 1960: 60)

Poets such as Nobel Prize winner Octavio Paz Lozano have also written about the bond that exists between the eye and the mother. Latin "pupilla," originally "little girl," referred also to the tiny image one sees of oneself reflected in the eye of another. In 1967, Donald Winnicott elaborated upon an infant development theory and pointed out that the "precursor of the mirror is the mother's face"; when the infant looks at the mother, what s/he sees is himself or herself. According to Winnicott, the infant depends on his mother's facial responses. In order to establish an authentic sense of self, to look creatively at the world around, the individual must first of all have internalized the experience of having been seen. In good-enough circumstances, this visual contact becomes "the beginning of a significant exchange with the world, a two-way process in which self-enrichment alternates with the discovery of meaning in the world of seen things" (Winnicott 1967: 112–13). "Apperception" is the term he used to capture the infant's subjective experience of merging with the mother, of seeing oneself through being seen by the mother.

The portrait of Mother Europa may respond to Europeans' quest to be seen, to experience transcendence, to merge with the mother, and to live moments of infinite pleasure. The ECB seems to have been receptive to Clercq's call, according to which the European elite must adopt a maternal approach—"Mother Europe must protect her children." Perhaps it endorsed Clercq's inspirational credo "together!" (1993) by placing Europa's portrait on the euro and allowing for citizens' symbolic reunification with the mother, for the restoration of the sacred primordial unity. A gift to celebrate the Eurozone's tenth birthday, the new banknotes were meant to be what Christopher Bollas called "aesthetic objects"—"transformational objects" that offer people the magic experience (see chapter 3) of wholeness and serenity. The awe-inspiring view of Europa's portrait on the banknote and the frequent encounter with her sacred gaze may periodically bring EU citizens back to the origin of their being where they may enter the primordial paradise through the powerful feeling of being seen by the mother and merging with her.

The decision to choose an aesthetically powerful version of a Greek image of Europa to ornament the new euro series was meant to indicate, also, the great extent to which art is cherished in Europe. The European Central Bank wished to convey the message that Europe's strength stems from its beauty and from beauty's transformative power. In *Civilization and Its Discontents,* Freud argues that valuing beauty is one of the primary characteristics of a civilized society: "We require civilized man to give reverence to beauty wherever he sees it in nature and to create it in the objects of his handiwork so far as he is able" (1930: 92). The British psychoanalyst George Hagman views the sense of beauty as a means of objectification of fantasy in which the anxieties and divisions of the internal world are transcended and a state of harmony, cohesion, and well-being may be accomplished (2002). He posits, for example, that beauty has a transcendent integrative function: it reconciles separation and polarization in the psyche and restores mental unity and harmony in the self. In the sense of beauty there is a feeling of wholeness, pleasure, and lessening of anxiety. The sense of beauty involves the experience of perfection, feeling alive, and lovability not only of the object but most importantly of oneself. Beauty reduces anxiety and stimulates hope. We call something beautiful because that is what we think when we see the triumph of life over death, the victory of hope over fear. He believes that the reason why Freud claimed reverence for beauty as a required trait of civilization is because beauty elevates human subjectivity and human values to a transcendental level. Viewing beauty as "one of the most exquisite forms of human meaning," he asserts that "a civilization that does not value beauty would be one that cannot hope and that cannot assert life over the inevitable and ubiquitous forces of entropy and death" (Hagman 2002: 672).

We could portray the reawakening of the intimate bond between aesthetics and politics in Europe as a response to contemporary society's yearning for rebirth and transformation, its desire to rediscover the meaning of sacred, to experience transcendence, to live moments that re-evoke the idyllic conditions of the primordial golden age, and to make life drives prevail over death drives. The most aesthetically interesting example of recently invented "sacred history" is the new euro series' blending of aesthetics with monetary politics. Unlike the first series of banknotes, the new Europa series was ideated to respond to people's nostalgia for paradise and evoke a profoundly ecstatic and moving, subjective, spiritual experience. The Europa myth, with its fascinating elements, contributes to the creation of the image of Europe as a chosen continent, elevated by its contact with the numinous. Allowing for the encounter between the natural and the divine serves to assign the much-desired spiritual and religious dimension to the euro. As a result of the ECB's politics of transcendence, the Eurozone becomes a sacred area imbued with divine powers, with the new euro, a par excellence anagogic symbol, serving as a ladder for elevation to the realm of the holy. The Europa series of banknotes promises to help people distance themselves from nationalist sentiments, experience enlightenment, purification, and ascent to the realm of the eternal through the discovery of their new "European identity." It offers the existential and metaphysical rite of "homecoming"—a reestablishment of the mystical union with the mother and finding a new home in the European Union.

CHAPTER 6

THE EUROPEAN CENTRAL BANK'S FABLES OF ABUNDANCE

IN BETWEEN SACRED RITUALS AND POLITICAL MARKETING

The new euro banknotes were introduced progressively—the €5 euro in 2013, the €10 in 2014, the €20 in 2015, the €50 in 2016. The unveiling ceremonies launched by (slightly different versions of) the "Illuminating the Europa series" video represent a yearly ritual. During these moments of storytelling, European Central Bank representatives provide verbal, visual, and acoustic versions of the *palingenetic* myth, the numinous story about a new Europe coming to life. These rituals, with both standard and new elements, disclose supranational policy-makers' omnipotent fantasies and their endeavors to attribute a transcendental nature to the European integration process. If the new euro series is the visible and tangible (sacred) symbol of new Europe's (and new Europeans') coming to life, the gradual unveiling of the new banknotes is a process of initiation where secrets are gradually disclosed to novices, progressively leading them to enlightenment. The unveiling ceremonies tell a fable of abundance, the cosmogony story that ends with the Eurozone becoming the center of the land of paradise and the new home for reborn EU citizens.

In the hope of building a European collective memory and guaranteeing the European Union's fusion with the divine and its ascent to the top of the global community's Olympus, at the unveiling ceremony of the new 5-euro banknote on 10 January 2013 at the Archaeological Museum, museum expert Egon Warmers spoke about the ancient Greek myth of Europa and her love affair with the "CEO" Zeus (ECB 2013a). Warmers is a storyteller devoid of pathos: he reads the tale as a solemn news broadcast rather than as an exciting tale of seduction that led to the birth of Europe. Though insisting that "nobility, divinity, beauty, and love stood at the cradle of our continent," he fails to convey the nostalgia, the excitement, the awe, and the reverence a similar emotionally charged foundation myth may deserve. "This *krater* brings us to the beginnings of Europe"—Warmers portrays the launching of the new euro as a rebirth of the sacred moment of creation and the new currency as the reappearance of the ancient *denarius* introduced in 794 AD by the Emperor Charlemagne as a new currency for the entire empire. He draws particular attention to the closeness in locality of the senate of 794 and the unveiling of the new euro banknote, suggesting not just an affinity but also an overlapping between the two (sacred) places. The *denarius* "was something like the first, the primary euro," closely linked to the city of Frankfurt, very well-accepted throughout Europe (including England) and valid for more than four hundred years. "If you want to save the euro for more than four hundred years, bring it to Britain!" is the moral of his story. After President Draghi's remarks, the ritual event concludes with the ECB president ceremoniously signing the new 5-euro banknote with the anthem of the European Union, "Ode to Joy," playing as he does so. The location of the museum and the ancient pillars in the background reinforce the religious milieu for the ceremony. The display of antiquities contributes to connecting the history of European currency to *illud tempus* and adds validity to the sacred bond that supposedly links today's Europe to antiquity.

The "Illuminating the Europa series" videos are presented officially once a year, each time a new totem, a new banknote, is unveiled (ECB 2013a, ECB 2014b, ECB 2015b). Their central motifs are the magic figure of Europa and the cosmic rays, bridges, and arches that reach and connect all corners of Europe. The first video (launched to celebrate the unveiling of the 5-euro banknote) begins with a pass through computer-generated, classical architecture, arches, and aqueducts. Although the architecture is classical, it has been re-created in a modern context. The arches and aqueducts are symbols of foundation and triumph that have been repurposed as proof of Europe's ability to propagate and innovate. Amid these structures and various other lines and nondescript images, cosmic light rains down from the sky to illuminate the face of Europa. The feeling is that through the encounter with the "sacred gaze" we have entered into the banknote; it is as if the Eurozone has become a mystic space that we are invited to explore. The sharp lines, basic colors, and computer graphics are broken by the magical appearance of stars. The constellation of stars takes shape and the *vera icona* is clearly visible before the light again disperses. The cosmic formation of Europa generates an atmosphere of excitement and awe, a magic moment of re-creation. Once Europa enters the microcosm of the Eurozone, she transforms it into a truly paradisiacal place. Color is introduced as the face of Europa gives way to a hologram strip. The bright colors reveal the mechanism of the hologram that includes the number 5, an arch, and the face of Europa. The next image illuminated by the celestial light is the emerald number 5, which sparkles and glitters from deep green to sapphire blue. The features highlighted in the video stand apart from the basic background imagery in blue and white. The hologram, glittering 5, and portrait of Europa transform the space from ordinary to extraordinary. The colors blue, green, and purple are associated with royalty and wealth, and we can understand from the video that the new 5-euro banknote represents the sacred source of abundance and idyll. At the center of the Eurozone dwells Europa; we are all invited to enter this space and reunite the umbilical cord to her. We traverse again the ancient architecture, which fades and gives way to the watermark image of Europa's face, followed by the hologram image, and finally the emerald 5 once more. Clearly written across the watermarked face of Europa is *M Draghi,* the signature of the ECB president—the piece that was missing to remake the vase of Pandora has been added. The new European family will not lack parents; reunification is complete. The architectural structures are reduced to basic, artificial, computer-generated versions of the original. The Eurozone is not a real, organic space, but a virtual paradise. The dramatic music, computer imagery, and use of light and the colors blue and green give the sensation of being in a divine realm; they evoke feelings of awe, excitement, and fascination, allowing us to experience a sense of unity and pristine pleasure.

The video iconography plays on the motif of the *vera icona* and portrays Europa as the "all-seer," "the icon of God" in a Cusan sense (1453/1988)—a figure that is painted with such a sophisticated technique that it seems to look at everything in the vicinity. Europa's gaze is represented though the web of multiple lines, rays, and bridges, as well as in movement that reaches out to every corner of Europe, resulting in the progressive constitution of a labyrinth not of things but of gazes and paradise dreams that meet. Observers' gazes encounter the gaze of Europa, and their nostalgia for paradise is fulfilled. The ECB rays are symbolic of the restorative rays emanating from the all-seer's eye, without which everything would be immersed in an apathetic and miserable obscurity. In Cusa's vision of the universe, the center (the gaze) is everywhere; its circumference is nowhere (De Certeau 1987). The ECB videos show that in supranational policy-makers' cosmographic symbolism, the gaze is a vector, a line, a shining ray that, like an arrow, implants itself in each EU citizen and enlightens them, revealing the sacred core of the federalist soteriology. Europa fixes her numinous gaze upon us; we'll be astonished by the *movement* of her *immobile* eyes.

These images are meant to generate in people what Horst Bredekamp called an "affective raptus" (2015) and create for them a new (paradisiacal) reality. Through Europa's sacred gaze, they promise to bring citizens together and transport them to another realm, thereby giving birth to Europe's new "fantastic family." Europa's gaze is meant to conjure up a social space, a collective consciousness, and a shared identity through bringing into coexistence the eyes of "true Europeans" (whose eyes have been captured by the sacred gaze). It is the domain of surprise, awe, and enchantment that will be the birthplace of Europa's fantastic family, of a European home based on cooperation, mutual understanding, and empathy, but also on the unconditional belief in the power of the gaze. In the digital world, old archetypes return in the form of artifacts that live in the realm in between dream and testimony (Belting 2014). The ECB's Illuminating the Europa Series videos are a fine example of this new type of cyber-utopia. They are digital works of art that give the audience the impression of being in front of an apparition, the feeling of being elevated to another dimension. Europa's portrait is a digital mask that immerses her face in a virtual aura.

When it comes to verbal announcements, the mission of the European Central Bank is often defined in more prosaic terms—*selling* a *product.* At the unveiling ceremony of the 5-euro banknote, Mario Draghi said of Europe's new totem: "Besides our core function and mandate to guarantee price stability, ... one of our tasks is to develop what we could call 'our product,' the euro banknotes" (ECB 2013a). Without much speculation, the new series of the euro banknotes could be seen as the last product of the ECB. The videos, "Europa, the New Face of the Euro," the Illuminating the Europa series, and other campaign spots are essentially the commercial ads through which the ECB seeks to *sell* its "product" (the new euro), and, its sacred essence—the *palingenetic* myth.

Advertisements show up everywhere, even in the special world of the European Central Bank. They have several functions: they urge people to buy goods, they validate a certain way of being in the world, they focus private fantasy, and they sanction or subvert existing structures of economic and political power (Lears 1994: 1). Advertising often offers "an image of things to be desired, people to be envied, and life as it 'should be,'" conjuring up a "potential place or state of being situated not in the present but in an imagined future" (Sturken & Cartwright 2009: 189). Advertisements (similar to any other images) interpellate their viewers to see themselves within the ad in a particular way and try to tether the viewer to the image through the Medusa effect.

ECB ads attach meanings to the euro that it would not necessarily bear otherwise, such as the intricate emotional attributes and special sacred aura. The currency acquires human and godlike qualities; it is presented as sexy, romantic, maternal and/or divine. ECB ads speak through particular written or audio texts that address the viewer directly, describing the euro as "your" money and suggesting that the ad (and its producers and European policy-makers in general) know what "you" desire and yearn for. More than selling products, advertising sells signs in the semiotic meaning of the term (Sturken & Cartwright 2009: 205). ECB ads create a special relationship between signifier (the new euro) and signified (its iconological meanings) to produce signs in order for Europeans to purchase not just the common currency but also the encoded meanings and the political connotations supranational policy-makers attach to it. Advertisers seek to turn their product into a recognizable brand and, for this reason, to add value to it, to attribute particular characteristics to it, and to construct an image of its potential consumer and his/her lifestyle. The communication experts of the ECB also aim to make sure that the new Europa series becomes a brand product recognizable by both Europeans and non-Europeans and that it is associated with the European Union and "Europeanness." The campaign gives the euro—and through the euro, Europeans—the added value of being sophisticated, cultured, and even superior.

The ideological function of many advertisements takes the form of speaking a language of patriotism and nationalism in order to equate the act of purchasing a product with the practice of citizenship. Because the idea of family is central to most national ideologies, Euro-federalism included, the euro is presented as the means by which the family is held together, affirmed, and strengthened. It is portrayed as a tool through which we can participate in the art of unification, in the recreation of Europe's fantastic family. The slogan "feel, look and tilt" promotes the euro and functions as a means to create emotional attachment. Although possessing (and spending) the euro often gives us pleasure and satisfaction, it can never entirely achieve the promises of fulfillment that advertisements offer.

As Sturken and Cartwirght point out, "ads create and speak in the world of fantasy. The world presented by an advertisement is fictional" (2009: 208). Ads promise (and ultimately fail) to fulfill emotional needs. Similar to advertisements in general, which all "speak the language of transformation" (212), the ECB ads imply that with the new euro, Europeans' lives will change for the better; this new product will alleviate their state of dissatisfaction. Europa's glamorous figure and the paradisiacal setting in which she appears and performs her role present a world that is both enviable and nostalgic. These videos conjure up a fantasy world and promise to turn this world into reality through the act of possessing Europa (the euro); perfect unification with the mother and with other EU members appears attainable. As John Berger wrote in *Ways of Seeing,* "Publicity is essentially eventless … situated in a future continually deferred" (1972: 153); it mixes and simplifies human yearnings, depicts the present as lacking in some way, and offers vague but magical promises. Our primal fantasy is to return to primal paradise, to reexperience the (imaginary) state of wholeness and infinite pleasure. The ECB, with its campaign, seeks to fill our structural lack and respond to our most intimate pursuit. In fact, "it is our drive to fill our sense of lack that allows advertising to speak to our desires so compellingly," to foster fantasies of perfect ego-ideals and regression to the childhood phase (Sturken & Cartwright 2009: 217). Over the last two hundred years, advertisements have acquired a powerful iconic significance. Fabulous and didactic stories have proliferated, evoking fantasies connected to the ancient dreams of abundance (Lears 1994: 2). As rhetorical constructions, ads do more than generate desire; they also seek to shape it and respond to it by containing dreams of personal transformation and yearnings for paradise.

Advertising is a symbolic art form. Its aesthetic and emotional appeal derives from the imagery, symbols, color, tropes, and fantasies it relies on. The use of subliminal messaging in the aestheticization of politics entreats people's emotions and stirs up unconscious desires, anxieties, and fantasies. Some marketing strategies correspond to the dream processes described by Freud (condensation, displacement, representation, and secondary revision): "the ad maker, like the dreamer, condenses several figures, images, or words into one, or splits, displaces, and decomposes one thing into several, or represents one thing symbolically by another" (D'Angelo 1986: 163). In *The Joke and Its Relation to the Unconscious,* Freud encourages us to read some kinds of ads the way we might read the manifestations of the unconscious (1905/2002). The interpretation of an ad thus becomes "a kind of tropical exegesis of the unconscious, a rhetorical act in which the reader tries to deconstruct the text and to unravel its myriad possibilities," moving back and forth between unconscious scanning and self-conscious analysis (D'Angelo 1986: 164). In order to decipher the mysterious illustrations, we may need to rely on our nature as *homo ludens* and use a psychoanalytically informed approach.

Both change and continuity have characterized the EU's marketing strategy. Europe is still, as Mabel Berezin diagnosed in the year 2000, occurring not only through the market but also through (American-style) marketing. The same phrase, "To be credible and effective, communication actions must be shaped by the culture, language and concerns of the citizen," appears in the 1997 Euro Papers and in a communication published by the European Commission on the implementation of an information and communication strategy on the euro and economic and monetary union (2004). Since 2002, supranational institutions, through evocative iconography and the use of an aggressive marketing campaign, have been seeking to conquer Europeans' hearts and convince citizens that the currency is worthy of their trust and love. The euro is still a product that must be sold; EU officials still seek to create brand loyalty for the euro, referred to as "our money." The main goals of the communication strategy are still 1) to define the meaning and the mission of Europe, 2) to reinforce a sense of Europeanness while meeting the (psychological) needs of various target groups, and 3) to respond to citizens' nostalgia for paradise.

The new euro has to be something that everyone can appreciate; it has to appeal to an inner yearning that most Europeans share. Recognizing the quest to leave behind today's unsatisfactory present and experience transcendence as perhaps one of the main (unconscious) concerns of citizens, the campaign advertising the new Europa series of euro banknotes has as its goal to respond to the nostalgia for paradise by telling a fable of abundance, where the image of Europe is one of the "chosen continent" and where the Eurozone reevokes the land of paradise, generating in viewers the feeling of wholeness, peace, and pleasure.

ECB videos provide a visual representation of federalists' eschatological fantasies: Europa in all of her various roles promises a paradise of effortless nurturance. The ads tell the story of a new beginning, of a new community coming to life, of the mythical journey of the hero. They narrate the same story of success Europeans are supposed to be proud of (told and retold by the European Commission): the euro has "become a symbol of integration and cooperation" and members of the Eurozone have no reason not to see Europe's future with "hope" and "confidence." The videos do not provide room for weeping over the debt crisis or the social and economic consequences of the financial turmoil that hit the EU. They evoke an Eden-esque atmosphere and depict the last product of the ECB as the elixir that will guarantee citizens' return to paradise and the center of the circle.

To share with citizens in the joy of celebrating the first ten years of the euro banknotes and coins, the European Central Bank released a six-minute video (ECB 2011). In the spot, a queenly figure donned in a flowing dress and veil, adorned with a string of elegant pearls, and characterized by a weightless frock and seductive recline emerges from an Ancient Greek *krater.* She transforms into a stylish modern woman, lovely face and long flowing hair in motion, on a mission. The video fits well in the category of advertisements that uses the codes of classical style to attach to products both a sense of lineage and historical tradition (hence approval of ancestors and legitimacy) and nostalgia for the (fantasied) past, as well as an aesthetic value of ideals meant to evoke tradition, authenticity, and prestige. The world created by this ad appears to be precious, artistic, and treasured. The classical pose and style of the model evokes the history of painting female nudes and thus attaches to the euro the qualities of art and upper-class taste. Her sensuality is heightened by the sheerness of her clothes that reveal her naked breasts underneath, visible as she comes to life. The dress, the pearls, and the hair of the model are all signifiers of the past and tradition. The ad suggests that we can all experience moments of seduction, love, and transformation if we acquire the attributes of classical art through the possession of the euro.

She walks with determination and the world materializes around her. She is *the* creator; the materials are drawn directly to her; bridges are being constructed following her magic footsteps. The lush rolling hills in the background are bathed in the glowing golden light of a new day. The landscape brings to mind a beautiful dawn. The atmosphere is both energized and peaceful, and the green hills and riverbed promise fertility and opportunity. The computer-generated images we see belong to a transcendental experience. The heavenly light does not fall on ordinary hills; these are the hills of paradise. Her walk through the beautiful landscape under a blue sky is enhanced by the hopeful, persistent music in the background. The rhythmic beat of the drum urges the figure forward, and mystical chimes interrupt the upbeat and energetic melody of promise. With every key change the anticipation grows, and one begins to wonder where the road may lead. She crosses under the classical arch, materializing before her, and looks skyward with a smile of satisfaction. As she approaches the newly formed arch the shot zooms out, and we see that the bridge assembling before her is not singular but is part of a network of roads and bridges being formed and connecting various parts of the continent. The shot zooms back in and she is transported from her Italian landscape to the Baltic Sea, which she crosses with ease as a modern bridge of concrete and wire erects before her. This Europa could easily find immortality in poetic form and represent a contemporary version of Gradiva, a figure from the realm in between dream and reality:

> There runs—no, that is not the word, there flies, or rather there hovers—the object of my dreams, which slowly assumes the proportion of a harming nightmare. A fantastic figure—should I call her a servant girl, or rather a classical nymph? … This lively, light-footed and rapid gait,

> this striding step, ... what is the meaning of it all? ... My condition varied between a bad dream and a fairy tale. ... I lost my reason. It was always she who brought life and movement into an otherwise calm scene. Indeed, she appeared to be the embodiment of movement ... but is it very unpleasant to be her lover? ... Who is she? Where does she come from? Have I encountered her before? I mean one and a half millennia earlier? Does she come from a noble Greek lineage, and did her great-grandmother have an affair with people from Asia Minor, Egypt or Mesopotamia? (Gombrich 1986: 107–8)

Through the ECB video, antiquity resurfaces. Viewers receive a contemporary (computerized) version of the mysterious nymph. The walking figure of Europa may have something in common with the handmaid who carries a basket of fruit in *The Birth of St John the Baptist* by Ghirlandaio. Both nymphs walk with determination while their clothes are moved by an invisible breeze. Europa's light movement contrasts with the common perception of an inanimate, passive, bureaucratic, technocratic European Union and announces the upsurging of an antique grace, of the original sacred, into the profane realm of contemporary Europe. In the mind of Aby Warburg, the nymph was the embodiment of the "move towards the ancient," an elemental spirit, a "pagan goddess in exile" (Gombrich 1986). This German art historian believed that what seduced his friend, André Jolles, in Ghirlandaio's painting was the alterity intruding in the ordinary space, the "survival of antiquity" as an "imaginary breeze," an "accessory in motion," and its charming and uncanny effect. Europa's clothes, hair, and light movement are expected to have a similar haunting and seducing power. The computerized representation of the Greek mythological princess is supposed to generate in citizens love and infatuation.

The very first shots of the video foreshadow the core message: the metamorphosis of the ancient Greek image of Europa into a living (modern, self-confident, and seductive) young woman is there to indicate the ECB's mission (and ability) to transform dreams into reality. She provides a visual representation of magic metamorphosis, the ECB's transformative and unifying power, the passage from one stage to another, the resurrection of an inhuman organization as a community with divine attributes and citizens' rebirth as true Europeans. As the ancient image transforms into a real woman, her robes and head cover are discarded for modern attire, but her pearl necklace remains. While the image provokes a sense of a new, changing Europe, her necklace remains in reference to a regal past, suggesting that new Europe is the heir of ancient Greece; its renaissance is a rebirth of the Sacred. As the modern depiction of Europe walks, a bridge materializes before her, eventually connecting all corners of the European continent. The bridge as a symbol is used both literally, suggesting the prospect of a more connected and interdependent Europe, and metaphorically when the narrator declares that "with its common heritage and history, shared values and achievements, Europe builds bridges and inspires hope" (ECB 2011). Her self-confident demeanor and forward-looking stride represent the progressive nature of the "new Europe" and evoke a sense of confidence in both Europe and the euro. The idea of a stable and prosperous Europe is reiterated in Mario Draghi's assuring words: despite the challenges Europe must face, "the people of the Euro area can rest assured that the European Central Bank will remain faithful to its mandate of maintaining price stability" (ECB 2011). From the classical to the modern, the architectural imagery promises progress and innovation. The foundation of classical history paves the way for advancement and modernity. The images elude space and time. We have the sense that the pathways are permanent, new, and omnipresent. The yellow bricks bring to mind the Yellow Brick Road that guides Dorothy to the Emerald City. And, just like in *The Wonderful Wizard of Oz*, there is only one pathway one can follow in the federalist narrative to reach the promised land and achieve wholeness.

The central theme of this commercial ad is Europa building bridges, crossing them, and reaching the far shores. Why is the bridge the most predominant design feature of the euro banknote, a key motif in the videos, an omnipresent element, and a sacred totem in the discourse of European federalism? The bridge has always had a great impact upon the fantasies of man; it has appeared innumerable times in literature and poetry from antiquity until today. According to Hungarian psychoanalyst Sándor Ferenczi (1950), the bridge represents an important vehicle between the "beyond" (the condition of the unborn, the womb) and the "here" (life); it may symbolize a formal representation of "transition" or "changes of condition" in general, a longing for a return to the womb and Mother Earth in particular. Following Ferenczi, we could see the bridge as (another) powerful symbol of the European art of unification that expresses the longing to reunite what has been divided and to re-establish a mystic union between Europeans and Mother Europa. Such union would defy the very act of creation and disregard the limits and prohibitions imposed by the Symbolic Father.

The ECB's cosmogony project could have gained inspiration from a number of stories from various cultures; in all of them we find the dream of reunification by magic, supernatural bridges, division, and a threshold guardian that needs to be defeated in order to gain access to the special world. In tribal cultures, rivers reflected the divine intention of drawing a boundary between tribes and their territories; their sacred nature derived from the divinity that was responsible for presiding over it (Friedman 1952). To cross the threshold, the transgressor had to pacify the river spirits by performing a sacrificial act. Folklore teaches us that without a bridge sacrifice the bridge could not be built and the other shore could not be reached. The excessive desire to reunite what has been separated (intrinsic in human nature and therefore a constant yearning since the dawn of civilization) has always been disturbed (and reinforced) by the fear of the other shore, the fear of defying the act of creation and violating the primal prohibition.

For Ferenczi, bridge dreams fall into three groups: 1) those in which the dreamer fears even attempting a crossing; 2) those in which a partial crossing is achieved; and 3) those in which the dreamer is successful in crossing the bridge and reaching the other shore (1950). As the video reflecting federalists' dream of Europe shows, Europa has no problems whatsoever in crossing the bridge and reaching the other shore. She builds bridges without much effort, and she shows no fear crossing seas and conquering foreign territories. Europa is neither anxious nor fearful; she is determined in her willingness to move beyond limits and cross all boundaries. For her, reaching the other side does not even require the payment of a sacrifice.

We might imagine her as a contemporary counterpart to members of the Collegium of the Pontifices of ancient Rome, who were in charge of the administration of the *jus divinum.* Her task is to govern the relations of the European community with the deities—she is the builder and guardian of Europe's bridges, the only one capable of pacifying the river spirits and making the structure of the bridge secure. Bridge-building has emerged as the key pillar in European politics of transcendence. A key focus in this religious enterprise is the sacralization of space through the enlargement of the microcosm (EU) and its holy center (Eurozone). Europa personifies the ECB as EU's bridge builder, the one who has access to the divine and who can guarantee citizens' return to the mother. We may also imagine Europa as personifying the hero of the primitive rebellion, the defiant adventurer who never stops seeking new exploits and for whom everything is possible. Through the building of numerous, beautiful, all-reaching bridges ready to withstand the vicissitudes of centuries, the ECB has offered clear, artistic, illuminating examples of its cosmogony project and its politics of *jouissance.* The overall design serves to nurture illusions of omnipotent organization, to defy the imagination of Europeans and non-Europeans alike by erecting structures that were once literally inconceivable, to inspire eschatological expectations, and to make perceptible to all the advent of the golden age (which is linked with the celebration of the tenth anniversary of the euro).

In the second part of the video, Europa reaches the other shore and arrives at paradise. She is no longer alone. The computer-generated images are gone; she is a "real woman" surrounded by "real people"—the (illusion of) the EU's metamorphosis from a bureaucratic artificial organization into a fantastic family is complete. To eliminate every doubt about Europa's and euro-users' final destination and to make sure that the other side of the bridge is nothing but the mythic land of paradise, the ECB chose as the scene a bustling marketplace. Europa appears in all her beauty available for the viewers' desiring gaze. The ad is selling an image of a "new woman," confident as the object of the "male gaze" (a female figure men can gaze upon and regard as a possession). In her active stance and determined behavior there is perhaps an attempt to challenge the traditional power dynamic of the gaze described by Laura Mulvey (1975). Europa seems to possess the "master eye." On the one hand, she is the central object that nails the gaze of the people in the market and captures the gaze of the viewers of the ad; on the other, she scrutinizes, controls, and dominates everything and everyone. With her penetrating look and with the medusa effect she generates, her power is presented as absolute.

For centuries, since the great commercial fairs of early modern Europe, market exchange has been associated with a carnival atmosphere. Commodities and events provide magical connections between the material and the spiritual realms; markets represent a mix of the miraculous and the carnivalesque. The ECB seems to suggest that once we possess the new euro, we gain the right to participate in a carnival, to be among the privileged and experience moments of transcendence and magical self-transformation. In the video, market transactions leaven the imagery of abundance and carnivalesque confusion. Citizens' dreams of a full belly are complemented by the fantasy of participating in an exotic cosmopolitan world, the European Land of Cockaigne, a space with a religious aura, and the vision of an earthly paradise, all of which are associated with maternal nurturance and the divine. The market is a symbol of the imaginary place of perpetual abundance, the paradisiacal land of plenty, the fulfillment of all desires, the resolution of all traumas, the symbol of infinite existence. In the Land of Cockaigne, food, sexual liberty, and opportunity to play are constantly and unlimitedly provided, allowing for the direct and immediate satisfaction of survival, pleasure, and ludic drives. In this special world everything is possible; there are no rules and no limits to enjoyment; life seems a permanent carnival. Unlike other countries, it has no borders. Not only the spatial but also the temporal dimension of liminality is fixed in the imaginary country. Time is suspended. Every day is a holiday. This fantastic land provides an alternative possible world and may be associated with the golden era. The video suggests that to enter the special world, one has to perform the ritual of "feel, look and tilt," holding in one's hands the sacred object.

As Ugo Fabietti explains, it is in the bricolage of the ritual, through *doing*, that human beings come to realize the sense of their religiosity. The rite is certainly not only the manipulation of objects, the so-called "paraphernalia," but a way to enter into contact with those objects, spaces, and materials that make the religious experience concrete (2015: 153–54). With this video and many other ads, the ECB wishes to educate citizens to recognize the totem of its new community. It seeks to teach people how to identify the special signs on the currency and remember the sacred image of Europa in hopes of putting them in the right mood. In other words, it seeks to convince them about the absolute truth represented by the United States of Europe and to make them feel that the Eurozone is the sacred center of the European microcosm.

Notwithstanding all the efforts put into the staging of the scene, the video itself anticipates the betrayal of the promise. Europa's carnival, as presented in the spot, is not an authentically communal experience; it is an individual show. Some scenes reveal that what Europa is seeking to generate is a commodity rather than a gift exchange. This realization is destined to provoke the opposite effect in respect to the official goals, reinforcing feelings of scarcity, dissatisfaction, and renewed longing rather than a sense of abundance and harmony. The people are a part of the scene only in necessity; they are the background props publicizing the dogma of togetherness. Integration is a stretch because everyone looks exactly the same. Europa must be set up alongside other "real" people so that we cannot see her as "one of us." Europa confidently strides up to a vendor and wordlessly indicates that she wants to purchase a loaf of bread. She hands the vendor a 5-euro banknote—emphasized by the phrase "our money" in the commentary overlaying the music. At the end of the video Europa accepts the change from her purchase with a half-smile, and without making eye contact with the woman vendor, she immediately scrutinizes the bill she receives. She handles the bill with perfectly manicured nails and holds the 5-euro note away from her to better examine it. The tilt of Europa's head and vague expression on her face give the impression that she is satisfied with the magic experience of taking possession of the desired object, and she gives a self-assured nod. The video shows another transaction between Europa and a waitress. Again, her interactions seem artificial.

Her preoccupation with her money removes her from the human experience of exchange and interaction.

These scenes reveal that what is really missing from federalists' idyllic community is the very idea of community. By following the trend of the personalization of politics, Europa embodies what the EU officially opposes. Her acting seems to serve the purpose of allowing her to parade as a celebrity—an idol, an object of love to be adored and identified with. The crowd is not the renewed collective body that the ECB wishes Europeans to feel part of; Europa has little or no interest in the people around her. The ritual of "feel, look and tilt" has a contrived rather than a sacred nature; Europa is not the nymph that euro-users could fall in love with; the Eurozone (market) is not the land of paradise that citizens yearn to enter.

When the territory of Latvia was "sacralized" (with the country's integration into the Eurozone), an information campaign was launched by the ECB and Latvian Central Bank. To give the campaign "a human touch" and "a face" (2013b), actress Lelde Dreimane was chosen to play the role of Europa. Officially her task was to teach people how to check the euro banknotes and coins for authenticity and to highlight "the close ties between Latvia and the rest of the EU." In reality, however, the undeclared goal of the pervasive and stylish personification of the Eurozone was perhaps to guarantee Europa's (the Eurozone's) rise to stardom. Image icons evoke pleasure and desire (Sturken & Cartwright 2009: 38). The image of Europa is proposed by the ECB as an icon of glamour. It is the first time that the figure of Europa has been associated with an entertainment icon. This decision seems to reflect a trend we can observe in France where the role of Marianne has been played by sex symbols such as Brigitte Bardot, Mireille Mathieu, Catherine Deneuve, Inès de la Fressange, Laetitia Casta, and Évelyne Thomas, and in 2013 by Inna Shevchenko, the highest-profile member of the Ukrainian feminist protest group FEMEN.

As Jackson Lears shows through his exploration of the American advertising culture since the nineteenth century, ads have offered a profusion of exotic imagery (1994: 10). Twentieth-century advertising iconography, he claims, redefined the source of abundance from the fecund earth to the efficient factory. In the developing corporate iconography where the industrial model of abundance prevailed, women were reduced to the conduit for corporate-sponsored largesse, or, more commonly, to mere passive consumers, and the machine replaced the nurturing earth as the representation of the cornucopia (1994: 18, 19).

ECB marketing experts seem to be driven by the ancient impulse to symbolize the source of plenty as female. Exotic imagery plays the central role in the new ECB communication campaign; utopian fantasies of abundance are central in the federalist discourse. The Eurozone is publicized as a terrestrial paradise; it is personified and portrayed as female with both erotic and maternal connotations. While the desire for magical metamorphosis and the yearning to return to the mother are expressed though the symbols of the bridge, the market, the pearls, etc., the dominant symbol of Europe is not the nurturing *Tellus Mater* but a young, modern, and aggressively seductive *femme fatale.* An icon of sexuality seems to have replaced earlier emblems of freedom, union, and progress.

The Ara Pacis is one of the most powerful visual representations of the set of iconographic motifs used by Augustus to explain the political project of reconciliation and rebirth. The programmatic will to raise the idea of a lasting happiness has the maximum effect in the image of the maternal divinity—the *Tellus*—sitting on a rock with two playful newborns in her arms searching for her breasts; the developing patterns of rhetoric and iconography construct a powerful, seductive female. Despite their determination to draw a thread connecting antiquity to the present, the model used by the ECB today is a seductive Europa, not a maternal one. In place of the traditional symbols of abundance, we meet with the fashionable woman (an active, independent, desired subject) who is central to the popular discourse of commodity civilization. The ECB seeks to inject some glamour into what is perceived by most as a boring, lifeless institution, and to turn the euro into an erotically charged commodity. The hope is to stimulate euro-users' fantasies and add luster to their deeply felt yearnings. The new euro that is being sold is not a product but an elixir that is meant to empower those who possess it with quasi-magical influence.

These videos suggest that not much has changed in communication policy; the ECB is still using the same (US-inspired) marketing strategy to sell its product. The euro donned with Europa is like Packard's "hidden persuader" (1957), a kind of "subliminal pill to the subconscious in order to exercise an hypnotic spell" (McLuhan 1954/2011: 13). Through "seductive Europa," the ECB seeks to appeal to Europeans' primal (unconscious) fantasies.

To offer a special (virtual) interactive experience and to ensure "that relevant information is easily accessible online and on mobile devices," the ECB launched the Euro Cash Academy (available in more than twenty languages and downloadable as a free app) on its "user-friendly" website called "Our Money" (www.new-euro-banknotes.eu). Citizens are invited to watch the video, answer the quizzes about the security features of the banknotes, and undertake a journey to a town in cyberspace to better explore the characteristics of the new (sacred) object. The very first thing we see when we enter this magic realm is Europa. Her presentation is dramatically different from the Europa depicted on the ancient *krater* and from the female figures that appear in ECB videos. Mario Draghi's seductive Europa is gone. She has lost all sensuality, flirtation, maternity, and divine gaze; Europa is in fact a robot. The implicit sexuality and purity of Europa's pearls have been replaced by gaudy costume jewelry explicitly exploiting the symbol of the EU, which may better be envisioned as an albatross hanging around the neck of the once glorious Phoenician princess. The *krater,* visible to the right, lacks the image of Europa. Are we to believe that she stepped forth from the vase in the form of this robotized, sexless girl? Her mouth does not move when she speaks; she is lifeless. In the introduction to the site Europa states, "I will be your guide." The guide, presumably, for our magic journey.

The ECB's politics of intimacy performed through the Euro Cash Academy may call to mind Spike Jonze's film, *Her* (2013). The movie is the story of a man, Theodore Twombly, in love with his operating system, Samantha. Samantha becomes his "guide" both in his work and in his private life. They embark on an emotionally intense journey through which Theodore discovers that even though she is "just a voice in a computer," she seems like a person. Samantha is magically voiced by Scarlett Johansson. As the cinema critic Christopher Orr asserts, "Her voice—breathy, occasionally cracking—warms the entire film"; she is "one of the more recognizably human characters of the movie year" (2013).

With the same ease that Theodore purchased Samantha, citizens can acquire their Euro Cash Academy app, call their guide Europa, carry her everywhere they go, and establish with her a special (virtual) love affair. Yet this (robotic) computerized reproduction of the Phoenician damsel is unlikely to inspire in viewers visual piety, excitement, delight, or even some fascination. The Europa robot has been deprived of her sacred gaze and seductive body. She is devoid of Scarlett Johansson's transformational voice, too. She does not say the words herself, but rather there is a disembodied voice explaining that she is Europa who will lead us on our journey and who we are to trust. The stylized image and the mechanical voice are courteous and removed. The app is neither provocative nor engaging. Unlike Samantha who "can be anywhere and everywhere simultaneously," and notwithstanding euro designers' will to provoke with currency iconography the feeling that the euro is everywhere around us, Europa's absence is evident; she is nowhere. After the short introduction she disappears. She is not present in the town that the viewer is invited to explore and her presence cannot be felt even when she is the protagonist. The computer Theodore falls in love with is not an *ordinary* computer. The ECB's app, with which Europeans will *not* fall in love, is banal. In *Her,* it was a voice that made the movie more about love and humanness than delusion and machinery (Schroeder 2014). In the ECB videos, it was Europa's sacred gaze, desiring face, and flirtatious movements that conveyed the presence of either the divine or the seductive. In the Euro Cash Academy, Europa's voice and appearance as a no-frills guide who will not lead us to paradise undermines the image of Europa as desirable; she is in fact a perfect representation of the bureaucratic, inhuman nature of the EU. Unlike Theodore, we would not close our eyes and let ourselves be guided by Europa to the land of infinite pleasure.

This new virtual, robotized version of Europa seems to foreground the betrayal of the promises made by the ECB: transforming an inanimate, bureaucratic, and technocratic organization into a European family; generating in citizens a strong affective attachment to the EU; and regaining (together) paradise lost. While in the previous video (ECB 2011) we saw Europa walking on the Yellow Brick Road, confident to arrive soon at the Emerald City, in this game we discover that the Wizard does not exist. Europa is neither a femme fatale able to generate desire nor a protective god/nourishing mother able to guarantee redemption and rebirth; the "seductive Europa" Draghi identified on the Greek *krater* and publicized through various videos is a lifeless robot. As it happens in cyberspace, where faces often transform into phantoms (Belting 2014: 297), the "true image" is revealed as fake by the app; the Eurozone is a mask without a face; the paradise it promises is counterfeit.

Policy-makers often make use of fairy tales in their rhetoric, sometimes explicitly and sometimes implicitly, to have a greater emotional impact on their audience. The ECB seems to have opted for *The Wonderful Wizard of Oz* but made flawed interpretations, ignoring the tale's real messages.

The reasons why L. Frank Baum's novel, written in 1900, has entered the story of the Eurozone could be many. When conceived, the tale was intended as a subtle political satire on the monetary reform of the United States of America and the populist movement that swept across the Midwest in the 1890s (Littlefield 1964: 50). If the monetary and fiscal reforms that supranational policy-makers have in mind are inspired by the myth of the United States of Europe (and the myth of the USA), what better source of mythical narrative than *The Wonderful Wizard of Oz,* the American fairy tale par excellence? What's more, Baum's story, just like the federalists' cosmogony story, is centered on the theme of finding a *home* and achieving *wholeness.* Finally, both stories seem to be structured on what Joseph Campbell described as the "monomyth," the model of the hero's journey (1991).

In *The Hero with a Thousand Faces,* the author argues that all important myths share the same structure; the stages of the hero's journey follow the same pattern:

> The standard path of the mythological adventure of the hero is a magnification of the formula represented in the rites of passage: separation-initiation-return, which might be named the nuclear unit of the monomyth. A hero ventures forth from the world of common day into a region of supernatural wonder: fabulous forces are there encountered and a decisive victory is won. The hero comes back from this mysterious adventure with the power to bestow boons on his fellow man. (Campbell 1991: 30)

According to Christopher Vogler, author of the best-selling guide for screenwriters *The Writer's Journey,* with this model "you can construct a story to meet almost any situation, a story that will be dramatic, entertaining, and psychologically true" (2007: 3). While Hollywood filmmakers have acknowledged on several occasions their debt to Campbell, storytellers that promise collective transformation and rebirth from the stage of politics have not. Yet the underlying fantasy of European cosmogony projects seems to revolve around the hero's journey. The Hollywood storytelling technique that often puts to the fore the fight of good and evil and gives preference to happy endings and tidy resolutions seems perfect for the *palingenetic* ultra-Europeanist narrative in which, for Europe's "true" mythic heroes, everything is possible. In the post–World War II period (when the memory of Hitler, Mussolini, and other charismatic leaders was fresh), the European elite was not comfortable with the term "hero"; the idea of a magic savior was given a rest as leaders sought to redefine the concept of Europe and Europeanness. Until recently, dispassionate, cold-blooded, charisma-free civil servants and patient consensus-builders were called upon the stage of European politics. This trend changed when European federalism became a soteriology invoking the metamorphosis of the EU into the USE as the only way to save Europe from the disaster caused by the 2008 crisis and to guarantee the return of the golden age. The EU's hero-phobia was then replaced by the belief that mythical leaders were needed in order to transform the chaos into cosmos, the dream into reality.

Campbell portrays the hero of the monomyth as a personage of exceptional gifts who enjoys the respect of his society but who lives in a world that suffers from a serious deficiency. Today in Europe there is a pervasive perception that the Eurozone is on the verge of abyss—the physical and spiritual life of the whole European Union is represented by many as fallen, or on the point of falling, into ruin. In the imagination of many, Mario Draghi possesses those extraordinary qualities that are necessary to save Europe. It was on 26 July 2012 when the ECB president accepted the call to adventure and assumed the role of the warrior. He pledged to do "whatever it takes to preserve the euro" and expressed no doubts about the happy ending of his mission: "believe me, it will be enough" (Draghi 2012). While enduring the supreme ordeal, confronting the prospect of the collapse of the Eurozone, Draghi experienced an epiphany and realized suddenly that he was the chosen one endowed with special powers. His announcement of the inspirational credo "whatever it takes" is widely regarded as the turning point in the euro crisis. Super Mario is expected to bring back from his adventure not only the means for the regeneration of the Eurozone but also a message for the European Union in general. Many hope that his journey will end with the fulfillment of the European dream—that the European Union will represent again (or for the first time) the promised land of stability, peace, prosperity, and happiness, an archetype to emulate.

In Baum's and in Draghi's stories, Dorothy and Europa respectively undertake a journey to the magic land of the wizard (a symbol of an external agent imbued with magic qualities) in an effort to return home and find wholeness. In the video celebrating the euro's tenth anniversary (ECB 2011) there is no twister like the one in *The Wonderful Wizard of Oz* that symbolizes the populist cyclone sweeping across Kansas in the early 1890s. In the ECB video the weather is perfect; there are no traces of the effects of the 2008 crisis, nothing disturbs Europa in her march for paradise. There is no crossroad that leads right to the Emerald City, no doubt whether to turn left or right. She doesn't face any obstacles and she doesn't need to fight enemies. The social and political forces that are contrary to and challenge the federalists' cosmogony project seem nonexistent. Europa is confident in her ability to accomplish her mission—she walks alone and she needs no one, neither friends nor mentors. She is such a unique hero that she manages to cross the bridge and to gain access to the promised land without having to pass a trial and without paying a sacrifice.

In the federalist narrative, the microcosm of the EU, with its varied landscape and diverse inhabitants, is associated with the Land of Oz; its center, the Eurozone, with the Emerald City. In order to make the audience feel the stark contrast between the ordinary world and the special world in the film *The Wizard of Oz,* Kansas is depicted in black and white, in sharp contrast to the Technicolor special world of the Emerald City. For the same reason, to make Europeans feel the difference between the profane world of a bureaucratic and technocratic EU and Europe's idyllic Garden of Eden, in the ECB video ads "old Europe" is represented with computer-generated images and "new Europe" is portrayed though an intimate space of a colorful, sparkling market surrounded by human beings who are affectionate toward each other. The Emerald City of the Eurozone is depicted either through the multicolored hologram (in contrast to the grayness of previous euro series) or though the authentic live atmosphere of the market (in contrast to the computer-generated images associated with the other side of the bridge). While the Europe we knew might have been colorless, passionless, and artificial, the Europe that awaits us after the redemption is colorful, alive, and passionate.

Stories' opening scenes should create identification between the audience and the hero by giving heroes universal goals, drives, and desires, such as the need for recognition, affection, acceptance, or understanding (Vogler 2007: 92). Both Baum's and Draghi's stories revolve around the most basic human yearning—lust for transformation and rebirth. The federalist *palingenetic* myth (like most fairy tales) reflects people's searching for completeness and striving for wholeness. As in *The Wizard of Oz,* subtraction from the family unit sets the story in motion. The risk of losing one of the members of the European family (the painful and frightening scenarios of a Eurozone without Greece or of a European Union without Great Britain) and the need to fill in all the missing pieces to recreate the pristine harmony of the European family drive the story toward the final proclamation of "and all European citizens lived happily ever after."

One of the reasons why Dorothy is incomplete and doesn't feel at home in Kansas is because her parents are dead. Some believe that European citizens do not feel at home in the European Union because their forefathers have passed and the new leaders have not been able to continue the heroic deeds of Schuman, Adenauer, De Gasperi, or Monnet. For others, Europeans' forefathers never existed, in the sense that people have never identified with or had emotional attachment to supranational policy-makers. In Draghi's story, it is the union with Europa and the recreation of Europe's fantastic family that symbolizes (and promises) the reconstruction of lost wholeness. Just like Europa in Moschus's poem, Dorothy answers the call of adventure and abandons her original home to follow her unconscious drives. Not only do both Dorothy and Draghi feel that they cannot refuse the call, they are also aware of the fact that things will not remain the same; the new home will be different, and return to the old home will be impossible. In the federalist narrative the euro is irreversible; exit from Eurozone and return to the national currencies is not an option anymore.

Dorothy meets Professor Marvel who reminds her that she is loved and sends her on her quest for home, which in reality is much more than a Kansas farmhouse. Walter Hallstein, the mentor of the prophets of the federalist soteriology, conveyed the following message: "Anyone who does not believe in miracles in European matters is not a realist" (Draghi 2013b). Inspired by him, today's ECB president believes that the dream can be accomplished—creating the monetary and fiscal blueprint for the United States of Europe and remaking the Eurozone into a safe and cozy home for citizens is possible. Dorothy escapes from the wicked witch's castle with the witch's broomstick and the ruby slippers, the key to getting back home (Hollywood changed the silver slippers of the novel into ruby slippers because of the use of Technicolor—they wanted them to be more visible and distinct). In the federalists' fable it is the unconditional faith in the dogma of the USE that represents the compass in citizens' journey toward the Emerald City. This religious faith is a gift that Europe's enlightened supranational elite give ordinary people to help them discover their "true self," their unique, sui generis nature as "European citizens."

Yet citizens' enlightenment, their conversion into faithful followers of the federalist soteriology, has yet to occur. Being "rejected" and "isolated" are key stages in the development of the myth of the hero, and Mario Draghi's story is no exception. After announcing the Outright Monetary Transactions program, he flew to Potsdam to receive a prize from Wolfgang Schäuble, a German finance minister, for promoting European understanding and said: "At a time like this, praise is a very scarce commodity. … So you can understand what this means to me" (Steen 2012). Draghi's hero credentials are still disputed. The moment of epiphany, the abrupt realization of divinity, has not occurred yet. The chain of divine experience that starts with enthusiasm (meaning being inspired, visited, or possessed by a god) and leads to apotheosis (becoming a god) and then to epiphany (being recognized as a god) has not been completed. His solitude is represented in the video by the figure of Europa walking alone. It is as if the European elite were ready to enter paradise without European citizens, as if the prophets of federalist soteriology were willing to pass the sacred threshold without their community of believers (betraying the official promise of *co-creating* new Europe *with* citizens). Unlike Dorothy, who gets acquainted with her fellow adventurers and learns of their hopes, supranational identity entrepreneurs ignore the fact that a great number of EU citizens do not share their dreams and goals. Proponents of the cosmogony project have failed to establish a bond of human feeling; the videos provide a powerful representation of the *lack* of heroic skills in this sense. What Draghi knows is that, in his mythic journey, he has arrived at the "approach stage" (the threshold to the innermost cave) and therefore has to make final preparations before taking that fateful leap. The team must be reorganized and rededicated to its sacred mission (in 2014 citizens elected a new European Parliament; EU's new leaders became consecrated). At the same time, the audience must be reminded of the ticking clock or the "time bomb" of the cosmogony story: the urgency and life-or-death quality of the USE must be underscored; the intensity of the (already catastrophic) discourse must grow to raise awareness that either further steps are taken to accomplish the goal of federal Europe or the EU will cease to exist as a community.

In *The Wonderful Wizard of Oz,* the treacherous journey plunges Dorothy into misadventure. Upon her arrival in the Emerald City of Oz, by accident, the all-powerful Wizard is exposed and his true identity is revealed. Dorothy discovers that the great and powerful Wizard is nothing but a fraud; a common conman using smokescreens and parlor tricks to deceive the citizens of Oz. He is neither great nor powerful; Dorothy has been betrayed. The main characters of the tale all turn to the Wizard to fulfill their most precious desires: the Lion wants courage, the Scarecrow wants a brain, the Tin Woodman wants a heart, and Dorothy wants to go home. The Wizard provides elixirs: a diploma for the Scarecrow, a medal of valor for the Lion, and a windup heart for the Tin Woodman. Yet these objects are not the elixirs themselves. Neither the Scarecrow nor the Tin Man nor the Lion truly lacked what each believed he was missing; each character finds within himself that which he desires most. In fact, all of the characters already possess the qualities they seek and the means to their own fulfillment. The true all-healing elixir is the achievement of inner change, but the scene acknowledges the importance of receiving outward recognition as well: hearts, brains, and courage are inside them and always were, but the physical objects serve as a reminder (Vogler 2007: 184). Dorothy may return to Kansas with the elixir that she is loved and that "there is no place like home." During her journey she learned to look for her "heart's desire" in her "own back yard"; she understood that happiness and the possibility of experiencing wholeness are within her (Vogler 2007: 211).

Whatever the videos may suggest, the ECB president has not passed the trials and he has not gained access to the special world. Draghi hasn't taken possession of an elixir to share with EU citizens, revealing how feelings of death can be overcome, how life can be restored, and how metamorphosis can be accomplished in the EU. The Nobel Peace

Prize is not an object symbolizing the success of finding the elixir but an outward recognition of federalists' cosmogony project; it is something concrete that is meant to remind citizens that the EU is an omnipotent organization ready and capable of transporting citizens into the Emerald City and bringing back the golden age by giving birth to a new Europe. European federalists seem to ignore the true message of *The Wizard of Oz.* The most important missing peace in the European narrative is the understanding that there is no collective rebirth without individual rebirth.

PART III

European Festival Tales

CHAPTER 7

The Promise of European Rituals

This part of the book discusses some of the special events through which the European supranational elite have been seeking to tackle the EU's "emotional deficit" and reinforce its democratic credentials and legitimacy. Through the staging of old and new European rituals, they have aspired to conjure up ecstasy and home-feeling, build an intimate community, change attitudes, transform citizens, and elevate them to the realm of the sacred, thereby completing the European art of unification, the federalist project of cosmogony. Similar to other political communities, the EU sacralizes politics by trying to place citizens' everyday reality within a transcendental realm.

If in order to understand a religion, one must start from the rituals (Durkheim 1912/1995); for us to gain some insights into the political soteriology of Eurofederalism, we must continue with the study of (at least some of) its rituals. There can be no politics without symbols or accompanying rites (Kertzer 1988: 181). For *palingenetic* ultra-Europeanism to seize power, to remain true to its core myth, it must legitimize itself by generating an elaborate civic liturgy. European politics, just like national politics, is reproduced, dramatized, and sacralized through symbols and rituals. A key pillar of the European politics of transcendence has been the restructuring of the ritual calendar through the creation of special events. Carefully staged political dramas play a central role in the European doctrine of *palingenesis*: in a period of flux, turbulence, and pessimism, they are meant to evoke feelings of purification and rebirth and guarantee (the illusion of) salvation by transporting citizens to the pre-trauma idyllic home. Ad hoc rituals have been designed to create "collective effervescence," the ideal condition for individuals to internalize the meaning of sacred symbols of European federalism. The hope of staging old and new political-cultural performances is to create "new human beings" (truly European citizens) and to restore the sacred unity of Europe's fantastic family. The supranational elite seek to add transcendental connotations to the EU and emerge as powerful "masters of ceremonies" capable of guaranteeing a successful rite of passage.

For our journey into the realm of European rituals, Geertz's words will be a great companion:

> At the political center of any complexly organized society there is both a governing elite and a set of symbolic forms expressing the fact that it is in truth governing. They justify their existence and order their actions in terms of a collection of stories, ceremonies, insignia, formalities, and appurtenances that they have either inherited or, in more revolutionary situations, invented. It is these—crowns and coronations, limousines and conferences—that mark the center as center and give what goes on there its aura of being not merely important but in some odd fashion connected with the way the world is built. The gravity of high politics and the solemnity of high worship spring from liker impulses than might first appear. (Geertz 1983: 124)

Rituals perform several social, political, and psychological functions. Émile Durkheim's theory of solidarity, his concept of "collective effervescence"; Victor Turner's notion of "communitas"; and Mikhail Bakhtin's idea of carnival will help us reveal more about the EU's politics of transcendence. According to Durkheim, ritual behavior is concerned with the sacred; like sacred objects, these sacred acts are symbolic representations of society. Rituals play a key role in producing and maintaining solidarity and a feeling of oneness and strengthening and propagating collective ideas and sentiments:

> There can be no society which does not feel the need of upholding and reaffirming at regular intervals the collective sentiments and the collective ideas which make its unity and its personality. Now this moral remaking cannot be achieved except by the means of reunions, assemblies and meetings where the individuals, being closely united to one another, reaffirm in common their common sentiments; hence come ceremonies which do not differ from regular religious ceremonies, either in their object, the results which they produce, or the process employed to attain these results. (Durkheim 1915/1961: 474–75)

This human yearning for "social communion" can, therefore, only be fulfilled through some form of common action able to bind the members of the community together: "It is by uttering the same cry, pronouncing the same word, or performing the same gesture in regard to some object that they become and feel themselves to be in unison" (Durkheim 1915/1961: 262). Symbolic actions allow for the externalization and enactment of one's deepest feelings and longings. Rituals offer people a psychosocial orientation. They confirm and strengthen social identity, representing an important means through which people experience community. For dispersed members, rituals provide occasion to reconstitute the community (Cohen 1985: 51). They could be seen as a set of symbolic actions and displays of symbolic objects representing the premises, core values, and norms of a particular culture that, due to their "multivocal" nature (i.e., representing many things), endow ceremonies with multiple (related to both cosmological and social dynamics) levels of meaning (Turner 1967, 1975). In theory (and often in practice), people can participate in the same ritual yet find different meaning in it: "It is the very ambiguity of the symbols employed in ritual action that makes ritual useful in fostering solidarity without consensus" (Kertzer 1988: 69).

For Clifford Geertz, it is in ritual that the "conviction that religious conceptions are veridical and that religious directives are sound is somehow generated"; it is in ritual where "the world as lived and the world as imagined, fused under the agency of a single set of symbolic forms, turn out to be the same world, producing thus that idiosyncratic transformation in one's sense of reality" (1973: 112). According to René Girard, myths, god, religion, Greek tragedy, and culture originate in rituals and not vice versa. At the source of all human societies there is always a religious element: all great institutions of mankind, both secular and religious, spring from ritual, and all religious rituals, he asserts, spring from the "surrogate victim" (2005: 321). The function of rituals is to reenact the surrogate-victim mechanism and, as a result, to keep *violence* outside the community (Girard 2005: 98). Ritual practices conform to the needs of a community while ensuring the purgation of violence. Ritual, which as Roy Rappaport points out, "establishes, guards, and bridges boundaries between public systems and private processes, is the basic social act" (1999: 138).

David Kertzer in *Ritual, Politics, and Power* (1989) provides a comprehensive analysis of how rituals function in modern political life and how power is sacralized in contemporary societies. Ritual is a "symbolic behavior that is socially standardized and repetitive," representing a powerful "means of channeling emotion, guiding cognition, and organizing social groups" (9). Rituals may be used by the political elite to preserve the status quo, by emerging political leaders to assert their power, or by revolutionaries to delegitimize those who hold power and to create a new source of political identification—"ritual is used to constitute power, not just reflect power that already exists" (25).

Rituals are useful for masters of ceremonies and also for participants. Participation in ritual is driven by psychological needs; it generates emotions and shapes people's sense of reality and worldview. Through participation citizens may identify with a larger community (which, thanks to symbolic representation, becomes easier to love), give meaning to a complex reality, find orientation in a chaotic world, play certain roles, unveil their "Homo performans" nature (Turner 1987), and reveal their true selves.

While it is important to emphasize the polysemic nature of rituals, the idea that through rituals "solidarity is produced by people acting together, not by people thinking together" (Kertzer 1989: 76), it is equally essential to point out that rituals are often used to engrain in people's minds particular political beliefs. Far from being neutral or open to different interpretations, rituals may carry aggressively encoded symbolic messages, serve specific political interests, and function as tools for propagating political myths. Social dramas, when particularly effective, have an emotionally compelling quality and manage to generate an emotional excitement focused on the sacred symbols, discouraging critical inquiry or subjective interpretations (Kertzer 1989: 99). Rituals excite in order to better instruct. In order to achieve the maximum effect on participants' cognitive and emotional state, various kinds of sensory devices are employed. The goal is to create an emotional state that makes the message uncontestable and to present "a picture of the word that is so emotionally compelling that it is beyond debate" (Kertzer 1989: 100).

Finally, perhaps most importantly, the sacralization of our sociopolitical environment responds to people's yearning to live transcendental experiences. In many rituals, not just in initiation rites when a man undergoes a metamorphosis and is given a new name and a new self, feelings of individual and collective transformation play a central role. Rituals attribute cosmological meaning to the political order and allow people to imagine their society as something that has been divinely ordained and reflects some higher purpose. Political leaders position themselves at the center of political ceremonies and surround themselves with appropriate symbols to lend their performance a magic aura. Socio-dramas serve to establish the elite's public image not just as bastions of morality, tireless servants of the collective interest, heroes guaranteeing peace, stability, and prosperity, but also as masters of ceremonies with mystic power able to transport people to the realm of the holy and restore the lost idyll of perfect harmony and pleasure. They wish to be seen (and felt) not as ordinary policy-makers but as leaders who enjoy special knowledge and exceptional powers to administer the magic elixir people are in need of, allowing them to leave behind the present's profane and overwhelming conditions. According to Arthur Maurice Hocart, "perhaps there were never any gods without kings or kings without gods" (2004: 7). Contemporary politicians too project their invincibility and perform on the stage as if the source of their authority was still divine (not just derived from popular consent or institutional framework) and sacred.

The term "supranationalism" itself carries not just a legal meaning but some normative assumptions too. A driving force behind the idea is that by reinforcing "European identity," it is possible to transcend the logic of nationalism, and that "Europe's de-territorialised and de-nationalised supranational civil servants embody a 'higher' and more noble set of principles: a distinctly 'European' ethos and morality that stands above the more primitive nation state" (Shore 2001). Like the rulers of the past that used rituals to stir up popular emotions and respond to people's yearning for transcendence, thereby strengthening public allegiance to the polity and their legitimacy, the European elite, through the staging of social dramas, make important efforts to (as Geertz puts it) "demonstrate sovereignty to skeptics."

These "European rituals" are meant to "help the citizen visualize the presence of the Community in everyday life" (Shore 1993: 789); they are closely associated with the exercise of domestic and foreign policy and seek to communicate "European values" such as social solidarity and sustainable peace in the "free world" (Manners 2006: 78). While often perceived as boring, bureaucratic, and artificial, European politics is not immune to the extraordinary—the power of supranational rulers is also meant to exalt (and to intoxicate). Supranational elite seek to endow the EU with mystical values, transport citizens to the realm of the sacred, and offer a system of values that is beyond criticism or revision. The staging and dramatic presentation of their sacred image serves to reinforce what is asserted verbally in official documents.

Throughout the European integration process the creation of symbols has gone hand in hand with the invention of political rituals. Symbolic markers of time and space and ad hoc patterns of symbolic legitimization have been developed; new anchors for a collective European imaginary have been invented. European institutions, in line with the rest of its cultural policies, have used as a model (and often emulated) the symbol politics adopted by nation-states. The (failed) Constitutional Treaty refers to three symbols (the flag, the motto, and the euro currency) and two rituals (the anthem and Europe Day). In order to punctualize time differently, the Commission introduced a new ritual calendar celebrating "Europe Weeks," "European months of culture," and the various "European Years" (public campaigns dedicated, since 1983, to the promotion of "European issues," meant to educate and change the attitude of the widest possible audience). The dramatization of European governance also occurs via European ceremony, the European Parliamentary elections, and the physical performances (verbal declarations and missions) of "representatives" of the EU (the presidents of the Commission, the Council, and Parliament, and the EU high representative for foreign affairs and security policy).

In 1985, supranational policy-makers invented something apparently similar to national holidays. To allow European citizens to give meaning to the flow of time, to enact a set of collective rituals each year on a specific date, to commemorate not just one of the "decisive moments in the history of European integration" but the (sacrosanct) moment of foundation, May 9 was consecrated as "Europe Day." The "official historiography" of the European community was made public—the moment of birth of the European family was identified as May 9, 1950, the day when the Schuman Declaration was released (Larat 2005). The declaration's status was upgraded; to ingrain in Europeans' minds that it all began when the French foreign minister outlined his plan for European integration and to draw a red thread irreversibly linking together post–World War II Europe and today's Europe, Europe's founding fathers and today's political elite, the Schuman declaration received the status of the foundational document. The hope was to give Europeans the possibility of reenacting every year on May 9 the heroic acts of their ancestors, the possibility to return to the sacred moment of creation. The goal was also to propagate European values and educate citizens about European affairs. Schools and universities have been identified as key spaces to raise awareness of the sacred beginnings and the glorious evolution of the European project through multicultural meetings, conferences, and cultural festivals.

According to Johan Fornäs, Europe day serves as a cultural tool to create what Ricoeur identified as a "third time," something in between the lived (subjective, experiential, concrete) and universal (objective, cosmological, abstract) time, thereby "cosmologising lived time and humanizing cosmic time" (2012: 4).

Unlike on national holidays, on 9 May European citizens work and do not adopt specific behavior patterns of public and private sociability (participation in processions, meetings, or family events). They do not gather to remember Schuman as founding father of their European family. No processions or events of popular rejoicing take place. The power and majesty of EU institutions is not displayed via military parades or staging of exciting political events. Unlike traditional rituals, Europe Day lacks a center, a focal point for a symbolic setting that would give the event an overall meaning. For Foret, Europe Day is a communicative event rather than "a potential matrix for European identity" that shows EU institutions' failure to dramatize the unity of the European family through popular celebrations (2010). It satisfies only one of the four attributes that, according to Elgenius, characterize classic national days (2005: 365): while representing the commemoration of a historical event and thereby contributing to building and shaping collective memory, it is not a public holiday prompting people to perform collective or private rituals. As an annual meeting of the community it fails to be a shared experience, remaining unknown to or unexperienced by most citizens; and it is not effective as the symbol of the human collectivity because collective imaginary is still connected to sovereign nation-states (Foret 2010: 69).

The veneration of Europe's founding fathers and the reenactment of the sacred creation of the European community constitute another pillar of the EU's politics of transcendence. In 2013 eleven "visionary leaders" were officially consecrated as founding fathers of the European Union: Konrad Adenauer, Joseph Bech, Johan Willem Beyen, Winston Churchill, Alcide De Gasperi, Walter Hallstein, Sicco Mansholt, Jean Monnet, Robert Schuman, Paul-Henri Spaak, and Altiero Spinelli. According to the official narrative they accomplished the magic transformation of Europe:

> The Founding Fathers were a diverse group of people who held the same ideals: a peaceful, united and prosperous Europe. … Without their energy and motivation we would not be living in the sphere of peace and stability that we take for granted. (European Union 2013)

As part of the process of the ritualistic veneration of these "fathers," the homes of Monnet and Schuman have been turned into places of worship to European integration (Kølvraa 2012). These museums could be seen as what Foucault portrayed as "heterotopias," real spaces that represent "a kind of effectively enacted utopia in which the real sites, all the other real sites that can be found within the culture, are simultaneously represented, contested, and inverted" (Foucault 1986: 26). They may also be considered as sacred spaces for hierophany, immune to the activities of everyday life, liminal spaces that create a communication between the sacred world and the profane realm where one can experience the feeling of "eternal return" (Eliade 1959) to the founding moment and values of the European community.

The traveling exhibition called "The New Face of the Euro," which presents the Europa series banknotes, the new sacred icon of Eurofederalism, is another example of the EU's attempts to sacralize space. This moving hierophany allows citizens living in different parts of Europe to encounter Tellus Mater that similar to Europe's founding fathers, is attributed to possess a unifying, transformational, and seductive power for which she deserves to be cherished. As José Manuel Barroso affirmed at the Denmark exhibition,

> I think it is very good that the exhibition starts with the kidnapping of Europe. As you know Europe was a very beautiful princess that was kidnapped by Zeus, the god of gods, the head of gods, from what is currently Lebanon. I think Europe, as a beautiful princess, should be treated with respect and admiration. It is great that during this period of your Presidency, you can meet personally Europe at the beginning of this exhibition. (Barroso 2012a)

The success of political rituals is generally determined by the degree of popular enthusiasm they generate. In fact, the elite's goal is always to design political rites that will get people emotionally involved and generate feelings of mystic metamorphosis and a sense of pristine harmony. According to Ian Manners, the EU's rituals are more deeply embedded than the "symbolic totems" of the 1980s and 1990s (2006: 74). For Foret, instead, there is no transcendental dimension to the European polity sufficiently strong enough, neither religious nor political, that could generate a "European liturgy"; symbolic "acquis communautaire" could presently exist to a limited extent, only at the level of supranational elites (2010). Using Bouchard's thesis (2007) that designs the evolution of a successful myth in three stages—diffusion (dissemination of a particular narrative), ritual (when the myth becomes a symbolic practice periodically enacted), and sacredness (when a myth assumes sacred attributes)—Della Sala argues that "the record is mixed with respect to the ritualization and sacralization of myths about the European Union" (2010: 9). European leaders have a hard time becoming a source of sacrality. Their aura is still devoid of the power to bless or maim, to link European citizens to the heavens. If, as Kertzer argues, "the greater the divisiveness in society, the greater the need for compensatory ritual to hold the society together" (1988: 63), then after the 2008 crisis the need for social dramas became even more deeply felt. Rituals maintain order, but when order dissolves, new rituals emerge (Wydra 2009). Instead of waiting for rituals to emerge from below, EU institutions have launched rituals from above to transcend the dividing lines and counteract the troublesome tendencies that plague citizens' daily social lives, bringing all members of the European family together, sanctifying their unity, and restoring the feeling of primordial idyll.

Ritual dramas are becoming core elements in the theater of European politics, with emotions being constantly manipulated on the stage. The goal of Europe's masters of ceremonies is to give rituals a means of generating powerful feelings through the use of various aesthetic elements. EU officials play central and backstage roles in an endless series of public spectacles. Notwithstanding their efforts, relations between supranational policy-makers and the European public are minimal and not dominated by ritual encounters and displays. The EU Commission president's State of the Union addresses and the ECB president's unveiling ceremonies of the new banknotes have not turned into dramatic, effective, public rituals. While carefully staged, they do not attract much attention. Though the euro-bureaucrats are able to pit themselves in ritual combat against the forces of evil, these rituals fail to encourage the belief that they are working on behalf of European citizens, protecting them from the forces of darkness. They fail to shore up confidence in and strengthen the legitimacy of the EU itself. Most European rituals are weak political witch-hunts, seeking to strengthen the sacred community of Eurofederalism and eliminate enemies threatening its success.

To enlarge the community of believers of the political religion and make people internalize the myth of European *palingenesis,* the prophets of Eurofederalism encourage the organization of events that may generate what Durkheim described as a "collective effervescence" and give birth to what Turner portrayed as "communitas," to offer room for carnivals (in a Bakhtianian sense) and generate those liminal moments where the new united and democratic Europe could generate. New forms of rituals had to be invented to allow Europeans to get together, communicate in a shared language, and participate in the same action. This togetherness should generate a strong group feeling—a high degree of emotional excitement, the sensation of being elevated and transported into a new, ideal realm, and the perception of being reborn with extraordinary qualities and power as European citizens. In *Elementary Forms of Religious Life,* Durkheim asserts that the rituals promoting collective effervescence involve the suspension of social norms, allowing new concepts and beliefs to emerge:

> It is no longer a simple individual who speaks; it is a group incarnate and personified. … There are some periods in history when, under the influence of some great collective shock, social interactions have become much more frequent and active. Men look for each other and assemble together more than ever. That general effervescence results which is characteristic of revolutions or creative epochs. (Durkheim 1915/1961: 241)

Events that generate "collective effervescence" have a strong impact on participants' psychic activity. The ritual mobilizes all our active forces, and as a result of the relief of vital energies, it also rallies our passions and strong sensations (some never experienced before): "Man does not recognize himself; he feels somehow transformed and in consequence transforms his surroundings" (Durkheim 1915/1961: 469). At the same time, all the other participants of the ritual feel themselves transformed as if they were transported into a special, ideal world.

Victor Turner's conceptualization of "communitas" (which he developed by elaborating on Arnold Van Gennep's concept of liminality) is intimately linked to Durkheim's notion of collective effervescence. *Communitas* describes a society during a liminal period that is "unstructured or rudimentarily structured [with] a relatively undifferentiated comitatus, community, or even communion of equal individuals who submit together to the general authority of the ritual elders" (Turner 1969: 96). It entails "the liberation of human capacities of cognition, affect, volition, creativity, etc., from the normative constraints incumbent upon occupying a sequence of social statuses" (Turner 1982: 44). People or societies in a liminal phase are a "kind of institutional capsule or pocket which contains the germ of future social developments, of societal change" (Turner 1982: 45).

In Wydra's view, the self-limiting revolution of the Polish Solidarity movement can be seen as a liminal *communitas*: a complex process of spontaneous mobilization, eschatological hope, and reaffirmation of national subjectivity where Poles lived out a short period of empowerment and collective spirit (2009). Elzbieta Matynia identified in the same movement a masterpiece of "performative democracy" where "the self-discovered, autonomously speaking 'I,' the citizen-actors, engaged in an authentic dialogue with the regime, replacing the anonymous, impersonal and 'institutional' way of speaking with concrete, individual, and distinctive voices" (2009: 5). Matynia's performative democracy, "a locally conditioned process of enacting democracy in politically varied contexts" (2009: 3), is similar to carnival as described by Mikhail Bakhtin.

In *Rabelais and his World* (1968), Mikhail Bakhtin portrays carnival as a moment when everything (except perhaps violence) is permitted. It is a type of communal performance characterized by displays of excess and grotesqueness with no boundary between performers and audience. For this Russian thinker carnival creates a situation in which social categories are abolished and everyone is equal, where diverse voices are heard and interact, breaking down conventions and enabling genuine dialogue. Carnival allows for the emergence of an alternative social space: the dominant culture is replaced by an unconventional way of living, marked by freedom, equality, abundance, and playfulness. It provokes an intense feeling of wholeness, unity, metamorphosis, and rebirth, the sensation of being part of a collective body that is continuously renewed. Through these moments of transcendence, the golden age is experienced in thought (and on the emotional level) and enacted by the body.

This carnivalesque atmosphere allows for the overthrow of hierarchic relation; new leaders can emerge. The unofficial becomes official. It can endow people with performative capacities, allowing them to leave behind their fear and frustrations and live joyous and subversive experiences; it releases a robust civic creativity. According to Matynia this particular dimension of political life can occur in democracies (to keep democracy vibrant) or as the early stages of a democratic project, construction sites for embryonic public spheres (2009: 8).

Proponents of the neofunctionalist theory believed that the process of gradual integration (step-by-step moving toward the United States of Europe) would automatically stimulate the transfer of loyalties from the nation-states to the federation. This "unflinching confidence" in the inevitability of the "spillover" effect—the famous "Monnet Method"—explains why EU elites felt little need to involve the peoples of Europe in their project of political engineering; their "passive consent" was deemed "sufficient" (Shore 2001). The prophets of Eurofederalism changed strategy and engaged in the continual creation of a cultic social environment. They attempted to forge the "sacred" through the constant invention of public ceremonies and rituals imbued with symbolic significance and theatrical elements that could allow for the (re)birth of the European community. Some rituals are overtly political (State of the Union addresses), while others appear apolitical (sporting events, exhibitions, or the Eurovision Song Contest) or quasi-religious (Europe days). The old political ceremonies had to be reorganized and new rituals of exorcism had to be invented to provide people not just consolation but (symbolic) empowerment. An aura had to be created where people would see the incarnation of the European family in federalist leaders, the embodiment of a sacred creed, and perceive themselves as actors rather than passive audience members. EU institutions were in desperate need of symbolic mechanisms to restore the illusion of control, participation, rebirth, and return to paradise.

"Carnival," "collective effervescence," "communitas," and "performative democracy" emerge spontaneously and represent temporary phenomena. They have intrinsically creative aspects through which society can be renewed and revitalized; yet they can be as destructive as they are creative. Representing temporally and spatially determined transgressions, they are followed by the restoration of the social order. The theorists of liminality emphasize that such unstable and potentially dangerous conditions, even when created through the performance of a ritual, require the presence of a special kind of "master of ceremonies," an "elite" that is able to keep the sentiments escalated under control and provide leadership for the successful return to normality and order (Szakolczai 2001).

The supranational elite have assumed the role of the master(s) of ceremonies. Their goal is to produce (artificially) from above what should (but does not) emerge spontaneously from below: a European *communitas*. They organize events hoping to provoke a collective effervescence. As we will explore, the 2014 Eurovision Song Contest and the 2014 European Parliamentary elections were seen as rituals that would serve as liminal sources of a new European democracy. The goal was to awaken sleeping citizens and sweep them into a purifying carnival that would exterminate and renew all. These and other rituals have been supposed to create a new meaning of political revolution and popular sovereignty and form the discursive basis of Europe's new political order.

CHAPTER 8

"Rise like a Phoenix"

A New Anthem for (Federal) Europe

Beethoven's "Ode to Joy," known (but not codified) as the European anthem, does not perform what we have identified as rituals' primal function. Its *passive* enactment (citizens can listen to but not sing it) can hardly offer moments of transcendence; except for wholehearted Eurofederalists, few would feel transformed and *one* with the European family upon hearing the score. Conchita Wurst's song "Rise like a Phoenix," winner of the 2014 Eurovision Song Contest (ESC), seems to have a better chance in enhancing a sense of individual and collective purification and rebirth through music. The song contest, more than the official celebrations where Beethoven's "Ode to Joy" is performed, may allow for the (long-cherished) European carnival to take place, reinforcing the emotional bond necessary to make the fantastic European family resurrect and become *whole* and *home* again.

Musical festivals in general construct and/or reinforce cultural meanings, social structures and popular music personas, and/or create icons and myths in the process (Shuker 2013: 51). While the Eurovision Song Contest is no exemption, little attention has been paid to the particular examples of utopian thought and practice it offers, to the fantasies that are evoked in ESC producers' staging of this festival and in singers' performances on stage. Conchita Wurst's "Rise like a Phoenix" embodies today's *zeitgest*: it symbolizes harmony and rebirth that so many long for as well as the ethos of our era—"nothing is impossible." Furthermore, the Austrian singer's performance offers a powerful musical and visual interpretation of the old *and* the new narrative of Europe. With its pathos and ethos, the song engenders in many feelings of ecstasy, harmony, and idyllic pleasure.

While the Eurovision festival offers a wide collection of different musical images and narratives of Europe, it has in recent years endorsed much more explicitly than in the past the cultural dogmas of the European Union. The winners of the 2013, 2014, and 2015 contests have all conformed, to a certain extent, to the federalist narrative and internalized the federalist doctrines: these performances are revealing of a willingness to promote through music the new European ethos and make the new, still top-down-constructed, mythical story accessible to European citizens. More than in the past, the ESC seeks not just to disseminate "European values" but also to strengthen the emotional bond linking together the members of the community. The protagonists of the festival play a central role in the European art of unification; they complement supranational identity-makers' politics of transcendence, conjuring up a fantastic family and creating a *Heimat* where citizens' yearning for wholeness and harmony may be fulfilled. By interpreting the textual, musical, and performative symbolism of the winning song of 2014, I will invite readers to see Conchita Wurst's (partially artificially-generated) mythological figure as the successor of Europa, "the new face of Europe," and as the ideal personification of the federalist dogma who offers with her performance a suggestive ritualization of the supranational cosmogony myth, the sacred anthem that supranational policy-makers have long been searching for.

Throughout history both religious and civic authorities have been aware of the strong power of music on the psyche and have used it for propagandistic purposes (i.e., to disseminate and popularize their messages among the people). Already in Ancient Greece reflections on the metaphysical function of music on human character were circulating. Pythagoras contends that music, like mathematics, offers the soul moments of harmony; it performs a purgative function. Taking inspiration from Orphic religions where music played a central role in rites of purification, he elaborated the idea of catharsis by music and put to the fore its therapeutic function. Pythagoras held that, if used skillfully, music could greatly contribute to health, and he called the medicine that is obtained through music by the name of "purification" (Harap 1938: 155). By producing movements similar to the movements of the soul, music in general was held to exercise a beneficial effect on human manners and lives and even to induce desirable states of the soul. The aim of music is not simply to provoke aesthetic emotions but to transmit a sense of harmony that changes the person who hears it. As Plato points out in the *Timaeus*:

> Of sound and hearing once more the same account may be given: they are a gift from heaven for the same intent and purpose. … All that part of Music that is serviceable with respect to the hearing of sound is given for the sake of harmony; and harmony, whose motions are akin to the revolutions of the soul within us, has been given by the Muses to him whose commerce with them is guided by intelligence, not for the sake of

> irrational pleasure (which is now thought to be its utility), but as an ally against the inward discord that has come into the revolution of the soul, to bring it into order and consonance with itself. Rhythm also was a succour bestowed upon us by the same hands to the same intent, because in the most part of us our condition is lacking in measure and poor in grace. (Timaeus, 47 D-E, in MacDonald Cornford 1997)

In this spirit, Plato called for songs appropriate for men and women, respectively, saying that the state "must assign to them their proper melodies and rhythms." For these reasons, music came to play a central role in education.

Pythagorean and Neoplatonic views on musical aesthetics, in particular on the metaphysical function of music, may help us better understand the use of music in the European politics of transcendence and the choice for a song for Europe.

As Sebastian F. Moro Tornese illustrates, for Neoplatonists, besides producing measure and grace and organizing those thoughts in musical phrase, music evokes emotions that may "open up the receptivity of the soul towards a cosmic openness" (2013: 32). In the context of Neoplatonism, the transcendent unity exists *beyond* the duality of cosmic principles. Through music, the original harmony may be reexperienced, and the primordial unity formed of *peras* and *apeiron* (*limit,* the male aspect; and the *unlimited,* the feminine or motherly aspect) may be restored. Listening to music may become a ritual where the human soul may reenact the creation of the world, as a harmonic process, and restore what Plato defined as order and consonance with itself, thereby returning to the sacred unity and recovering the primordial essence and the spiritual health of the soul. The Pythagoreans practiced purification of the body through medicine and purification of the soul through music. For them, purification had two stages: a hermetic or alchemical healing through music, and a second, higher, purely spiritual or theurgic level inspired by the "anagogic art of Apollo and the Muses" that favors the ascent of the soul, the reopening of a connection between heaven and earth that allows for a deeper spiritual transformation of the soul on its way up toward the One (Moro Tornese 2013: 44). This process of transformation of the soul can be seen as a reenactment of the cosmogonic process, a journey of return to the primordial paradise.

The European art of unification also makes use of music to restore pristine wholeness and bring back the golden age. Supranational policymakers also seek to exploit the inner connection between musical sound and metaphysical principles and consolidate rituals where (sacred) music may function as a privileged, transformative, spiritual tool. In European politics of transcendence music is meant to contribute to restoring harmony in the spirit of Europeans, conjuring up the illusion of a pristine European family, united, peaceful, and joyful. The first European "ritual" that relied on the power of music to perform transcendental functions was the European anthem.

In their 1971 report, the Consultative Assembly of the Council of Europe declared,

> At this crucial hour in Europe's search for her identity, the time has perhaps come to provide her with what she still lacks in the trilogy of symbols by which our States identify themselves: like them she needs her Flag, her day and her Anthem. These will give her the new impetus she needs in order to advance on the road to unity, and she will find therein a resounding expression of her driving force and of her faith. (CACE 1971: 15)

The secretary-general of the Assembly pointed out that similar to the European flag the anthem would represent not just a symbol but "the expression of a myth," and like other symbols and myths it would "lead the world" and "have a profound effect on men" (CACE 1971: 8). The committee could have opted for the "Chant de la Paix," written by a French woman with the goal of appealing to "everyone in the world who desires peace unreservedly and aspires to join forces to bring about the United States of Europe" (quoted in CACE 1971: 3), or for the Prelude to Marc Antoine Charpentier's *Te Deum,* which acquired an iconic status by virtue of its use by Eurovision to introduce numerous broadcasts of political, cultural, and sporting events since 1950. Their choice, however, fell on the "Ode to Joy." Beethoven's *Ninth Symphony* was seen as the musical composition that could best "propagate the ideal" of European unity, spread "the European idea," "inspire the peoples of Europe … with a genuinely European spirit, compounded of generosity, of faith and of fellowship," and "prepare the citizens of Europe to live together in a spirit of solidarity and fraternity" (CACE 1971: 6). The hope was that the "divinely sweet, pure and innocent human melody" (as Wagner described it in his essay in 1870) would enact through music the foundation myth (a *new* European community founded on peace, unity, and prosperity) and perform the above-mentioned purgative, transformative, and integrative functions. To avoid possible fiascos on the journey back to paradise, the Berlin Philharmonic's conductor Herbert von Karajan (whose Nazi past made him a controversial figure) created an arrangement for an instrumental hymn version, eliminating the thunderous opening terror fanfare and the first instrumental recitative of the symphony. While he reduced Beethoven's composition to "a pompous, solemn and almost sacral background to official ceremonies" in his attempt to elevate Europeans and Europe to a higher sphere

(Fornäs 2012), his version also reveals that "the council capitulated to a certain cultural indoctrination" (Clark 1997: 801).

In 2013, president of the European Commission José Manuel Barroso declared that the old European narrative based on peace, fraternity, and prosperity was to be replaced by a new one and shared with European citizens *before* the European Parliament elections of 2014. The European elite recognized that this new story had to be written by authors outside (at least seemingly) of the official realm of Eurofederalism. The New Narrative for Europe, released in 2014 (see chapter 3), reflects the collective thinking of a group of intellectuals and artists; it emphasizes Europe's eternal regenerative force, its ability to resurrect each time it undergoes periods of destruction and trauma. Since new political myths need new storytellers, the new European narrative (still of a top-down construction) also required new storytellers who could induce people to make the myth their own and to keep it alive. The story had to be told in a certain way to fulfill myths' transcendental function. Anthems, including the "Ode to Joy," that tell the old European narrative have capacities for emotionally embodied community-building, but these capacities are typically confined to ceremonial events and do not extend and integrate into everyday life. Awareness emerged that the classical European high-culture tradition had to be transcended. Popular music can perform the affective function of music and triumph where the official anthem fails by appealing to people's emotions and reinforcing collective identifications, but even more importantly by exciting and transforming, thereby creating a fantastic European family where citizens' longing for rebirth may be fulfilled.

The European Broadcasting Union was founded in 1951 with the clear goal of connecting the various parts and people of Europe through media. It launched the Eurovision Song Contest in 1955 to establish a new political community (Pan-Europe) and reinforce the emotional bond that links its members together with the help of music. Popular music was identified as a new tool in the European politics of intimacy despite the fact that it quickly became evident that, while enhancing feelings of togetherness and attachment to Europe, the festivals also revealed and reinforced old ruptures or created new ones, provoking splits in the fantastic European family. In the fifty years of its existence, the Eurovision Song Contest has evolved into the most important European popular festival (with debatable artistic quality of its musical content), besides the UEFA Champions League perhaps, and become a key media event; in 2015, nearly 200 million people watched it (Eurovision 2015). The song contest represents, perhaps, the most effective European ritual. Performed and enacted once a year on a Saturday evening, it interrupts the everyday routine; it performs the function of circus in ancient Rome (Jauk 2015: 21) and creates a carnivalesque atmosphere that allows people to experience moments of transcendence. The tune of Marc-Antoine Charpentier's Prelude to *Te Deum* is the sign that one has to prepare for the magic transformation that will result from hearing and viewing the musical performances. Moments of ecstasy will be experienced while viewing and listening to the performances, voting for and betting on them, or commenting on them by phone or via the internet while celebrating together at parties and special events connected to the festival. Music and entertainment together play important integrating and transformative roles. Collective effervescence, the sensation of being a part of the new pan-European community that is about to be born anew and reflects the primordial idyll, is among the expected outcomes.

Analysis of the Eurovision festival allows us to gain insight not just into how nations view and perform themselves but also into the changing understanding of Europe: "it materializes concepts—Europe and Europeanness—which are otherwise quite abstract and complex" (Fricker 2015: 8). The Eurovision Song Contest has both reflected and served as an engine driving changes in the meaning of Europe and producing a sense of feeling European (Fricker & Gluhovic 2013). According to Cornel Sandvoss, who explores the affective bond that television audiences have built with the ESC by relying on Donald Winnicott's object-theory, the ESC serves as a space of illusionary belonging that challenges the homogenous constructions of home and belonging prevalent in national identity through the disillusionment of a shared and negotiated cultural space, thereby allowing for the formation of a "good enough" Heimat (2008: 190).

At the conference titled "The Promise of the EU," organized by the Italian Department for European Policies and the European Commission in Rome in September 2014, president of the European Broadcast Union (EBU) Jean-Paul Philippot highlighted the role of the European public service, media, in creating a European public sphere and promoting cultural diversity and informed citizenship. He added, "We cannot serve as a mouthpiece of the EU Institutions, but we promote the values that shape the European public sphere and thus provide the EU Institutions with a vital asset for the future" (Philippot 2014).

My argument is that the festival, as much more than a democratic open forum where different definitions of Europe and Europeanness can be playfully performed and debated, seeks to celebrate the official agenda of supranational institutions. Not only does its schedule (defined in yearly mottos) reflect the federalist dogma, it also promotes the federalist credo through an often veiled marketing strategy and by awarding singers that best conform to this narrative. Media commentator Paul Jordan is right in arguing that Eurovision represents a unique form of public diplomacy; it represents "a form of living nationalism" (at a European level). It encapsulates some of the key debates of our time and reveals how the European Broadcasting Union seeks to instill and cultivate certain shared cultural values through its programming (2015: 34–35). The EBU and its core media product, the ESC, *do* endeavor to serve as the mouthpiece of supranational institutions; the winners are among the storytellers of the new European narrative.

The declared mission of the EBU is ambitious. The mission comes from the 2012 "Declaration on the Core Values of Public Service Media," and in the spirit of universality it seeks "to reach … everyone, everywhere," to create a public sphere "in which all citizens can form their own opinions and ideas," and to foster inclusion and social cohesion by enabling all its viewers to engage and participate in a democratic society (EBU 2012: 4). Denoting diversity as one of its core values, the EBU promises to be diverse and pluralistic in the genres they program, the views they express, and the people they work with to support and give voice to a plurality of competing views, thereby contributing to the construction of a more inclusive and less fragmented society (5). The Eurovision Song Contest has been identified as the most suitable arena to perform and promote these ideals and to achieve these goals. The program, in fact, has a mandate not just to entertain but also to educate people about how to become democratic, European citizens. The EBU handbook prepared for the media reveals how this mission is to be accomplished. It defines the ESC as "a strong, clearly defined brand that appeals at an emotional level to millions of Europeans." Its "brand vision" is portrayed as bringing together Europeans through the "ultimate musical event of the year." The "brand values" that singers are supposed to embody and spread are: "SURPRISING: Magical, distinctive, fun; CULTURAL; CONNECTING; EMOTIONAL; and COMPETITIVE" (capitals in the original). Its "brand personality" is described as "a modern classic," while its "brand essence" consists in offering a "positive cultural and emotional experience" (ORF 2015a).

Since 2002, yearly slogans used to publicize the festival and convey its spirit also covertly market political objectives. These mottos are symbols that encapsulate cultural and political messages; often they reflect federalist imperatives. The first slogan, "A Modern Fairytale" (2002, Estonia), was perhaps an invitation directed at participants. At a time when the myth of a reunited Europe (during the preparation for the 2004 enlargement: central and eastern European countries' "return to home") was emphatically diffused by supranational identity-builders, their version of Europe's modern fairytale was reflected in the invitation to create a second (virtual) reality where the "European dream" and people's nostalgia for paradise could be fulfilled. "Share the Moment!" (2010, Oslo), "Feel Your Heart Beat!" (2011, Düsseldorf), and "Light Your Fire!" (2012, Baku) can be seen as solicitations (in evident crescendo) for citizens to feel passionate about Europe.

"We Are One" (2013, Malmö) seems to be the motto of the European art of unification; it was probably meant to convince Europeans that, no matter what people perceive in the turbulent era of crisis (fragmentation, uncertainty, turbulence), dividing lines do not exist; the European family constitutes one whole. Singers' solo performances on the grand Eurovision stage resonated with this European imperative for togetherness/oneness (Bohlman & Tragaki 2013). The internalization of this sacred federalist dogma is best reflected in the spectacle of the winner, Emmelie de Forest. Her song, "Only Teardrops," tells the story of a community torn apart by selfish interests. Emmelie's answer to the dilemma of European unity—"How many times do we have to fight? How many times till we get it right between us? Only teardrops, only teardrops"—may leave us puzzled. It is the music more than the text of the song that seems to provide an answer and facilitate her consecration as the best storyteller of the European tale. The sounds of the military drumbeats evoke the strong vibration of the European soul in times of sweat, tears, and blood, a soul that has lost its original harmony. These drumbeats, however, are followed by the melodic music of the flute. Aristotle maintains that there is a "proper time" for playing the *aulos*: "when the performance aims not at instruction, but at the relief of the passions" (Harap 1938: 161). The melodic lines of the flute (a core element in Dionysus's cult) in Emmelie's song help the Europeans who hear them to restore their soul's lost harmony, reestablish the idyllic conditions they have been deprived of, and reexperience wholeness and pristine pleasure. The Danish singer's *aulos*, as a par excellence organ of pathos, acts as a vehicle that transports Europeans to the gates of paradise with the promise of rebirth, sacred integrity, and the harmonious and joyful existence of the European family.

The motto of the 2014 festival "#JoinUs" (Copenhagen) can be interpreted as a call to action in the year of European Parliamentary elections, a desperate attempt to increase electoral turnout. It can be read as an imperative to join the community of Eurofederalists and as an invitation to singers to provide a visual and musical interpretation of the European narrative of *palingenesis*. "Building Bridges" (2015, Vienna) further strengthens the idea that *crossing the bridge* (see the symbolism of the bridge in chapter 3.), thereby accomplishing a return to paradise, is possible once one adheres to the European soteriology. The logo of the event, The SPHERE (with capital letters), conjures up the fantasy that the contest is a magical place where cosmic changes can occur (including the creation of a European democratic "public sphere" in Habermas's sense). Emanating from Vienna (thanks to the magical light of Europe's new star, Conchita), the event promises to reenact, together with singers and audience, the moments of creation. The SPHERE and the motto epitomize this promise and emphasize not *the thought* but *the fantasy* underlying the motto of "building bridges." The three-dimensional sphere signifies both "the endless versions of this diversity" and the ethos of living without limits in a space where everything is possible. It *is* a unique branding for the sixtieth Eurovision Song Contest, a perfect signifier for the supranational cosmogony project, indicative of federalists' politics of *jouissance.*

The winning song of the 2015 contest explains to "ordinary Europeans" that the heroes who are just about to accomplish the magic acts of transformation and rebirth are "ordinary Europeans" themselves. Måns Zelmerlöw sings what he calls "the greatest anthem ever heard"—"We are the heroes of our time." His inspirational credo is likely to receive a warm welcome in an era characterized by widespread social discontent, disillusionment, and pessimism. It also fits perfectly in the intense political communication campaign launched by EU institutions with the declared goal of facilitating the emergence of a European public sphere and empowering Europeans by making them the protagonists and co-creators of the European family and its magnificent accomplishments. While the phantoms of the past still haunt us—"we're dancing with the demons in our minds"—Måns Zelmerlöw encourages us to rediscover in ourselves our generative and transformational power. Europeans, by identifying themselves with him, will restore their lost inner force and "make worms turn into butterflies." Those who are ready to embark on the mystic journey must be aware of the moment and maintain a sacred silence in anticipation of the return to *illud tempus*—"It's life's creation." They are invited by their hero to pursue their wildest dreams, "Wake up and turn this world around," and sing all together "The greatest anthem ever heard": "We are the heroes of our time."

It is not *only* homosexual spectators who create "an alternative family" and transform the festival into a celebration of values and aesthetics that they hold dear: glamor, fabulousness, underdog stories, and high drama (Fricker 2015: 13). European federalists also use the festival to create *their* fantastic family, to celebrate old and new federalist dogmas, giving birth to a close-knit emotional community where there are no limits to what we can yearn for and what we can reach. Through the (federalist) mottos (that singers are invited to perform) and the performances, the goal is to conjure up a second (virtual) reality, a fantasy world where Europeans can find refuge from the overwhelming circumstances of the present and achieve all that they have been yearning for. The linear crescendo of the list of themes, the 2015 logo, and the winning songs tell the story of Europe in a teleological fashion, as a lineal process toward paradise. More than fostering a mere acceptance of the European *palingenetic* myth, these elements are aimed at making people *feel* its sacred (metaphysical) truth.

"Europe needs a new face"; we hear this repeatedly from supranational identity entrepreneurs seeking to fire Europeans' imaginations and make them feel emotionally attached to the European Union. Neither José Manuel Barroso's face, Herman Van Rompuy's face, Mario Draghi's face, Jean-Claude Juncker's face, nor even Europa's face have managed to evoke in citizens strong enough feelings or offer a powerful personification of "new Europe." In 2013, the Danish European Movement named Emmelie de Forest, winner of the Eurovision Song Contest, "European of the Year" for bringing Europeans together. Yet Emmelie, while performing well as storyteller of the European cosmogony myth, has never been recognized as an icon; an unpleasant fact considering that Europe needs not just a face but an *iconic* face. The European elite have remained faceless to the average citizen. Reflecting a trend that sees committed pop stars (or generous benefactors) rather than accountable politicians emerging as key public figures of a new order, Conchita Wurst, Emmelie's successor and winner of the 2014 festival, triumphed where Emmelie had failed. Conchita was welcomed at the United Nations by Secretary-General Ban Ki-moon as an ambassador for basic human rights as "the star of the world" (United Nations 2014). Her/his victory was ratified by Google Trends as one of the top stories of the year worldwide; her/his books are sold in most libraries and considered by many as useful manuals for individual transformation.

One performance was enough for her/him to emerge as an iconic figure. Similar to the winner of the 2013 contest (and later, the winner of the 2015 contest), Conchita brings onto the stage her/his vision of the European myth of rebirth. The title of the song itself, "Rise like a Phoenix," foreshadows the feeling that what we are going to hear and see is a magic story of sacred resurrection. The text could be seen as an explicit endorsement of the "New Narrative for Europe" document, otherwise called "The Mind and Body of Europe," according to which "The European integration project was born like a phoenix out of the ashes. … But, since the end of World War II, the ideal of a Europe united by the principle of mutual respect and the values of freedom and democracy has brought redemption" (Cultural Committee 2014). Conchita, too, assures us that while her/his past is painful, s/he has transcended the horrors; s/he is back, born anew and ready to "rise like a phoenix out of the ashes" and fly as never before. Trials and transformations, splendors and miseries, traumas and triumphs characterize the body and the mind of Europe and Conchita. The "New Narrative for Europe" document mentions the two world wars, communism, and the 2008 crisis; Conchita refers to a suffering perpetrated by neighbors and otherwise unidentified offenders. Her recounting of the past—"No one could have witnessed/What you did to me," "You threw me down," "neighbors say we are trouble"—calls to mind the deep-rooted European (universal?) tradition we see in verbal and visual (national and supranational) narratives that manifests itself in mythical accounts, the romanticization of history, the externalization of responsibility, the construction of self-image as victim and/or hero. The audience is invited to be part of the performance, to identify with Conchita, and to feel like they are on the right side of history. The song is an ode to (absolute) freedom: it launches a battle against limits, it demands a total liberation from internal and external obstacles, and it invites us to live in an illusionary world and "Act as if [we're] free." Symbolic of her/his longing for infinite and perfect pleasure is her/his flight that knows no limits; she promises to triumph where the builders of the Tower of Babel failed—"Once I'm transformed/ Once I'm reborn/ I rise up to the sky." There are no limits to what she, i.e., Europe and Europeans, can achieve. For those who are hesitant to accept the dogma of absolute politics, for those who fail to feel the anagogic power of the song's text, for those who do not believe in the European promise of rebirth and return to paradise, s/he adds: "you have got to *see* to believe" (my emphasis). This hint brings us to the analysis of her/his *look*.

Her appearance is a real epiphany. She is standing alone at the center of the stage; she *is* the source of light that irradiates from her toward the sky, hieratic, almost immobile, yet passionate in deploying her voice. She is filmed from a distance, a distance that is not just appropriate but compulsory when one has to deal with a godlike figure. We have the impression she shields a mystery or a surprise. The secret is gradually revealed by tracking shots that close with fast zooms on her face and tracking shots from behind that alternate with panning (panoramic) shots on the mass of her adoring believers. The music intensifies slowly, with a catchy crescendo, rich in pathos, representing, together with the scenography and the choreography, a perfect accompaniment of the exhibition. Her plentiful and elaborately styled mane is symbolic of femininity and fertility. She is wrapped up in a white-golden dress, a look that is reminiscent of a siren, a hybrid divinity that in popular imagination has *ittiomorph* features, but that some sources describe as originally *ornitomorph.* Finally, a close-up. The full light reveals the face of this dame. Her eyelashes are extremely long; the lineaments are regular, and, here is the secret: her lips and cheeks are decorated by a virile and immaculate beard. S/he brings onto stage a carefully constructed image of the sexual merging of feminine and masculine elements. Her/his look *and* her/his voice all serve to evoke in the audience the liminal figure of a hermaphrodite. In the successive scenes flames and lapilli rise toward the sky, and tongues of fire behind her/him design two wings. These effects reinforce the perception of experiencing the birth and rise of a phoenix. Neither the performance nor the official narrative reveals the circumstances that led to this magic transformation; no details are provided about the injustices suffered, and thus the roots of the *palingenesis,* too, remain unknown. The audience is comforted by the prophetic figure of Conchita announcing the beginning of a new era on earth. Her/his divine (and monstrous) figure is calm, emotional, strong, tolerant, and determined, and, thanks to the special effects of smoke and wind, s/he flies.

Conchita uses music in conjunction with her/his look and acting on stage to reinforce her/his image as symbol of the herald of a new era of pristine harmony and paradise in Europe. According to Timothy Martin, there is nothing seemingly special or sophisticated about the song. Its structure follows the traditional ABABA form (verse/chorus/verse/chorus/slight bridge/chorus/cadenza). Her/his singing voice is valid as an instrument, and s/he has vocal talent. While many claimed that if it hadn't been for the beard she never would have won, a careful analysis of her voice confutes the idea that her music offers nothing and that the iconic figure of pristine harmony rests only in her look. What is exceptional, says Martin, is her/his unique, androgynous voice characteristic. The voice sits comfortably high; s/he sings effectively soft and full toned. However, the quality of the sound, the timbre, is rather sexless. Although there is warmth and roundness of tone, which one would associate with an adult singer, there is something pubescent about her/his voice. Again, even though her/his voice doesn't lack in vibrato, one doesn't hear a strong core of tone at the center of her/his vocal production. The lack of which resembles that of a *voce bianca* (a child's voice before the age of puberty), the preferred voice type for the sacred singing of the Catholic Church. All of this confounded by her/his look, an angelic voice coming out of a bearded face. As it was for the great castrati of the sixteenth century, her/his sound and physical appearance contradict one another, leaving the audience captivated and spellbound. Certainly, a major aspect of her/his allure is that while s/he performs as a hermaphrodite, a siren, and a phoenix, s/he is neither fish nor fowl, so one can project onto her their wildest imaginations.

Conchita, like other performers on the stage of the festival, seeks to awaken her/his listeners to idealized emotional states. Every aspect of her/his musical composition must reflect the romantic and fantasized vision of paradise and generate in the audience feelings of harmony, hope, love, and joy.

Her/his style evokes sixteenth-century church music. It is as if the 1562 directives of the Council of Trent recommending intelligible words to transport believers into a realm of the holy have inspired her/him.

> But the whole must be managed in such a manner that Masses should be celebrated either simply by the voice or by a chant, so that all should be pronounced clearly and distinctly and make its way undisturbed into the ears and hearts of the hearers. What is customarily rendered with musical rhythms and instruments should have intermingled with it nothing profane but only the divine phrases of hymnody. This entire scheme of psalmody with musical measures should be arranged not for the mere delight of the ears but in such a way that the words should be apprehended by everyone and that the hearts of the listeners should be ravished by longing for heavenly harmony and by contemplation of the joys of the blessed. (Theiner, Acta Concilii Tridentini, 1874, II, 122, cited in Fellerer & Hadas 1953: 576)

Conchita's music follows the sense of the text, and the harmonies adeptly move the heart toward religion and piety and arouse people to devotion. Her/his vocal delivery shows clear enunciation of text and beauty of voice. The ancient doctrine of affects and modes (cherished during the period of the Renaissance) seems to have impacted Conchita. It seems that also the styles, forms, and compositional techniques of Baroque music, and in general, the "theory of affects," have prompted her to carefully plan the emotional content of her/his work and to use all the devices of her/his craft; scales, rhythm, harmonic structure, tonality, melodic range, forms, and instrumental color work together to draw from her/his audience the desired response (excitement, sense of rebirth, and then pristine harmony). S/he sought to sing and perform in an artful and graceful manner so as to move the heart of the listener and to move the affects. Similar to a speaker using the tools of rhetoric, Conchita uses musicality as a musical-rhetorical means to add dramatic musical stress to the song's content and to appeal to her viewers' thoughts, emotions, and fantasies. The musical composition was carefully prepared and put on stage to support effectively her persuasive point. To persuade her audience about the truth of her/his (the European) story of rebirth and return to paradise, s/he had to create an atmosphere with her/his performance that would make people *feel* transformed and united with the sacred.

Those who believe that Conchita won *only* because of her/his beard may be right. The question is: in what sense? The singer made no secret of the fact that s/he felt s/he had a (heroic) mission to perform in Europe and that with her/his song s/he wanted to deliver important political and moral messages. Two months *before* performing on the stage, s/he explained the essence of her/his creed and task:

> For me the most special and honoring thing is that Austria shows tolerance and acceptance and I'm so happy to be this statement. I'm allowed to be the voice of their beliefs during this time and this really makes me very proud. We, and not at least myself, want to stand for a society without hate and discrimination. And if I'm honest, I think everyone of the contestants should stand for the same, cause we are joining a very opend minded [*sic*] project, so they should be open minded too. ... Besides that, I really hope that I get the chance to change some minds all around Europe. I want to show them that you can look whatever you want and that everybody must have the right to live their life however they want it, if nobody gets hurt. (Conchita 2014)

Conchita's clearly defined ambition is to have an impact on people's emotions, behaviors, and even morals. S/he has achieved her/his goal, and today s/he is celebrated as a moral authority, a guide who has received through her/his music a sacred gift from the Muses and the responsibility to restore harmony in the soul and promote civic virtues across Europe (and not only). Her/his "moral competence" emerged (was constructed) during the various televised music and celebrity-based reality shows in which s/he participated in Austria. Her/his ethos became evident as s/he came to be seen as the national icon of tolerance (perfect to banish the counterimage of a country with people nurturing deeply embedded feelings of intolerance and hatred). It is perhaps her/his iconic characteristics that prompted the Austrian national public service broadcaster (ORF) to make less of providing a national selection by *choosing* her to represent Austria in the 2014 Eurovision Song Contest (provoking outrage in many and shedding some light on the EBU's rhetoric of promoting democratic values and the construction of a public space).

Conchita's transformation from national to European hero, her/his consecration as a new moral authority for Europe, occurred with her/his coronation as victor of the 2014 Eurovision Song Contest. The song was probably perceived as beneficial to the European "polis" for its promise of strengthening and spreading "European values" such as freedom, diversity, and tolerance. Many believed that perhaps with her/his music (in line with Plato's beliefs about song) s/he could help cultivate civic virtues, have a purgative effect, teach people to be more tolerant and congenial, more harmonious (in other words, "more European"), and thereby reestablish personal and collective inner harmony in the self and in the European family. Conchita's European triumph reached a global dimension. The reach of her/his sacred mission extended from the European family to include the whole "human family" when Ban Ki-moon transformed her/him into a universal icon. The UN secretary-general called Conchita's victory an "electrifying moment of human rights education" and expressed his delight for her ability to spread her "powerful message" from a Eurovision platform to a global audience (2014). At the (coronation) ceremony he cherished Conchita's promotion of respect for diversity, a "core value" of the United Nations Charter, and talked about the song as a possible anthem for the twenty-first century.

Gender- and sexuality-related issues have always been performed on the stage of the Eurovision festival, and often these issues become important political instruments. Many who support the "beard theory" (which identifies Conchita's immaculately sculpted beard as the primary cause of her/his cultural, political, and/or marketing success) believe that her/his gender narrative, while complex to grasp, is certainly a call to move beyond the (antiquated) binary categories of male and female and to respect diversity. According to Karen Fricker, "tolerant, emotive, unconventional, subversive, progressive" are characteristics that make Conchita "the 'New' European Eurovision winner par excellence," and her performance a "watershed moment in the history of queer Eurovision" (2015: 15).

The term hermaphrodite has been introduced in reference to Conchita only by her critics as an insult. Yet, without using (and understanding the various meanings of) this term, it is impossible to decipher her complex gender narrative (a topic beyond the scope of this study) and to understand the strength of her *political* narrative.

Philosophical and religious traditions point to the hermaphrodite's *dual* nature, at once divine *and* monstrous. It has been seen as the perversion of nature but also as a symbol of perfect and harmonious existence preceding sexual differences. Through history the hermaphrodite's dual nature (perceived as both paradisiacal and hellish) has evoked diverse, often contradicting reactions (harmony as well as confusion), performing sometimes unifying, sometimes disintegrating functions. During the Renaissance, in the realm of medicine, the hermaphrodite was most often seen as an anomaly; it became associated with death, decay, and descent into chaos. This figure of transcendent power, for example, was twisted into a monstrous form and used to denigrate the king of France, Henri III (1574–89) and his court (Long 2006: 24). In a similar spirit perhaps, many depicted Conchita through the visual metaphor of the hermaphrodite to emphasize the degeneration that the singer evoked in them and to criticize Europe. They perhaps imagine the thread linking together her performance, the festival, and the projects of federal Europe. For instance, according to Vitaly Milonov, a deputy member of St. Petersburg's legislative assembly, "The participation of the clear transvestite and hermaphrodite Conchita Wurst on the same stage as Russian performers on live television is obvious propaganda for homosexuality and moral decay." According to deputy prime minister Dmitry Rogozin, "Eurovision showed the eurointegrators their europerspective—a bearded girl" (Golubock 2014).

Yet it is time to highlight that it is Conchita's hermaphroditic look and voice that has made her message as the harbinger of rebirth and the era of pristine harmony in Europe so effective.

The hermaphrodite plays a central role in various foundation myths: in several cosmologies it symbolizes the beginnings when all elements were united in harmony, the period before the cataclysmic rupture that split this unity into several fragments causing universal unhappiness and strife. In prehistoric cults the hermaphrodite "was a figure of divine power, of fertility and procreation, of the union of mother and child"; in Aristophanes's narrative, "in the beginning, there were three sets of double beings, male, female, and hermaphrodite" (Long 2006: 7, 8). African and Indian mythologies abound with images of the hermaphrodite invoking a universal order, a primal union. In Midrash Rabbah we find that before the split in half (before the creation of two separate beings, a man and a woman), "the Holy One, blessed be He, created Adam, He created him an hermaphrodite. … Male and female created He them and called their name Adam" (Gen. 5: 2) . In Hindu cosmology, the Sacred Hermaphrodite is half Father, Shiva, and half Mother, Shakti, complete in their eternal union. The divine nature of the hermaphrodite is emphasized in early Gnostic thought too, where it embodies the Creator of the universe. In the Renaissance, hermaphrodite was associated with the notion of the original, unfallen man. It was a symbol of pristine harmony in Neoplatonic philosophy.

From a psychoanalytical perspective, we could look at the hermaphrodite as symbolic of a pre-verbal, pre-trauma, pre-Oedipal, perfect idyllic stage and consider its appearance and disbursement as representative of (growing) nostalgia for return to paradise.

Conchita's hermaphrodite look *and* voice should also be seen as the reassuring image and the sacred sound of cosmic order and primordial paradise. This visual and musical metaphor helps to give a more effective staging of the European cosmogony project, to reinforce the narrative that depicts her/him as a phoenix, to have a stronger impact on her/his audience, and to better convey the promise of the restoration of the golden age in Europe. Conchita's role consists not just in promoting civic virtues but also in performing a metaphysical function: assisting supranational policy-makers' in their "art of unification" and contributing to their politics of transcendence. Her song may be seen as a result of divine activity that fulfills the primary task of music, recovering what Neoplatonists described as the "unified sound," the marriage of the female and the male aspects. In a period (of post-trauma) when Europe suffers from a "psychological crisis" and Europeans have lost the inner harmony of their soul and forgotten about the divine harmony that the European community had provided for them, Conchita's performance could be seen as a medicine for Europeans to awaken the spiritual seeds in their soul, a *pharmakon* that allows them to recover the primordial state of perfect unity and infinite joy. S/he may confront us with what Rudolf Otto described as "the numinous," the "wholly other," Other (i.e., the transcendent). It appears as a *mysterium tremendum et fascinans*—that is, a mystery before which man both trembles and is fascinated, is both repelled and attracted. Lower levels of the numinous seem to be present in her/his performance, which is "potent and strange, queer and marvelous, horrifying and fascinating, divine and daemonic, and a source of energy" (1958: 39).

Conchita can use her/his hermaphroditic look and voice to impact people's thoughts, feelings, and fantasies in order to strengthen the sacred dimension of her/his mythical narrative of rebirth. With her/his performance s/he can induce people's inner transformation and help them recreate a new cosmos within their soul. A song that can deliver us back to the primal paradise represents a "transformational object" in a Bollasian sense, a substitute for the mother that can return us to pre-separation wholeness and pleasure. It could create the feeling of being at home, where people's "emotional home" and Europe would coincide.

According to Kathleen Long, the hermaphroditic figure can be seen as "a symbol of the end of an order, an era, and of the beginning of a new era ..., the perfect figure for troubled times; an expression of both internal strife and potential solutions to it" (2006: 27, 2). Today, in (another) era of social disorder, uncertainty, and pessimism, the hermaphrodite may symbolize on the one hand a Europe profoundly divided by political and identity-related differences, and on the other the solution, the *puer* bringing rebirth after death, closing an era of crisis and inaugurating the new golden age. The project of the United States of Europe, like the figure of the hermaphrodite, has been described both as monstrous and paradisiacal. It divides citizens, policy-makers, and analysts into those who want *more* and those who want *less* Europe. As a result of the 2008 crisis, the project has turned into a doctrine of salvation, promising by those who profess it the "only solution for Europe," the only possibility for Europe to resurrect and be born anew, ending a period of turbulence and initiating a new era of divine harmony, prosperity, peace, unity, and perfect enjoyment.

Unlike the European Union's official anthem that was purposefully disencumbered of ambiguity, "reducing the hybrid mobility of the original to a unitary and static expression close to the idea of Europe as a closed and self-sufficient fortress" (Fornäs 2012), the unofficial anthem places hybridity and ambiguity on the altar. The "true" nature of her/his hybridity and ambiguity is and will remain debated. Some believe the hermaphroditic look and voice of Conchita represent the result of an authentic inner transformation; others believe they have been artificially constructed for show business following the tradition of marketing and fashionable "ethical norms," and some believe they are part of an artistic performance. However, since we are talking about a mythical narrative, we should not ask ourselves whether it is *true* or not, but whether it *functions* or not, and whether it evokes feelings strong enough to perform myths' (symbols' and rituals') transformational, integrative, traumatolytic, and anagogic functions. "Ode to Joy" does not resonate within Europeans deeply enough to affect their heart rate or breathing. The musical experience of listening to the official anthem does not strengthen the emotional bonds with others members of the European family. Neither does it establish for most of those who listen to it the feeling of being connected to the divine.

"Rise like a Phoenix," on the other hand, could be seen as a perfect musical accompaniment to the *new* European narrative, a sacred anthem for the new European political religion—an "Ode to the Eurofederalist myth of *palingenesis*." The elevating effect of the song is not confined to the supranational elite: "Rise like a Phoenix" is more likely to promote personal and group catharsis, the feeling of an individual and collective transformation, and transport those who internalize its dogma to the (long-desired) paradise. While most of Eurofederalists' archenemies (far-right supporters and homophobes) will deprive themselves of this transcendental experience and hence from access to Europe's nascent fantastic family, the anagogic power of the song for "true Europeans" (who uphold the European values s/he supposedly symbolizes) will be strong. Being a messenger of the divine spheres, s/he is ready to share with Europeans the gift of the Muses and transform them with her song, restoring Europe's body and soul, lost in the turbulent era of the 2008 crisis. Her/his overall performance (the text, her look, and the music) expresses harmony as a recovery of primordial unity, elevates Europe and Europeans to the realm of divine, and reconnects their soul with the sacred primordial paradise, bringing them back to Thalassa, the pre-trauma idyll of perfect unity with the mother.

Conchita and federalists conjure up a fantasy world in which everything is possible and where all dreams can turn into reality. As Tim Martin explains, the predominance of orchestrated string and percussive instruments give the song anthem-like, heroic qualities. These qualities, however, are overshadowed by melancholic minor musical chords that do not allow for a sonorous atmosphere of secure victory, a victory without more battles to come.

The federalist discourse based on the Manichaean division between good and evil leaves no room for beings with a complex, nondual nature. Those who have deified Conchita have silenced the ambiguity of her/his appearance and overlooked the monstrous side of the hermaphrodite. They have denied its *unheimlich* nature and chosen only to consider and cherish its paradisiacal traits. The moments of harmony offered by Conchita (just like the instants of idyll by the federalist project s/he symbolizes) appear to be uncertain, ephemeral, and hunted by uncanny elements.

CHAPTER 9

THE 2014 ELECTIONS OF THE EUROPEAN PARLIAMENT

PREPARING FOR A EUROPEAN CARNIVAL

EU citizenship policies, like cultural policies, offer federal institutions the means to control a process of socialization and enforce a sense of democratic legitimacy to conduct politics of transcendence. A sacred dogma in Eurofederalist discourse is EU citizenship. Defined broadly as an identity and an allegiance not just as a legal concept, it has come to be seen (together with common European culture) as one of the missing pieces of the puzzle, the last trial before completing the project of *palingenesis*. A massive communication campaign was launched via both traditional and social media to create the right climate for the 2014 elections to the European Parliament, to increase media interest and eventually electoral turnout, to raise awareness of EU citizenship rights and the functions of the European Parliament, and to kindle imagination. Video ads were released to allow citizens to experience in their real life and in the domain of the virtual the effervescent experience of being and acting like European citizens. The videos were meant to encourage people to participate in a European carnival and make them feel as though they had been transported, together with the other members of the community, into a special world.

For one of the key prophets of *palingenetic* ultra-Europeanism, Vivian Reding, citizenship is not just about an "action," the act of voting; it is a "state of mind," something that exists 24 hours a day, 7 days a week, 365 days a year (2013b). In scholarly literature, citizenship is seen as representing more than a formal arrangement or legal status granted by institutions; "citizenship is not just a certain status, defined by a set of rights and responsibilities. It is also an identity, an expression of one's membership in a political community" (Kymlicka and Norman 1994: 352). Citizenship is about being, acting, and enacting. It refers to a "lived experience" that involves multiple identities as well as individual and social practices. It is something that allows individuals to "enact" themselves as European citizens (Isin & Saward 2013: 66). According to a Policy Review that summarizes the conclusions of a range of EU-funded research projects in the fields of citizenship, European identity, political participation, and democratic governance, EU citizenship has three constant elements: appurtenance (the feeling of belonging to the polity), passive citizenship (protection by the polity), and active citizenship (participation in the polity) (European Commission 2013a: 14). It has affective, protective, and participatory aspects, and, unlike national citizenships that presuppose peoples' rootedness, it is intimately linked to citizens' mobility and to border crossings (ibid.).

Let's now open the window to psychoanalysis and political anthropology as lenses though which the affective aspects of EU citizenship, the feeling of belonging to the EU, could be examined. Szakolczai defines citizenship as a form of political allegiance based on the experience of being at home (2008b: 67). From the Hungarian social theorist's perspective, the concept of home incorporates spatial coordinates, material objects such as the room, the house, the physical surroundings, and also siblings, relatives, and acquaintances. The feeling of "home" is defined as the "centre and the background of the life experiences of any child, the place and the substance of what happens with him/her," whose lack has profound marks on any child (2008b: 62–63). Szakolczai reminds us that according to ancient Gnostic psychodramas, creation was the work of an evil demiurge; it represented the enclosing of the spirit into the prison of the body, which, as a result of its "fall," can never be "at home" in the "world" (2008b: 61). Drawing on Heidegger and Voegelin, he reiterates the argument that one cannot feel at home in the world, especially not in our modern world that turns liminality from a temporary into a permanent state (Szakolczai, 2000: 215–26). He portrays today's modernity as a peculiar form of "permanent liminality" that is characterized by continuous testing of limits, ceaseless drives toward overcoming traditional boundaries, and attempts to turn the world into a permanent carnival, which results in an existential sense of alienation and a prevailing sense of loss of being-at-home. The success and the ineradicable nature of nationalism, he says, stems from the valorization of the nation-state as a home.

The cultural and psychological dimensions of the meaning of our dwelling on earth and the attempt to explain the human yearning to feel at home in the world have been explored from a psychoanalytical perspective too (Hill 1996, Lichtenstein 2009, Seiden 2009). For Henry M. Seiden, home is a concept, a state of mind that "reflects belonging, safety, self-definition, comfort, and unquestioned acceptance," "a place, a time, a family, and a culture" (2009: 204, 200). Home is not something we have or possess but rather something within which we dwell, a spatial, temporal, and emotional enclosure. The analysis of heroic and quotidian sources prompted him to consider mourning for a lost home, and the real and the symbolic efforts to return home, as a universal human quest. He thus proposed the replacement of Oedipus with Odysseus as the figure from antiquity most representative of the universal psychological experience of human beings (2009: 191).

For Edmund Burke, the European home existed in the eighteenth century:

> In the whole form and fashion of life, no citizen of Europe could be altogether an exile in any part of it. There was nothing more than a pleasing variety to recreate and instruct the mind, to enrich the imagination, and to meliorate the heart. When a man travelled or resided for health, pleasure, business or necessity, from his own country, he never felt himself quite abroad. (Burke 1841: 299)

The European integration process has been driven by the goal of building a new house where citizens could dwell and feel at home; the idea of a European family has gone hand in hand with the understanding of the European community as a meta holding environment, a new home. Eurofederalism has always been modeled on the Homeric theme of the hero's quest for home and has spurred endeavors to bring citizens' souls back home into the world and to restore their inner harmony. Some have no doubts about the existence of a European home; "What European," asks Fontaine "would not feel at home visiting Europe's high spots of culture and savoir-vivre?" (1991: 44). Former Italian prime minster Enrico Letta seems to suggest that the Nobel Peace Prize was assigned to the EU for its transformational power and for its ability to offer a home-feeling:

> In 2012 we all were awarded with the Nobel Prize, though perhaps we were not fully aware of it. The European Union was awarded for its unprecedented political alchemy: the transformations of the remnants of a war-torn continent in a space of peace. … Together with the students who left in 1987 for the first Erasmus, we discovered that we have new homes and new families. Europe is our journey. … The port towards which our journey is directed is the United States of Europe, and our ship is called democracy. … We have the right to a dream which is called Political Union, and we have the duty to make it more clear. (Letta 2013)

When Vivian Reding asserts that the Treaty of Maastricht created an "incomplete union"—"We built a house without a solid foundation. And the crisis brutally exposed this fault" (Reding 2013c)—she apparently expresses her regret for European policy-makers' failure to complement the nascent monetary union with fiscal and political integration. Yet she might also allude to the fact that with the creation of the European Union in 1992, a new house based on three pillars was built, but this house did not offer its inhabitants a home-feeling. Maastricht invented the legal concept of European citizenship, but notwithstanding its benefits for private individuals, consumers, residents, students, workers, and political actors, most did not feel as though they were European citizens; the EU did not become a spatial, temporal, and emotional enclosure for people. A series of citizenship policies have been launched since Maastricht with the (implicit) promise of transforming Europe into a home. The hope has been to establish a sacred space that would lend a sense of history, boundaries, intimacy, and belonging to the people, evoking a certain back-to-home sentiment, a return to the mother, a restoration of the primordial idyll experience.

Today the federalist discourse seems to adhere to the definition of home (old and new) provided by Henry Seiden. According to Seiden, the elements of the story of leaving one's original home and finding a new home are: "an original home supporting an original, authentic sense of identity; [and] a necessary and inevitable leaving of one's home (and therefore loss of it) in the service of a new self and new authenticity" (2009: 199). Federalists seem to associate with the European home an "authentic sense" of "European identity" and consider return to Europe—i.e., homecoming—a religious duty. Their narrative is replete with the theme of making a new home with reborn citizens that transcends the elements of the original (national) home and of the original (national) identity, creating something completely new, sui generis: an authentic European home where citizens can experience an authentic European identity.

Yet David Lichtenstein is right in emphasizing that home and identity always partake of invention and imagination (2009). Lichtenstein refers to Jacques Lacan's theories to show that neither exists without the ideal, which is never real in itself. According to Lacan, the "imaginary order" emerges out of the mother/child dyad and manifests itself in the mirror phase, a fantasized realm of wholeness. During the first encounter with the mirror, the infant suddenly finds himself in front of his image as a whole in place of the fragmented entity he previously experienced. The image itself in the mirror is described by Lacan as the ego ideal, the "Ideal-I" (Lacan 1949: 2), an image of completeness and coherence. The ego is constituted through the infant's internalized image of the Ideal-I; thus, from Lacan's perspective, ego-formation is profoundly imaginary. Due to the denial of loss, fragmentation, and difference, it is based upon narcissistic misrecognition. This imaginary wholeness is the paradigm of identity throughout our lives. Our true being remains divided and only approximately coordinated at best. Our identity or self-image rests upon an image of wholeness and authenticity that is a fiction, albeit a necessary fiction. Lichtenstein, like Szakolczai, is right in emphasizing that exile and loss are the real conditions of life; unlimited satisfaction is the fiction (2009: 457).

Authentic European identity, something federalists call for, has more to do with Lacan's "imaginary" than with his "symbolic order." Like the mirror image, it provides citizens an ideal image of wholeness that is devoid of any relation to citizens' real, fragmented experience of being and reflects instead their yearning for pristine harmony. Federalists deny that, similar to identity, the very idea of the original sacred home and a new idyllic home are inventions, echoing and responding to human longings rather than factual reality. Not only will the new home never be like the old one, the new home will never match perfectly what we have been dreaming of. There is no return to primordial (imagined) idyll; the return is always to a new and transformed situation. As Seiden emphasizes, the ancient *Odyssey* is a metaphor for all our human odysseys, but the epic story also sheds light on the impossibility of these human odysseys to be perfect completions; Odysseus does return to Ithaca, but, significantly, to a home transformed (2009: 196). Supranational masters of ceremonies do not acknowledge the inevitable impossibility of a complete return; they cherish instead the logic that "nothing is impossible," promising to transform Europe into the paradisiacal land reflecting the sacred original idyll. The European home is part of a narrative that serves to create the feeling of a safe enclosure. Return to the European home is seen as a realization of the project of *palingenesis,* the fulfillment of the European art of unification.

Yet the valorization of the EU as a home has not managed to supersede the valorization of the nation-state as a home. So far, no authentic attachment has been established between supranational elite and people. Despite intense cultural and citizenship policies, emotional mobilization has not occurred. European policy-makers still continue to struggle to respond to people's lust for transcendence, to transport them into a special world. The EU does not seem to offer a special space where citizens could orientate themselves or feel safe and emotionally attached to the other members of the European family. With the beginning of the 2008 crisis, many experienced a shattering of the integrity of their already fragile European holding environment/home. Since then, citizens' gradual alienation from the European Union has deepened further, signaling the evaporation of the sacred space and people's moving away from a house that offers no home-feeling. What steps has the EU taken recently to build political allegiance on broad, social, emotional bases?

Modern-day elections may be seen as the contemporary manifestation of ancient rites of authority and "royal entry." Despite politicians' attempts to stage the transparent and uninhibited nature of the roles, modern-day political rituals, particularly the elections, evoke ancient rituals of installations and successions. Similar to nation-states where the most important ritual of legitimation is the election (Kertzer 1988: 49), in the European Union, on its way to becoming a mature democratic polity, voting is seen as the main source of legitimacy and the most efficient way to provide authority. The European Parliamentary elections and their preparation phase, including the selection of candidates, the selection of electoral manifestos, campaigning, and media coverage, have structured a liturgy. Many associate elections to a European ritual where European citizens, while discussing European issues and casting their vote, enact EU citizenship and contribute to the creation of a European public space and to the strengthening of a common sense of belonging.

Yet since 1979, EP elections have not turned into an effective, collective ritual. There is no standard European electoral system; the rules of the game are established following national rules. Each state can establish the day of the elections in a predefined period of time. EP elections do not solicit the same acts at the same moment because they do not follow uniform calendars and electoral rules, and because citizens do not cast their vote on the same European transnational groups but on national parties. In academic literature, EP elections are portrayed as second-class national elections. Citizens know little about the EP and about party groups, and candidates are rarely selected from the most charismatic policy-makers. Elections' attractiveness has declined. The lack of interest and lukewarm enthusiasm is manifested in low turnout (62 percent in 1979, 56.67 percent in 1994, 49.51 percent in 1999, 45.47 percent in 2004, 43 percent in 2009) (Finizio, Levi, Vallinoto 2011: 28) and in the weak media attention given to the election. The Europeanization of political discourses and the possible emergence of a truly European political vocabulary have been hindered by the weakness of transnational manifestos as well as language barriers, low levels of competency among citizens regarding European affairs, and the predominance of national factors in terms of the decisions of citizens. The level of the ritualization of European elections, according to François Furet, is weak because European elections do not create a specific temporality, a time of promises and projects; they do not break with normality (2010). The enactment of some forms of codified behavior does not provoke much effect (2010: 25). The vote does not have the role of sanction and revival. The ritual humiliation of rulers, as illustrated by anthropologists, does not occur; the relation of domination between politicians and masses is not inverted, not even temporarily. Finally, unlike national elections, EP elections have not produced specific discursive resources (metaphors, key words, slogans) with strong symbolic meaning.

The (partial) awareness of these weaknesses drove supranational institutions to launch a massive awareness and informational campaign in preparation of the 2014 elections. This was a desperate attempt to turn the EP elections into a sacred ritual, to evoke the feeling of a carnival (albeit only for the followers of the federalist doctrine), and to make the concept of EU citizenship come alive. The 2014 EP elections came to be portrayed by the prophets of the federalist soteriology as a ritual of installation (citizens anointing MPs and the president of the European Commission); an opportunity to enlarge the community of their believers as a means to retell narratives on the origins, the present, and the future of the European Union; a special event evoking collective effervescence and giving birth, at least momentarily, to a European *communitas*. The federalist narrative depicted the 2014 EP elections as a sacred purification ritual that would eliminate the enemies threatening the birth of new (federal) Europe. Speaking in Athens, Commission president José Manuel Barroso signaled that the EU would use the centenary of World War I to warn that Euroskepticism, far-Right, and populist anti-European parties could bring war back to Europe. In a speech to the EP in January 2014 he said:

> We are seeing, in fact, a rise of extremism from the extreme right and from the extreme left. We must, however, make sure this campaign is an opportunity for more genuine debate about Europe, not a festival of unfounded reproaches against Europe. (Barroso 2014)

Viviane Reding asserted that a campaign for the European Union to become a "United States of Europe" would be the "best weapon against the Eurosceptics" (2013 a). To increase tension and the illusion of a period of imminent catastrophe, where federalism represented the only salvation, she declared that it was decision time: "Europe is at a cross-roads," so much so that voting is "more crucial than at any other European Parliament election."

The official communication campaign launched on 10 September 2013 with the slogan "This time it's different, Act React Impact" lasted until the instauration of the European Commission president by the newly elected Parliament. It represented perhaps the most ambitious citizenship policy, the most evident attempt to transfer citizens' allegiance from nation-states to the EU. The campaign, designed with marketing tools and rich in cinematographic elements, had four parts

(European Parliament 2013a). Phase one started with the presentation of the inspirational credo "Act. React. Impact." and the introduction of the scene: the European Parliament was portrayed as the house of European democracy where citizens can dwell with serenity, feeling and acting like equal members of the European family. Phase two, from October 2013 to February 2014, was designed to address key family issues: the economy, jobs, quality of life, money, and relations with other members of the human family. Phase three served to prepare the event of the initiation ritual (EP elections). In the final phase, the coronation of Europe's new leaders was to take place.

The plot of the coronation drama is still accessible on the website of the European Parliament. The moral of its story is that the European Union is a human community by, of, and for EU citizens, and that citizens and the European Parliament represent a sacred dyad whose power, if the unity is solid, is virtually limitless. In terms of the language adopted, the most evident characteristic of the story is the use of the second person. The European Parliament

> decides on the European laws that affect *you*, … on how *your* money is spent. … It is *your* parliament who will elect the head of Europe's executive, based on *your* wishes. … *You* can influence the decisions that touch *your* own life. … *You* can start something or end something. … *You* can act and take all matters big and small into *your* own hands. Choose which Europe *you* want. In the end, *you* decide what happens. … The European Parliament represents each and every one of *you* and acts on *your* behalf. Our decisions are based on what matters to *you*. … *You* can make a real difference. … Share *your* thoughts and react. … The European Parliament is here to react to *your* demands and to fight for the things *you* really care about. … Through the European Parliament, *you* have more power than you think. *You* make a direct impact on everyone's future and more importantly: on *your* own and on the future of the next generations too. Each of *your* actions and reactions ultimately lead to results. … The European Parliament's responsibility is to make it work for everyone, including *you*. Not just to make a real difference for *you*, but with *you*. (European Parliament 2013b)

The language of this text is reminiscent of advertising discourse in which the use of pronouns is one of the most distinctive features (Cook 2001: 157). The EU narrative, like a publicity ad, is filled with second-person references either via second-person pronouns (you, your, yours) or through the imperative tone such "act react impact!" Using second-person reference creates an intimate atmosphere like a face-to-face conversation (Torresi 2010: 128). The frequent use of second-person pronouns in the EU communication campaign serves not just to involve audiences' attention but also to bring citizens closer to the European

Parliament, to create an intimate atmosphere between people and the supranational elite, to highlight the indissoluble link binding citizens to the European Parliament, and to conjure up the illusion of a close everlasting bond. The conversational tone established by second-person reference serves to fulfill people's yearning for recognition, protection, love, their need to communicate and be active participants of their community, and their desire to feel powerful. The endeavor to evoke the idyllic relationship between mother and infant through the creation of an intimate communicative situation becomes manifest in the continuous invocation of the term "together":

> This time it's different. *Together* we now have more power to make a difference. The European Parliament and *you*. *Together* we can act, react and have an impact. … No, not everything can happen overnight, but one thing is for sure: *together* we can get it done. … The decisions we make *together* have an impact on the day-to-day life of over half a billion European citizens. (European Parliament 2013b)

The oversimplified language, the use of succinct and short words, sentences, and paragraphs, the omnipresence of second-person pronouns, and the imperative tone are meant to engrain the supranational elite's vision of the European Parliament, EP elections, and European democracy in general in people's minds. The gratification of audiences' needs, their emotional involvement, and the illusion of political empowerment is meant to enhance the internalization of the advertised product—the EP as a democratic institution, of, for, and by the people—and to spread the ideology of Eurofederalism. While officially a call for action, the style transforms the call into a demand. Citizens are prompted to assume a monopolistic position and decode the message as it was encoded, i.e., to see the elections as an opportunity to act, react, and impact—in other words, to enact citizenship and to see the EP as a powerful and efficient democratic organ that acts in the "collective interest of Europeans."

To understand more about the fantasies underlying the EP's communication strategy, it's worth taking a glance at the poster publicizing the EP elections (European Parliament 2013b). The image on the EP's website ornaments the text that describes the plot of the campaign. It captures the (liminal) moment when a young woman and a man, whose bodies and faces are covered in mud, are just about to kiss each other. What is the promise of the European Parliament sealed in this picture? The poster grabs the attention of passersby and encourages them to look. It uses the saga's principle characters, young people, and establishes the plot through an iconic design. The image doesn't have a unique style; it borrows heavily from photos taken at the Woodstock festival, at the festival in Glastonbury commemorating the 1969 event, and the Eurowoodstock—the Sziget Music festival organized in Budapest every August on the Island of Freedom. Pictures of young couples covered in mud have assumed an iconic meaning and become symbolic of carnivalesque musical festivals. The EP poster gives a glimpse into what the story is about: the model for EP elections is not the Eurovision Song Festival but the muddy festivals of Woodstock, Glastonbury, and Budapest. The promise of the EP is to transform Europe, at least for the period of elections, from an ordinary space into a temporary, unique, spectacular, and sacred environment created for and by European electors. The hope was to give birth to another mud festivity based on the utopian ideals of peace, love, and happiness. EP elections were to become an event that would foster a sense of community, comradeship, and the sharing of experiences, and where the boundaries between different social roles and nationalities and the boundaries between the elite and citizens would be broken down. If what makes a musical festival a special and unique community is the "'youtopian' vision of people being themselves, together" (Larsen & O'Reilly 2009), then it comes as no surprise that between 22 and 24 May Europe was to become a social space in which electors were supposed to reveal who they are, what they believe in, and to express their views about the future of Europe.

The image of a couple covered in mud on the verge of kissing is certainly meant to emphasize the human characteristics of the EU and inject some emotions into what is often seen as a lifeless and boring technocratic organization. It may even evoke the atmosphere of Woodstock, vibrating with sexuality, and the atmosphere of carnival where there are no limits to enjoyment. For a few days Europe can turn into the Land of Cockaigne. Yet it also promises something sacred beyond the simple fulfillment of profane needs. The energies released in these festivals may be seen as divine, cosmic energies capable of generating the feeling of a return to paradise juxtaposed against the overwhelming conditions of everyday life. In the discourse of *palingenetic* ultra-Europeanism, the EP elections may evoke spirituality that could manifest in the presence of a mysterious, palpable, benign force able to gather every elector together for the event. This transcendental force would be strong enough to "neutralize" (even transform?) "populists" and "nationalists" who, it is feared, would threaten the collective rebirth as true Europeans. The poster seeks to trigger excitement and desire and create a strong incentive. The incentive is that in order to participate in the European carnival and experience moments of unlimited love and individual and collective transcendence, the person looking at the poster needs to participate in the elections. EP communication experts wanted to convey with one single, iconic image the central idea of EP elections as carnival, but they failed to produce a powerful marketing tool. The poster didn't become recognizable for electors; it hardly sprang to mind as soon as one was talking about EP elections.

The text describing the plot on the EP website is, to use Umberto Eco's term (1981, 1984), "a closed-text." To open it up (at least a bit), European institutions released various videos. Carefully arranged video ads heavily laden with well-choreographed symbols and reflecting the federalists' Manichean worldview were launched to bring the dramatic, staged story of *palingenesis* into people's homes and to spread the idea that Europe was at a crossroads and the Unites States of Europe presented the only salvation. The first video, "Nine Months and Counting" (European Parliament 2013c), tells the story of a special pregnancy that is supposed to lead to the (re)birth of European citizens. Othmar Karas, European People's Party (EPP, AT) and vice-president responsible for communication, underlines the need to provide people with information because "many misunderstandings exist about the decision-making role of the European Parliament." Anni Podimata (S&D, EL), the other EP vice-president responsible for communication, specifies that these elections are "the most crucial elections in European history, because of the difficult environment of the crisis." Citizens' (lack of) relationship with the EP is symbolically captured through the setting. In the video, interviews with EU officials are staged inside the building, and interviews with EU citizens are staged outside the building. However, the "strong message" the campaign seeks to engrain in citizens' minds is the opposite. The goal is to create the illusion that citizens are *inside* the building, that they "have the power and the possibility to reshape Europe" and work in close contact with MPs for the common good. No cathartic music, no carefully staged scenes, no special effects are used. The shots are simple, even amateurish. The video is more like a short documentary film showing life as usual.

"How It Works: Electing Europe's Future" (European Parliament 2013d) is a product from the first stage of the communication campaign; its goal is to the teach citizens the role of the EP in order to "eliminate the misperceptions" (i.e., visions of the EP that do not coincide with the image of a powerful, efficient, democratic institution). The video has the same structure of an animated educational video for kids. A reassuring female voice guarantees the presence of a mother who loves, protects, and imparts lessons. Every sentence is short and simple to make sure that cognitive barriers disappear. This video shows no real human beings but uses puppets drawn in the most elementary style. Citizens are depicted as faceless and emotionless. They all look the same. The only difference is in gender which is revealed by either a skirt or trousers. There is no background music that could distract viewers and divert their attention from the encoded messages of the video. For the same reason the scenes are left very simple; there is no room for details, complexities, or ambiguities. The journey toward the elections is portrayed through perhaps the most banal metaphor: the road. Each country is represented by a car. All the cars look the same; the only change is in their (uniform) color. It is as if countries were seen as unitary actors whose actions on the stage of international politics are not influenced by internal factors, as if countries represented homogeneous utopian units devoid of internal complexities and cleavages. In a similar, dull manner, a car race, signified with cars arriving to the finish line at different times, serves to explain that countries are free to set the election day within a fixed period (22–25 May). To demonstrate the act of voting, some stylized and anonymous shapes insert their ballots in a box, out of which the members of the European Parliament materialize. The imperative to vote (characteristic of some countries) is represented by a police car chasing some automobiles with its sirens on. A rectangular road sign stands for the 2009 European elections, while a triangular road sign indicates the average voter turnout.

The educational video then features a brochure to explain the rules of exercising passive and active electoral rights. The name that appears on this sheet is John Doe. MEPs are represented through the metaphor of the blue cars. Jubilant citizens stand beside the road as they pass and we see them celebrating MEPs who represent, as the video narrates, "the interests of all of Europe's citizens." Their magic metamorphosis, a change in identity, mentality, values, and interests, is symbolically portrayed through the uniform color of the blue cars. The final scene shows the shapes of the members with their briefcases ready to start their work for Europe. "The work can commence for those representing Europe's citizens"—anticipating the European leaders' coronation.

The reference to the name John Doe is an element that reveals once again the EP's preference for American marketing experts in the preparation of the communication campaign. John Doe is in fact the fictitious name widely used in the United States to indicate someone whose identity is either unknown or must not be revealed. Its use became obsolete in the UK (the only country in Europe where it had circulated) in the second half of the nineteenth century. John Doe may call into mind the American dramatic comedy directed and produced by Frank Capra, *Meet John Doe* (1941). Europe's supranational entrepreneurs might have found inspiration in the film in which a newspaper columnist unwittingly creates a political campaign and in which the John Doe philosophy has the capacity to spread across the country and develop into a powerful grassroots movement with the slogan "Be a better neighbor." Indeed, the goal of Europe's official storytellers is to appeal to the everyman with the motto "together" and produce a narrative that is eloquent and shows affection for citizens as well as sensitivity and responsiveness to their pain as the protagonist in Frank Capra's film.

Or, viewers familiar with American pop culture might recall the episode "Transfigurations" of the science fiction television series *Star Trek: The Next Generation* (season three, episode 25). The EP video perhaps suggests that we should draw a parallel between European citizens and the stranger in the show who wakes up with no memory of his life or identity. Though suffering from severe pain, John Doe is capable of emitting bright energy bursts and using this energy to heal injuries. Once he regains his memory he reveals that his race has reached a new stage in evolution in which they are evolving into beings of energy. John is the first to undergo this magic metamorphosis and to become invulnerable. The end of the episode suggests that John returns home so that his fellow Zalkonians have the chance to evolve and join him. Drawing a parallel between the European Parliament's and *Star Trek*'s John Doe, the video ad might put forward the idea that despite lacking a collective memory, and despite being unaware of their common roots, European citizens may still possess a magical healing power. The video seems to anticipate that once people recover their memory and understand who they are and where they belong (to the European family), they may reach another stage of civilization, have an anagogic power, undergo a true transformation, and have the ability to enlighten others.

A product from the second phase of the communication campaign that seeks to bring core European issues to the center of public debate is "Europe, your vote counts" (European Commission 2013d). It addresses topics such as the economic crisis, banking union, European financial transaction tax, European army, immigration policy, and environmental protection. Twelve people illustrate their views on these issues in a few seconds. The video follows a binary structure staring six common people in favor of greater integration and six against. The declared message of the video is that through voting we "can create the Europe we want." The encoded message is that the EP respects diversity (individuals differ in their opinion, gender, age, and physical aspect) and succeeds in creating unity in diversity. This feeling is emphasized with the jovial music and the twelve protagonists who are calm and peaceful, twelve symbolizing the number of stars on the European flag as well as cosmic unity and harmony. What disturbs this carefully created idyll is the static binary structure, protagonists' artificial (sometimes even embarrassed) posture, their emotionless expressions, and the impression that they are reading their comments rather than expressing their thoughts spontaneously. Everything is rigid; the video offers no room for authenticity, imagination, or playfulness.

The structure of the video and the attitude of the protagonists are revealing of the supranational elite's tendency to reason in dichotomous structures, in which one set of concepts tends to dominate and exclude the other (good vs. evil, unity of disintegration). The EU elections seem to be portrayed as a referendum about *more* or *less* Europe, as the definitive battle between two (utopian) visions—USE and populism. In the video, one position runs next to the other, and the binaries never meet. The protagonists do not have an exchange; they do not try to convince each other or let their own positions be challenged by others'. No room is offered for the exploration of the curves of inter-coexistence; the different positions exist next to each other but do not truly coexist. The protagonists stand on their own and do not form a community. Their performance is based on the absoluteness of the dichotomous conceptuality and is immune from the logic of play. The video offers no hope for a playful exchange where paradoxes are tolerated and dichotomous oppositions become interpenetrated by each other. It anticipates instead a split-off intellectual functioning, an aggressive fight with each side trying to impose its own self-identity to delegitimize and exclude the other.

With the great moment of transformation approaching, the campaign entered the third stage and made efforts to come out with more effective, creative, and evocative marketing products. The video "Act. React. Impact." (European Parliament 2013e) is a perfect example for dramatization of politics, a seemingly memorable piece of advertising. It can be watched anytime, anywhere, indefinitely. The video is not a simple commercial ad seeking to sell a new product; it is a cinematographic trailer. Its 16:9 aspect ratio reveals immediately that what we are watching has to do with cinema, not TV. It aims to encapsulate the story of the European Parliament in two minutes, exciting and seducing its viewers. As Stephen Garrett points out, a trailer, if cut well, is the stuff dreams are made of (2012). A good trailer must raise expectations, convey a promise, and provoke and beguile viewers by appealing to their emotional impulses. He believes that trailers lend themselves to a three-act structure: act one introduces the film's main characters, act two presents the obstacles to overcome, and act three intensifies the tension and the excitement without offering a resolution. If we apply Garrett's structure to the trailer of the EP we see that act one introduces the protagonists of the story, a mother and her newborn child, and anticipates the plot of the whole (cosmogony) story, the coming to life of new Europe and its inhabitants, the new Europeans. The calm and warm background melody serves to provide the necessary musical accompaniment to the narrative of *palingenesis,* evoking the atmosphere of pristine harmony. In act two, with his deep and resonating voice, the narrator launches short communications that are accompanied by flashes of images. Each piece encapsulates an element of the EU story: economic crisis, social unrest, mourning of past traumas, reconciliation, technology, environmental protection, preservation of local traditions, challenges of globalization, etc.

After "Begin!" and the image of the mother hugging her newborn son, the narrator's call "End!" is illustrated by an image capturing the moment of the fall of the Berlin Wall. "Win!"—a young girl gymnast performs her exercises with elegance and determination. "Lose!"—we see a father and a son who either live in their own car or are obliged to undertake a long and painful journey. "Hold on!" is accompanied by the image of two aged men using a calash. "Move on!"—the prototype of a car speeds down a road. "Think global!"—people working in the stock market. "Think local!"—an old woman sells her hen in a marketplace. "Dream!"—migrants jump from their boat into the sea. "Wake up!"—a young man alone in nature. "Agree!"—a marriage between a black man and a white woman. "Disagree!"—a violent protest that pits protesters against policemen. "Think big!"—a huge fishing boat in the sea. "Think small!"—two fishermen and their freshly caught (and impressively big) fish. "Change!"—a man looks at a huge landfill inhabited by seagulls. "Never change!"—a young shepherd and his herd. "Love!"—a young couple covered in mud is kissing. "Hate!"—a boy driven by anger and revulsion repeatedly fires his rifle as he yells out. "Forgive!"—an elderly war veteran. "Never forget!"—an old war clip shows soldiers charging out of the trenches. "Look back!"—two elderly men look at an old military barrack. "Look ahead!" introduces act 3. It features the same mother hugging her son who appears at very beginning of the trailer. This scene brings all family issues under the same umbrella, completes the circle of the narrative, and reaffirms its central theme—rebirth.

In this cinematographic representation, the European narrative is concentrated within two minutes and the sacred promise is encapsulated in two bookend images; EP elections represent a sacred ritual where the magic moment of birth can be reenacted by all citizens. The narrator summarizes the moral of the story by saying, "We all face many choices and many issues; we all have our own views. But in Europe every opinion gets a fair chance. The decisions of European parliament are driven by everything that matters to you. You have the power to decide." He repeats the title of the movie, "The European parliament: act, react, impact." The last shot is meant to reveal the real authors of the story, the imaginary co-directors of the European elections, "The European Parliament and you."

In the final sequences of scenes, all the protagonists are looking directly into the camera. They are perhaps seeking to both establish a direct communication with the viewers and to generate a mechanism of identification.

The music, the images, and the short imperative sentences dictate the feeling and structure of the film without revealing the whole story. The slogans are all imperative sentences (wake up, think big, think small). These apparently contradictory demands inject playfulness and promise to accept rather than aggressively get rid of the paradoxes and complexities that characterize twenty-first-century Europe. Though built in a binary structure (like the "Europe, your vote counts" video), the boundaries are more fluid; protagonists appear and disappear; a feeling of awe and playfulness kindles the imagination. Unlike previous emotionless videos, this video is centered on human feelings and yearnings. All issues are addressed through a human-centered approach; people are the protagonists of all scenes whether they relate to war, the economic crisis, social problems, the environment, or agriculture. The ad connects the (imaginary) past, the (imaginary) present, and the (imaginary) future. Music sets the tone while the short imperative sentences advance the story and set a mood. This binary structure lends a seductive rhythm that amplifies the excitement and anticipation.

The video raises expectations even more by featuring the muddy couple kissing vehemently, the same couple that appears on the election poster at the moment just before the kiss. It thereby promises to replicate the spirit of a music festival like Woodstock. The goal is to convey the message that European parliamentary elections will be a carnival; the moment when we can celebrate peace, love, and (infinite) freedom is nearer and nearer.

There is another iconic image that the producers of this video decided to recycle. The scene "Wake Up!" is a quick but explicit reference to the movie *Into the Wild*; its protagonist looks just like Emile Hirsch's Christopher McCandless. Why "wake up"? Why Alexander Supertramp (Christopher McCandless's pseudonym)? What does Sean Penn's movie have to do with the film about European Parliament? The fact that these are good questions, which therefore have no answers, should not discourage us from speculating on the filmmakers' possible motivations. The "wake up!" call follows the solicitation "dream!" The image of immigrants fleeing Africa and searching for a new home in Europe precedes the image of a young European man in the shoes of Christopher McCandless, roaming in nature, he too in search of a real home-feeling.

In Penn's film (based on Jon Krakauer's novel and inspired by a true story), Chris, a young man from a wealthy household, cuts ties with his family and wanders alone penniless, and after a long voyage he reaches Alaska. In the wilderness the young man establishes his new home in an abandoned school bus where he pens graffiti onto various surfaces. "Two years he walks the earth. No phone, no pool, no pets, no cigarettes. Ultimate freedom. An extremist. An aesthetic voyager whose home is the road." He dies after 113 days. The film (and the novel) can be seen as a critique of early 1990s American hyperconsumerist culture. In Chris's family, hypocrisy and well-being reign. The father has two families, one official and one clandestine. The conflict between the parents is denied; psychic pain and a sense of responsibility are entombed to safeguard the couple's professional success and appearances. This emotional environment becomes unbearable and pushes Chris and his sister to leave. Chris undertakes his journey in search of truth and an authentic home-feeling, sincerity, reciprocity, and affective human relations. Both in the film and in the novel, the uncontaminated places of nature become equated with beauty and pristine paradise. His odyssey is a journey toward the long-desired (idyllic) home. Chris dons the suit of the paladin of sincerity, truth, and authenticity but is unable to internalize and accept the ambivalence and paradox that desire and affective relations necessarily entail. During the journey he meets people with whom he first establishes a relation but from whom he soon feels estranged. The psychosis of Chris, the denial of the symbolic, is a response to the evaporation of the paternal function (Barracco 2011). His passionate idealism, his manic escape from society in search of perfect harmony, his journey back to paradise, lead him to extreme solitude (and death).

The EP video portrays immigrants and Europe's youth as symbolic mythic heroes undertaking an often dangerous journey and fighting against the forces of nature (their own and external) in the hope of finding a new home. Chris's drama may recall the anxiety and alienation of younger generations in respect to the credibility of the poststate model of the European Union. It may recall the anger and frustration of the followers of anti-European populist and/or nationalist movements. The trailer launches a wake-up call to the angry, disenchanted sons and daughters of the European family and a promise that if they abandon their rebellion against their fathers, they will find in Europe the home they have been yearning for. Viewers of this trailer, however, may not see these images as a tribute to Europe's tormented heroes. They may opt to see them as a critique of the European elite. If Chris is a metaphor for Europe's rebellious sons, the hypocrisy with which the supranational elite propagate their paradise dream recalls that of Chris's parents. The journey may be interpreted not only as a rite of passage, interior transformation, and the universal lust for home but also as symbolic of the messianic European integration process, of its "politics of *jouissance*," its chasing of *objet petit a*—the ever-closer union. Like Chris's parents, the supranational elite have failed to provide a real home for citizens and are therefore doomed to fail in their challenge of channeling back the extreme drives of their sons unless they renounce their religious dogma.

A good trailer should not reveal the whole movie, just the movie's potential to be great; a powerful trailer "pitches the promise of the premise" (Garrett 2012). While the images of the EP video hint at the plot, nothing is explicit. Everything serves to tell (and sell) the narrative of rebirth, the idea that EP elections represent a rite of passage from which citizens would emerge truly European and more empowered. Despite the fact that it offers a clear (albeit veiled) representation of the federalist narrative, the trailer leaves the key questions open, suggesting through the gaze the protagonists staring at the viewer at the end of the video and through the "signature" "the EP and you" that the answers will depend on and will have to be provided by citizens themselves. Far more intriguing and enthralling, and ultimately more powerful than previous marketing tools, this trailer keeps the audience wanting more.

The EP launched another "trailer" similar to the video "Act. React. Impact." (European Parliament 2013f). In it, we reencounter many of the permanent characters of the campaign: immigrants diving from a boat during the night, men working in a market, a father and his son living in their car, a man watching at a landfill inhabited by seagulls, a prototype of a car, a young gymnast performing her exercises, and a newborn son hugged by his mother. Some of the new characters include a man lugging his washed-up boat across the shore, a woman melancholically watching out of her rainy window, and a black woman viewing a panorama. One of the flashes shows a hippie-looking man in a wheelchair supported by a cheering concert crowd; he recalls Ron Kovic, the protagonist of the film *Born on the Fourth of July*. In the movie Kovic, a member of Vietnam Veterans Against the War (VVAW), irrupts into the 1972 Republican National Convention in Miami to speak out against the atrocities committed by US forces in Vietnam War and show empathy for a "proud people" fighting for its independence. He is brought away with force. The EP video seems to suggest that the 2014 elections will be a true festival where, unlike at the Republican National Convention, all voices, but in particular the ones in favor of peace, tolerance, and diversity, will be heard and celebrated. The final shots of the video, featuring the words "This time it's different. Soon in 28 countries," reverberates the title of the story and refers to the twenty-eight member states where the movie will be released.

As the elections approached, the supranational elite felt the need to launch clear and precise messages and therefore replaced polysemic trailers with simple commercial ads. The goal, again, was to encourage a dominant (or "hegemonic") reading, to adopt a language that would be perceived as "natural" and "transparent," and to make citizens accept and internalize the European Parliament's preferred reading. The official TV spot for the 2014 elections shows ordinary people from different parts of Europe in everyday-life situations (EP 2014b). It is short, concise, and offered in thirty-one linguistic versions. The narrator pronounces the text slowly, as clearly as possible: "An ad tries to tell us what to do. But this ad wants you to tell *us* what to do. Use that power, and choose who's in charge. Vote from May 22nd to May 25th." The language structure—the use of second-person pronouns, short words, concise sentences, repetitions, and the imperative—serves to establish an intimate communicational relationship between the sender (EP) and the audience (citizens) to strengthen the effect of the message. At first sight the choice of the thirty linguistic versions may seem revealing of the typical rigid bureaucratic style of European institutions. This panorama, one could bet, would surely include the twenty-four official languages of the EU. Yet it does not. The English (international as it is specified) is followed (rigorously in alphabetical order) by Basque, Bulgarian, Catalan, Czech, Danish, Dutch nl, Dutch be, English en, English ie, Estonian, Finnish, Swedish, Galician, German, Greek, Hungarian, Italian, Latvian, Lithuanian, Luxembourgish, Maltese, Portuguese, Romanian, Slovak, Slovenian, Spanish, Swedish, Turkish, and Welsh. The European Parliament, in defiance of the politically correct, leaves out from its selection the Croatian, the French, the Irish, and the Polish languages. It emphasizes the supremacy of English as the European family's common language. English appears three times (int, en, ie), twice exactly the same (int, en), with the narrator speaking American instead of British English. We can hear the ad in Dutch in two versions (nl and be), in Basque, Catalan, Galician, and Welsh, but not in Scottish. Luxemburgish was perhaps added to anticipate and celebrate in advance the election of Jean-Claude Juncker to the position of Commission president. Turkish is present as well, but not Russian, Ukrainian, Serbian, or other. It is well known that the borders of Europe can be subject to political and cultural debate. The video suggests symbolically that the borders of the European Union, the members of the European family, may also change; where they can find their home is not clear.

The ad promises to invert communication (and power) relationships by attributing the role of message-sender to citizens and the role of the audience to the EP. It may be seen both as an attempt to inject some irony and playfulness into the narrative and as (another) avowal to turn the EP elections into a carnival, where hierarchies turn upside-down and participants may feel not just empowered but omnipotent.

Yet the covenant was not fulfilled. Between 22 May and 25 May 2014, no carnival atmosphere spread across Europe; no *communitas* was created; no collective rebirth took place. The EP elections saw the *lowest* voter turnout on record—42.61 percent (EP 2014a). The majority of the European conservatives were renewed but weakened; the *royal* entry of Eurofederalists did not occur; Jean-Claude Juncker's coronation as the next Commission president did not entail popular jubilation. The result of the elections shows that there is little public appetite for federal Europe. The dream of the ever-closer union, the fantasy of the United States of Europe as a land of paradise, does not fire the collective imaginary. Not seeing in the supranational elite the embodiment of a sacred salvation, citizens did not sanction the birth of a civil religion. Though the Euro-bureaucrats tried hard to pit themselves in combat against the "anti-EU" and "Euroskeptic" forces, they failed to make European citizens believe that they were working on their behalf and protecting them from the forces of darkness. They did not shore up confidence in and strengthen the legitimacy of the EU itself. The elections turned out to be an ineffective witch-hunt that did not manage to enlarge the sacred community of Eurofederalism and eliminate enemies threatening its success; anti-EU and protest parties increased their power in most parts across Europe. Supranational policy-makers stopped trumpeting their plan loudly, but the mission of building the tower of ever closer union was not immediately removed from their agenda. After all, the four main pro-EU groups still controlled about 70 percent of the votes in the parliament and could count on forming a German-style grand coalition to pass laws.

What shook federalists' plan was the refugee crisis. Their archenemy, the populist and nationalist premier par excellence, the Hungarian prime minister Viktor Orbán, turned out to exercise soft power not just in Central Europe but also in "old Europe." His authoritarian stand, the idea of building a fence to keep immigrants out, initially received harsh criticism but then quickly started to gain more and more supporters. The refugee crisis made evident the numerous dividing lines that criss-cross Europe. The painful failure of the quota system (symbolic of the Commission's top-down elitist approach) forced Jean-Claude Juncker to face reality and declare that "one day we should rethink the European architecture with a group of countries that will do things, all things, together and others who will position themselves in an orbit different from the core" (Guarascio 2015). In February 2016, at the meeting of the ministers of foreign affairs of the six founding states, the taboo of the two-speed Europe was removed. The subsequent European Council meeting desacralized the dogma of the "ever-closer union" principle by allowing the United Kingdom an opt-out.

The introduction of "temporary" border controls in various parts of the continent and the outcome of the UK referendum on EU membership (where it voted to leave the EU) are likely to do away with another doctrine—the one that tells the story of the European integration as a teleological process, as the European family's linear march, starting in 1950 and advancing gradually but without interruptions and setbacks, toward a complete pristine union. In other words, what we are witnessing today, is citizens' judgment on the federalists' Tower of Babel.

Concluding Remarks

The European Union's (Magic-Less) Bridge-Builders

Europe's founding fathers, as the official narrative goes, created a *new* Europe out of the ashes left behind by the Second World War. We could use Eric Voegelin's theory of political order elaborated in *History of Political Ideas* and consider this *new Europe* a *cosmion* to expose the deeper meaning of the mission undertaken by today's supranational elite: protecting the integrity and the sacred nature of this European microcosmos by fighting their (perceived) enemies and converting the skeptical through their elaborate symbol politics. For Voegelin the cosmological and the political construction are interconnected: "The polity is conceived as a cosmic analogue, as the cosmion; and rulership and administration of the state are conceived in analogy to the thearchy and hierarchy of the cosmos" (1998: 204). The creation of the political *cosmion* is, in this sense, an "experiment to overcome the essential incompleteness and relativity of human life by means of an image of divine completeness and absoluteness" (Voegelin 1997: 227). Europe's "founding fathers" gave birth to a little world of order, a shelter in which Europeans could give to their life a semblance of meaning, where they could encounter the divine, feel at home, and use the community as a condition of their self-realization. While it is the nation that has become "the substance of the political cosmion" (Voegelin 1998: 250), today's supranational elite seek to persuade citizens that in the twenty-first century the true microcosmos that can offer for them an experience of sacred idyll is *not* the nation-state but the European Union.

Robert Bellah rightly points out the need to endorse "the Durkheimian notion that every group has a religious dimension" and the idea that "civil religion" has "its own prophets and its own martyrs, its own sacred events and sacred places, its own solemn rituals and symbols" (1970: 187, 186). It seems in fact not just reasonable but important to portray Eurofederalism as a soteriology and reflect on the religious qualities its prophets have been attributing to the European Union. Since the 2008 crisis, *palingenetic* ultra-Europeanism has emerged as a salvation doctrine. This political religion has been seeking to construct a utopian sense of community and promote the ideas of Europe's manifest destiny, the promised land, and redemption waiting at the end of the road, encouraging people to fight for the (sacred) "collective goals": giving birth to a new Europe, a "fantastic family," a perfectly integrated and democratic nation-like polity.

The extraordinary (liminal) conditions generated by the crisis, during which the sacred center of the *cosmion*, the Eurozone, was felt to be on the verge of disappearing, has reinforced the (already strong) elitist and technocratic nature of the European Union. Supranational policy-makers have made various attempts to teach citizens the "true meaning" of Europe and to convince them that the EU represented the most suitable shelter, the only place where they could find sublime home-feeling in today's chaos.

They have generated something similar to what Stanley Cohen described as "moral panic" (1973), identifying in populists, nationalists, and Euroskeptics the "folk devil," the contemporary image of evil. Throughout Europe numerous reports circulate; speeches are delivered, and conferences are held on the recent outbreak and dangerous spread of these monstrous epidemics. The behaviors associated with this disease are described as irrational, entirely emotion-driven, obsessive, destructive, and morally dissolute, thus anti-European. A supranational elite consensus has emerged that citizens' unrestrained exposure to populist and nationalist "propaganda" would infect the minds and the spirits of the young and the not-young, lead citizens lose touch with reality, and bring them back to primordial frenzy. The prophets of the federalist soteriology do their best to stir up citizens' fear of populism and nationalism as obscure, alien, and hostile groups threatening the public good and the very existence of the European Union. The fight against new Europe's internal enemies that aim at the destruction of the *cosmion* is seen as functional for marking out the boundaries of the community and reestablishing a sense of moral direction. Populism and nationalism today are seen by the prophets of *palingenetic* ultra-Europeanism as the Bacchanalia threatening the *cosmion* of the European Union. Similarly to the Bacchic cult (deriving from the Greek Dionysian festivals) in ancient Rome, populism and nationalism are associated with irrational passion, excess, and unrestrained lust and rage, in contrast to Eurofederalism, which is seen as the (only) heir of the enlightenment. Adoration of "ever-closer union" is the only legitimate political religion; nationalism and populism are seen as belief systems that belong to the past and have no place in Europe's new polis. Emotional attachment to nation-states, the pursuit of "egoistic impulses,'" and the neglect of "European interests" means the worship of primordial Europe, the dissolution of the rational individual into the Dionysian collective (which characterized Europe before the *cosmion* was created). Until recently, federal Europe's internal enemies were tolerated because they were seen as insignificant in size and strength. Today's supranational elite feel that the number of initiates converted by the Dionysian spirit is getting out of control and threatening to destruct citizens' moral personality, affecting in particular the young and the educated, those who could instead belong to the "Erasmus generation" and actively participate in the building of the United States of Europe. As a consequence, the protectors of federal Europe have decided to act. Similar to the suppression (religious persecution) of the Bacchanalia in 186 BC in ancient Rome, the fight against populism is justified by the need to protect the *cosmion* of the EU against an enemy that is (seen as) an illegitimate political religion, a phantom of the past that is ready to haunt citizens again. Now, in times of crisis, turbulence, and flux, the prophets of federalist soteriology feel the need to reaffirm the sacred nature of the European microcosm and strengthen its protective functions. The moral panic generated by supranational elite is structured around the thesis that if the EU does not defend itself against this alien element, populist leaders and their followers will offend the gods of the ancestors (the memory of Europe's founding fathers) and establish their own *cosmion* in which the virtuous and pious EU citizens would be an alien element: the absolute otherness would triumph, causing a return to the chaos of the pre-1945 period.

Victor Turner asserts that social life is a performance characterized by imagination, play, and creativity. Politics, one can claim, is a highly specialized and sophisticated form of playing, a contest for the best representation of people's fantasies, desires, and lust for transcendence—a competition between actors who seek to seize control over the illusions, the yearnings, and the phantoms that keep the polity of the "fantastic family" together (Salgó 2014). Nationalist projects triumphed in the past and are strong even today because they echo(ed) in the social domain processes of identity formation that individuals take in their earliest encounters with social reality, and because they manage(d) to conjure up in citizens a home-feeling and the perception of the nation-state as a family. Similarly to the Bacchic cult that offered an alternative way to find some fulfillment for people (including women and even slaves) who had no chance to participate in the administration of the republic (Riedl 2012), populist movements promise empowerment, a place in the social order, direct participation in the administration of the polis, self-realization, and a different kind of transcendental experience for people who feel excluded and marginalized. Both seek to help people escape the experience of meaninglessness and abyss by replicating the traditional, transcendental structures and offering refuge in the consoling milieu of awe-inspiring systems.

The *cosmion,* as Voegelin contends,

> is illuminated through an elaborate symbolism, in various degrees of compactness and differentiation—from rite, through myth, to theory—and this symbolism illuminates it with meaning in so far as the symbols make the internal structure of such a cosmion, the relations between its members and groups of members, as well as its existence as a whole, transparent for the mystery of human existence. The self-illumination of society through symbols is an integral part of social reality. ... Through such symbolization the members of a society experience it as. ... of their human essence. (Voegelin 1987: 27)

Fighting against the EU's "internal enemies" is one of the policies aimed at preserving and protecting the *cosmion.* Another is the cultural battle, fought with the use of the tools of symbol politics, for those whose souls can still be saved, those who can still be enlightened and converted to the federalist dogma. This book has explored some of the new (and old) symbols, myths, and rituals that supranational institutions have fashioned using visual sources with the hope of conjuring up the atmosphere of the numinous and making people who generally feel detached from and skeptical about the European Union have a religious experience. These symbolic tools are meant to inspire citizens by promising to fulfil their primal fantasies and yearnings and making them feel that they are the mythical heroes who (re)create with their daily acts Europe's democratically functioning family. The expected outcome of this new politics of transcendence is a reinvigorated *cosmion* that has deprived the nation-state of its emotional monopoly over citizens' hearts and has strengthened its core values, its borders, and the loyalty of its members.

To give life to the EU, to turn it into a both human and godlike entity, both delightful and adorable, Europe has come to be portrayed by the mythical image of the Phoenician princess. To give the symbol of the common currency a religious valor and to forecast the sacralization of the EU (and the deification of its leaders), the new series of euro banknotes has been presented as the symbol of a new era, of Europeans' salvation, rebirth, and return to paradise. Together with the other symbols that ornament the banknotes, the portrait of Europa seeks to relax fears about the euro crisis by giving Europeans an attractive image to dwell on: problems may remain but the "new face of the euro," through the sacred gaze of the *vera cona* and the loving gaze of the mother, offers a way to transcend them by conjuring up a new utopia. Europa's face is meant to become a medium of metamorphosis, a source of political and religious might, the symbol of the EU's power of transmutation. Fifteenth-century humanist thinker Leon Battista Alberti chose as his personal emblem a winged eye because "[It is] more powerful than anything, swifter, more worthy. … It is such as to be the first, chief, king, like a god of human parts. …" (1966: 63). In Europa's eyes, citizens are meant to see god and the mother, they are expected to feel transformed and be able to discover their true (i.e., European) self. The shining rays emanating from the sacred eyes (that we see on the official videos) seek to strengthen the divine quality of the (elite's) "all-seeing eye."

In the early seventeenth century the leviathan became the symbol of absolute power. It was a visual trick to affirm the legitimacy of a new form of power, a tool to "prescribe" much more than to "describe" the absolute exercise of authority (Stocchetti & Kukkonen 2011: 14). Its strength, according to Matteo Stocchetti, was made of the same substance as dreams: "so formidable while we sleep but 'melting—rapidly—into air' as soon as we awake" (2011: 15). Hobbes put the "visual strategies" at the center of his political theories. To understand politics, he believed, we have to understand the images. He introduced the visual metaphor of the leviathan to generate fear in people, because human beings will follow the "natural passions of man" if "there is no visible power to keep them in awe, and tie them by fear of punishment to the performance of their covenants and observation of those laws of nature" (1668/1994: 106). The image of "seductive Europe" serves to fire (rather than to restrict) passions, to evoke (rather than to restrain) love and desire. In the EU's contemporary mythology, the ambiguous portrait of Europa is a visual trick to affirm the legitimacy of Europe's *soft* power. Europa is represented as the contemporary manifestation of Peitho, the goddess who should be venerated for protecting and spreading (sacred) "European values," championing the "European way of life," in (and beyond) a new, perfectly united, and harmonious Europe. In Greek mythology, Peitho was the goddess who personified soft power, persuasion, and seduction; her role as a companion of Aphrodite was intimately connected to the goddess of love and beauty. Peitho was adored for the various roles she played in private and public life, for the virtues she represented. She was "the patron of civilized life and democratic institutions … the spirit of agreement, bargain, contract, consensus, exchange, and negotiation in a free polis" (Mourelatos

1970: 139). Europa, with her sacred gaze promising paradise, due to her magic ability to seduce, persuade, transform, and offer a magic experience of transcendence, has become the allegorical representation of today's Europe and its soft power.

The fantasy driving the prophets of the federalist soteriology is perhaps to make Europa occupy a role in Europe similar to that of Marianne in the French political culture. Though Marianne is devoid of a constitutional status as a symbol of the republic, in the imagination of French citizens (and not only) she is the official human face (and body) of the republic. She is one of the most popular symbols of the French Republic; we can encounter her figure on many government documents, the former franc currency, on French euro coins, postage stamps, wine-bottle labels, etc. The various styles and the colors of her clothing and her changing posture throughout the centuries have served to reinforce the image of her as the figure of liberty and reason. Similarly to Europa, who has had different representations and interpretations in different historical periods, Marianne has appeared in the form of a Greco-Roman goddess, a mother, a warrior, a mother, and a *femme fatale.* While Uncle Sam and John Bull have a relatively standard representation, Marianne (like Europa) follows political fashion: she seems to have many outfits just like a Barbie doll (Renault 2004). As Bronwyn Winter shows, Marianne became seen more and more through the French nation's sexualized political metaphor: it is "her association with icons of entertainment, fashion and media that has most decidedly assured Marianne's rise to stardom as the ubiquitous and glamorous personification of the French Republic, and this starisation" (2009: 232). We can see a similar trend in the use of Europa, in particular, in the official campaign videos.

Yet federalists' expectations seem even more ambitious; it is as if Europa was to perform in European *cosmion* the functions that the Virgin of Guadalupe performs in Mexico. Eric Wolf describes the Virgin of Guadalupe as a "master symbol" that enshrines Mexicans' most important inner yearnings, their political and religious aspirations, and provides a cultural idiom through which the tenor and emotions of salient social relationships of Mexican life can be expressed, a "collective representation" of Mexican society (1958: 1, 38). In his interpretation, the Guadalupe represents for Mexicans the supernatural mother and thereby embodies a longing to return to the pristine state of original idyll. To many, the symbol stands for life and hope, for political and religious salvation. The Guadalupe is a paradise myth that promises the abolition of hunger and humiliation, an assured place both in earthly and heavenly paradise, and a worthy place in and after life. Through this symbol, deeply felt human yearnings are projected onto the political scene: "The wish for a return to a paradise of early satisfactions of food and warmth, a life without defeat, sickness or death, gave rise to a political wish for a Mexican paradise" (Wolf 1958: 38).

For seventeenth-century ecclesiastics the Guadalupe represented the harbinger of a new order. For the prophets of *palingenetic* ultra-Europeanism, Europa is the herald of the return of the golden age. Like Guadalupe, the Phoenician princess may be equated with the apocalyptic woman of the Revelation of John, "arrayed with the sun, and the moon under her feet, and upon her head a crown of twelve stars" (12: 1), who is to realize Deuteronomy's prophecy by leading Europeans into the promised land. The apparition of Europa on the banknote is portrayed as a product of a divine decision, as a manifestation of Europe as a "chosen community." In federalists' salvation doctrine, true Europeans will finally possess the land of paradise.

Driven by the same intent (i.e., to offer believers and nonbelievers the possibility of sharing experiences of transcendence, thereby strengthening the stability of the *cosmion*), the supranational elite have launched their own sacred rituals.

They have identified in the audiovisual sector the ideal space to convey to citizens their cosmogony plan, to transport them to a new realm, to increase their community of believers, and to prepare the acts of European communion. While the euro-unveiling ceremonies represent mystical ceremonies for the elite only, the videos that were launched to celebrate the arrival of each sacred totem serve to create a virtual place where acts of Europeans' collective devotion can take place. Not just to introduce a greater degree of "face recognition" (as the official mantra states) but also to make the sacred core (i.e., the Eurozone) "visible" as the center of the European microcosm, the spots launched to celebrate the new series of euro banknotes seek to exploit the potential inherent in the female representation and in the "sacred gaze" of Europe. Actresses and models have been selected to don her mask, to reveal the "real" face (the "true image") of Europe and display it for citizens to adore. According to film critic Pascal Bonitzer, close-ups represent the iconic form of film and are meant to provoke in viewers an emotional shock: close-ups perform a terroristic, a revolutionary, role as they subvert the hierarchy of images, as they make big what is small and small what is big, as they launch a provocation, an attack on the spectator (1985). The "close-ups" of Europa in official spots are employed to stimulate an eruption of the divine, an explosion of affection, face-to-face (a body-to-body?) contact between citizens and the organization, a special encounter between the profane and the sacred.

The communication campaign preceding the 2014 elections to the European Parliament was launched with the hope of preparing the ground for a sacred rite that would be enacted by all citizens (with the right to vote). Supranational institutions' campaign ads publicizing the event were intended to offer a special occasion for the affirmation of the (sacred) "European values," an opportunity for citizens to rediscover (or renew) their devotion to these values and participate in an act of European communion. Citizens were to share something similar to what Shils and Young described in reference to the coronation ceremony as "the common sentiment of the sacredness of communal life and institutions" a "great act of national communion" (1955: 74, 80). Videos represented a virtual venue for celebrating the unifying presence of the supranational elite as defender of faith and guardian of European traditions of tolerance, openness, and unity. The hope was that citizens would come together in one great European family, express their devotion to the prophets of federalism, anoint the (pro-USE) members of the European Parliament with holy oil, and enthrone the (pro-USE) president of the European Commission. They sought to generate the feeling that citizens themselves were the protagonists who were enacting the sacred ritual and giving birth to new Europe.

However, the campaign videos with their structure and symbolism anticipated the betrayal of the promise of a new, democratic, idyllic Europe and revealed the supranational elite's authoritarian approach. The institutional visual narratives reproduce the binary structure present in verbal narratives. The opposition between two sides, the mythological fight between Good and Evil, and the legendary themes of the hero's journey (call to action, trials and resurrection) constitute the main framework for their plots. With their moments of trauma, suffering, defeat, triumph, and rebirth, the videos depict and display for EU citizens what Roland Barthes (1972) describes as "the spectacle of excess," the great drama of magic transformation. These videos convey and perform the potency of magic and the epic quality of the federalists' quest for justice, freedom, development, and unity. They present what Žižek calls "the politics of *jouissance*" where there are no limits to what the elite can achieve.

These videos reveal that supranational institutions defy contemporary conceptualizations of identity and culture (that emphasize identities' fluid, fragmentary, contested, and hybridized nature) and are inclined to fix the meaning of Europe and Europeanness. Similar to seventeenth- and eighteenth-century iconography, they portray Europe as a unique civilization whose heritage and identity stem from a glorious past (that goes from ancient Greece through Christianity, the

Enlightenment, the Scientific Revolution, to a model based on parliamentary democracy and social market economy). In its Eurocentric and chauvinistic conception of history, "European identity" is portrayed as a fragile, delicate entity constantly (but in particular since 2008) under the threat of dangerous and contaminating forces. Visual sources support a fixed or monologic view of the European Union; they depict the "ever closer union," a thick cultural European identity, as the only salvation and promise of redemption through the EU's power to transmute and create *ex nihilio.*

The videos do not point to the active role of the viewer in narrating and building Europe; they frame the viewers as passive. A canonical Euro-bureaucratic way of selling a complete (cosmogony) story seems to prevail. Umberto Eco makes a distinction between closed texts that "aim at arousing a precise response on the part of … readers …, at pulling the reader along a predetermined path … according to an inflexible project," and open texts, characterized usually by ambiguity, irony, and complexity that are designed to generate multiple interpretations, presuming a reader who is "able to master different codes and eager to deal with the text as with a maze of many interests" (1984: 8, 9). Applying this train of thought, supranational institutions' visual narratives appear as closed texts. The official videos do not provide citizens with considerable freedom in the interpretative process; contrary to the promise of empowering and involving people in the making of new Europe, the viewers are not drawn into the action; they are not invited to complete the narrative about Europe for themselves. The possibility of people's response has not been built into the communication strategy; the promise of correcting the historic imbalance in EU communication theory that had focused on the sender, EU institutions, is also betrayed. As Umberto Eco points out, "signs are open devices, not still armors prescribing a bi-conditional identity"; their very nature "postulates an active role on the part of their interpreter" (1981: 45, 35). Contrary to the official mission of telling the story of a European *cosmion* built by and for Europeans, videos seek to convey one rather fixed (romanticized and mythicized) vision of Europe and sell the federalist cosmogony myth. Citizens are users, not creators: they are invited to decode messages as they were encoded. The plots follow a predictable "sequence of moves," representing a device that Eco described as "typical of an escape machine geared for the entertainment of masses" (1984: 156, 161).

EU rituals seem to fit Steven Lukes's definition better than Emile Durkheim's. According to Lukes, rituals are not spontaneous collective celebrations but events staged by the dominant groups to pursue particular interests (1975). Instead of promoting value integration, rituals help these groups "exercise power along the cognitive dimension," representing "crucial elements in the 'mobilization of bias'" (Lukes 1975: 301, 289). In the European Union's politics of rituals, we can in fact detect the supranational elite's intent to spread the federalist ideology, gain loyalty for the sacred mission of the United States of Europe, and expand the community of believers of *palingenetic* ultra-Europeanism. Rituals serve the purpose of fostering citizens' shared-value commitment toward the sacred core of the EU and generating collective effervescence that would help unite citizens around predefined dogmas. Through these special events the prophets of federalist soteriology draw people's attention toward their powerfully evoked representation of the European Union and encourage them to make it their own.

The European Union's project of elite-driven identity-building, inspired by the model of nation-states and based on the use of symbols, myths, and rituals, has many critiques in academic literature. According to Chris Shore, the idea that culture can be used as a tool of political integration and that cultural unity can be "injected" into the masses, thanks to the efforts of bureaucrats and marketing professionals, reveals a top-down, elitist, and typically "Jacobinist" approach, one reminiscent of Leninism (2001). As Rosi Braidotti points out, to rethink and relaunch a diverse European imaginary, the link between citizenship and identity and the dualistic system of oppositions between us and them should be dissolved. A postnationalist European space, from her perspective, requires a flexible citizenship, a "nomadic" (rather than a "unitary") subject (2008, 2011). Bo Stråth stresses the need to leave behind chiliastic utopias in favor of pragmatism: the image of Europe should be an image of openness; the idea of a linear development from the European nation-states to a single European nation-state at an imagined higher level of polity, the idea that history has a direction, the conviction that a unified collective identity would represent an immediate solution to Europe's "identity crisis" should be rejected (2000b: 41). For Luisa Passerini, too, the challenge of the absence of Europe should not be met by a quest for identity (understood as harmony) (2000). We had better substitute "identity" with "identification" (as used by Freud) and focus on the relationship between the individual and various collectives, on the dynamic element of personal choice, on the emotional attachment, the feeling of belonging and "being possessed" (Passerini 2000: 47, 48). In regards to the supranational elite's symbol politics, she emphasizes the impossibility and the undesirability that out of the myths and symbols a new and "clean" European identity could emerge directly and linearly. Passerini stresses the need to recognize that symbols belong to everybody and that they can bring together rather than separate continents and cultures (Passerini 2003a: 32, 33).

Hayden White adheres to the idea that "identity" applied to a nebulous and unspecifiable entity, such as Europe, that has never existed anywhere, except in discourse, is a mystification (2000: 67). Kalypso Nicolaïdis and Janie Pélabay also criticize the policy of turning norms, principles, or political ideals into mandatory "European values"; they warn against "a single European narrative, in a new collective myth, handed down from above, and then drummed into children in civics classes" and emphasize the risk that the official narrative of a "European past" could one day lead to "religious, moral or cultural 'rearmament' of Europe" (2009: 182, 183). While normatively undesirable, it is also questionable to what extent a "pan-national Europeanism," based on homogenizing narratives and a unified cultural identity, could find a solution for the identity crises Europe faces (Ransmann 2006: 154). Albrecht Sonntag further elaborates on why the Commission's decision to mobilize symbols and invent traditions to enhance the legitimacy of the EU following the model of nineteenth-century nation-state building is both flawed and counterproductive (2011). Instead of clinging to something that is neither possible nor ethically desirable, he believes that it makes more sense to admit that the EU will never be "a fatherland," "to openly, almost aggressively, assume the boring side of European politics and abandon attempts to 'brand' the EU with an objective to create affective connotations and 'brand loyalty,'" and accept it as it is: "boring, unsexy and slow, but necessary" (Sonntag 2011: 127).

My argument is that the concept of a playful European public space should replace a thick European cultural identity as a precondition of a democratic European polity. For the supranational elite to perform the functions of the mythical "masters of ceremonies" and succeed in giving birth to a new democratic Europe, they must undergo an inner transformation, shift from a dichotomistic-dualistic way of thinking to a tripartite one and conduct democratic politics based on the spirit of play and the logic of the impossible as conceptualized respectively by Donald Winnicott and Jacques Lacan (Salgó 2014). They should take the value of diversity seriously, endorse the Dionysian dimension, and internalize the true legacy of Athenian democracy. Visual narratives should resist the supranational elite's straightforward, authoritarian reading and offer instead an "amphibolic" reading. Similar to an Isocratean text, which resists simple appropriations by any particular political or artistic tendency (Ober 2005), images portraying the European Union and EU citizens should be openly designed so that different subcommunities and individuals can read them differently.

The tendency to reason in dichotomous structures, in which one set of concepts tends to dominate and exclude the other (right and wrong, life and death, friend and foe, similar and different, etc.), prevails in human societies. Dualistic thinking reflects people's need to use dichotomous logic in order to transcend the complexities of reality; it has developed as a kind of defense mechanism that can foster the illusion of grasping the meaning and taking control of reality. Yet, as Arpad Szakolczai elucidates, processes of transition demand a nondualistic approach, because the "period of transition is a third, temporary, intermediate situation between two different stable states" (2001). Transitional periods, characterized by instability, flux, and uncertainty, require the presence of "special guides," exceptional, charismatic individuals and leaders "who both possess a special kind of knowledge and preserve a distance from the events, are able to maintain their stability, concentration and composure amidst the disturbing, unsettled conditions," and therefore can administer successfully the rites of passage (Szakolczai 2001). Today's Europe indeed is going through a liminal period. The 2008 crisis has entailed the dissolution of stable structures; its economic, political, social, and identity-related effects that are felt to be a threat to the entire community have reinforced in many the quest for a new era. Supranational policy-makers, contrary to what they promise and wish to suggest, do not perform the task of masters of ceremonies with demiurgic ease and struggle to end the emergency situation. They seem to ignore the warning made by one of the most erudite metaphysical thinkers, Béla Hamvas, a few year after the Great Crisis:

> Statesmen and economists make a pathetic attempt when they strive to resolve the crisis, to guide humanity and to force on people renewal … while themselves have not risen above their own crisis … while they have not been born again. (1936/1983: 61)

Europeans may find themselves in a *permanent* state of crisis, deprived of the possibility of having an elite capable of leading them out of this situation. What is needed in order to avoid liminality becoming permanent, to pass to a new stage where citizens are co-creators of Europe, is leaders' metamorphosis. The supranational elite need to see, think, and act with new eyes and new minds; they need to play a different role in Europe's social drama and perform perhaps the functions of Donald Winnicott's "good-enough mother."

To pass from dualistic to tripartite thinking they should internalize the spirit of play as conceptualized by this British psychoanalyst. For Winnicott, the first experience of playing belongs to the potential space between infant and mother, to the "transitional space" (the land of play) that can emerge as a result of "good-enough mothering" (1960). Primary maternal care, which from his perspective consists of providing a "holding environment" that meets the physiological and the psychological needs of the infant and which is reliable due to the mother's strong empathy, allows for the infant to immerge in an illusionary feeling of omnipotence. The British psychoanalyst's transitional space is the realm of illusion, the land of play. It is however not a magic land, an idyllic land of absolute and ideal happiness; it is interpenetrated by separation, loss, and absence. The space of imagination is the "area of yearning" where bridges can be formed and borders between me and not me, us and them, reality and fantasy can be transcended, where the inner subjective world and external reality seem to coincide.

Jeffrey Prager applies Winnicott's theory on "transitional space" to modern politics and conceptualizes "healthy politics" as politics that fosters the realm of freedom, the realm of illusion (1993). From Prager's perspective, imaginative societies are committed to enhancing the realm of freedom, they foster and support illusion, encourage individual autonomy, and promote the feeling that the object world is a world of individuals' own making (1993: 573–74). Only democratic politics is illusionary; only in democratic communities are members capable of playfully defining the meaning and purposes of the community in relation to the democratic structures (i.e., objects) that self-consciously stand in relation to the subjects they serve (1993: 577). In authoritarian systems, coexistence between political forces is either repressed or turns into an aggressive fight with each side trying to impose its own self-identity, to delegitimize and exclude the other from the "fantastic family of full-fledged members." Democratic politics moves beyond the politics of negation; in it, play implies neither the loss of identity nor the aggressive definition and fixation of identity. It is characterized by the peaceful coexistence of oppositions: opposites are not considered either contradictory or complementary, paradoxes are tolerated, dichotomous oppositions become interpenetrated by each other.

Democratic politics represents the most sublime form of playful politics: the political elite performs a spectacle in the original sense of the words—they strive to enhance the illusion of a different, more beautiful, more uplifting reality. Democratic politics is an "art of theater," which demands a world of players rather than a passive audience, giving responsibility for the play's success not only to the directors but also to the actors. Democratic politics allows for the emergence of a playful public arena, in which people and the political elite are not two distinct entities but coexist peacefully and playfully on the stage. The political game is founded on playful relations among actors whose playgrounds are no longer perceived as contradictory, but rather as interwoven. Rather than a rigid repressive order that must be maintained through coercion, playful politics is capable of creating graceful, harmonious order by imposing law and at the same time fostering illusion (as defined by Huizinga). Playful politics has the ability to transform, for temporary periods, the imperfect world, the confusion of life, into a limited, fragile perfection. Human relationships underlying the machinery of democratic systems are elastic and allow for easing those tensions in society that would otherwise be unbearable or dangerous.

Through visual and verbal narratives, the supranational elite seek to convince citizens that they are conducting democratic politics that allow citizens to feel as though they are the creators of Europe. However, their campaign videos anticipate the betrayal of this promise and prove that what prevails in federalist discourse is certainty and surety of vision. These visual tools offer no possibility for persuasion, no playful interactions, but rather preformulations and irreconcilable hostilities between pro-Europeans and those against. The EU's symbol politics reflects federalists' fantasy of a world devoid of the ambiguity of illusion. It represses contestatory politics and aims to construct a like-minded community where all members have the same perception of external reality (from which others with whom members do not identify are excluded), and it aspires to foster a strong collective identity. The supranational elite do not perform the functions of the "good-enough mother"—they fail to conjure up an enabling environment that would facilitate the development of illusion and playfulness and autonomy and make citizens feel that they are the ones who build Europe. The "transitional space" between the individual and leadership is absent. The Winnicottian illusion is reified; while omnipotent fantasies, aggressive rhetoric, and depreciation of difference characterize political leadership, anger, frustration, and intolerance grow in European societies. Contrary to what they wish to achieve, supranational elite deny subjects the possibility of identifying with them. Politics in the European Union is experienced as something external to citizens' own social experience, something they cannot even imagine to change.

European institutions' visual narratives about Europe seek to reinforce the (already widespread) belief that ancient Greece represents an archetypal role model, a holy area, predestined by fate, in which the greatness of European spirit had first appeared. Many arrived to the conclusion that by virtue of its sacred nature and its inexhaustible magic source of generative energy for the rest of the European family, Greece cannot be separated from the European *cosmion.* Negotiation efforts seeking to avoid bankruptcy and exit of the country from the Eurozone can be seen as a symbolic manifestation of the mythical attraction toward a "sacred center" and a desire to cling to its divine power. Yet today's Greece, while seen as sacred by some, is portrayed as monstrous by others. The country became associated with the epitome of populism seeking to destabilize the European polis. It came to be seen as responsible for the sacrificial crisis—that is, responsible for the disintegration of distinctions within the community, for violating Europe's norms and rules. The artificially created moral panic is centered on Greek populism as a disease that could spread and weaken Europe. To regain its (lost) sacred nature and to contribute to the strengthening (rather than the weakening) of the European *cosmion*, it had to play the role of what René Girard described as the "surrogate victim," the sacrificial victim that has to die so that the entire community, threatened by the same destiny, can be reborn in a new cultural order (2005: 269). In popular imagination, sacrifice is associated with some form of deprivation that will entail moments of transcendence. In traditional societies, the ritualized forms of killing human beings represented the quest for salvation as a response to the disaster suffered (Wydra 2015a). The sacrificial crisis and its resolution are intimately linked together; the crisis is inseparable from its happy ending (Girard 2005: 129). The drama provoked by the Greek debt crisis offered EU citizens the promise of establishing contacts with transcendence and strengthening their polis by means of the sacrifice of the surrogate victim. Greece seemed perfect to play this role—it is perceived by many as a monster and not as a real member of the community, neither outside nor inside the community but marginal to it. Greece, whose relationship to European community is neither too close nor too distant, seemed a suitable subject for exercising a cathartic effect: exploiting the ambiguity deriving from its liminal nature, relieving the community of its burden of violence, and effecting its purification through her sacrifice. The debt negotiations and the packages of austerity measures, like ritual practices, were felt to be conforming to the needs of the European community. These acts were to guarantee the purgation of violence (its transference to the victim) and the reestablishment of Europe's communal unity. The word *pharmakon* in Greek means both poison and antidote for poison, a substance that can perform both curative and destructive functions (Girard 2005). The packages of austerity measures represent a *pharmakon* that can both kill and heal. But again, the realization of the rite of passage, the administration of the *pharmakon* "had best to be left by ordinary men in the hands of those who enjoy special knowledge and exceptional powers" (Girard 2005: 100).

European supranational elite seem to be lacking special knowledge and exceptional power. They desperately cling to an archetypal role model and to the artificially created umbilical cord that is supposed to link today's European Union to ancient Greece, and they seem unable to grasp the real lessons to be learned from the Athenian city-state.

The Athenian city-state was an internally diverse, democratically governed community that was not based on a common cultural matrix. According to Josiah Ober, the success of Athenian democracy lies in its "commitments towards diversity and coherence within Athenian political culture and within Athenian 'souls'" (2005: 8). The Athenian polis tried explicitly to foster a "proper Athenian-ness" through the enactment of the "All Athenians" Panathenaic Festival and by promoting an idealized conception of Athenian past; but at the same time, it let these expressions of ideological coherence be challenged by acknowledging diversity and conflict in Athenian drama, legal process, and religious ritual (Ober 2005: 4). In some ways, the EU resembles the ancient Athenian polity. "European" may be seen as an umbrella term that covers a wide range of social identities; the official motto "unity in diversity" is a symbol expressing the ideal of recognizing in diversity something precious that enriches rather than threatens the community and that can transform into productivity and creativity. We should not expect from the supranational elite the complete abandonment of the romanticization of the European past and the promotion of the idealized vision of European identity. But we may expect them to internalize the true spirit of their official motto and, rather than treating the European Union as a neutral space where diversity, inequality, and conflicts are finally resolved and disappear, adopt what Ober described in relation to the Athenian polis: "democracy as diversity management" and the "politics of going on together." European supranational elite must recognize the goal to accomplish a perfect unification and a return to pristine idyll as impossible and potentially dangerous. It is unlikely and undesirable that the EU marches forward to a fully integrated federal United States of Europe. Likewise, it is unlikely and undesirable that the EU returns to a loose association of autonomous states devoid of a common currency. Europe's fantastic family should remain an illusion—yet, an illusion in the Winnicottian sense—necessary (when it is not overpowering) for healthy, playful politics.

As Cornelius Castoriadis outlines, one of the paradoxical aspects of the "impossibility" of politics is that there can be no democracy without democratic individuals (and vice versa). The autonomous society becomes meaningless if it is not at the same time the project of bringing forth autonomous individuals. There is no reflective community without reflective individuals: "An autonomous society, as a self-instituting and self-governing collectivity, presupposes the development of the capacity of all its members to participate in its reflective and deliberative activities" (1997b: 132–33). European citizens need to follow Athenian citizens' example, which "constructed appropriately democratic souls for themselves" (Ober 2005: 26). We can expect democracy to function once policy-makers *and* citizens have undergone transformation and constructed for themselves "democratic souls," once they have accepted and internalized that democratic politics is the "art of the impossible," the "art of autonomy," the "art of playfulness and imagination" (Salgó 2014).

Matthias Riedl points out that the mythological enemies Dionysus has to constantly fight for his acknowledgment as a legitimate god in Olympus are predominantly rulers who try to ban him from their kingdoms: Perseus of Argos, Lykurgos of Thracia, and Pentheus of Thebes (2012). The political elite of the European Union also seek to deny the legitimacy of Dionysus (with populism being its contemporary embodiment) and expel him from the European polis. Symbolic of this suppression is the ECB's decision to celebrate Europa, who appears on one side of the ancient Greek *krater*, and negate the existence (and the importance) of Dionysus, who appears on the other. Similar to Pentheus, who wants to stop the Bacchanalia but falls victim to the Dionysian dimension in himself, the supranational elite have launched a crusade against populism, becoming populist themselves. Stavrakakis and Katsambekis are right in emphasizing that the antipopulist critique is often articulated in a very populist and Manichean manner (2013). The conflict between federalism and populism is staged as a clash between Europe, portrayed as intrinsically democratic, moderate, benign, and the cradle of sacred values, and populism, conceived of as inherently undemocratic, extreme, malignant, exclusionary, and aggressive. It is as if mechanisms of splitting, idealization, denigration, and denial, as described by Melanie Klein (1975), have taken hold of the prophets of *palingenetic* ultra-Europeanism. The "good object" (the United States of Europe and its members) is idealized and granted supreme and unquestionable legitimacy, while the "bad object" (nationalists and populists, but often Euroskeptic voices in general) is feared as a terrifying, destructive persecutor. Extreme splitting is linked with the mechanisms of denial and omnipotence; with persecutory phantasies stemming from the desire to get rid of the personality's unwanted parts.

Cornelia Isler-Kerényi deserves credit for confuting the theories that see Dionysus as alien to the Homeric pantheon and bringing instead evidence to show his central role as a god of the polis in the wider and deeper sense of the term, his function as a civilizing force (2007). In her conceptualization, the polis is the antithesis of, but also intimately connected to, the wild nature. She draws a parallel between the individual and the social levels and asserts that in both cases the civilized human condition constitutes one of the many possible modes of being; a return to wild nature is always lurking behind the corner. The very function of Dionysus, she claims, is to prevent individuals and communities, especially in critical moments of transition, from regressing into the primordial realm (Isler-Kerényi 2007: 213). Besides serving as a platform for ritualized transitions, the symposium was a symbol of civil life that contrasted with life in the wild. As the Attic vases express it most clearly, Dionysus assumed the crucial role of promoting the process of stabilization and civilization on occasion of the symposium:

> Guaranteeing order and continuity of the polis was possible only because, in the setting of the symposium, space and time were granted for escape, for periodic "lapses" into a pre-civilised condition. Therefore, the presence of Dionysus is not limited to the sphere of order and civilisation, but is extended also to savage nature, and, logically, to the intermediate, transitional zone of the countryside and manual labour. (Isler-Kerényi 2007: 104)

The *krater* Draghi chose was used on occasions of symposiums. It contained a mix of wine and water (and often a bit of honey), suggesting perhaps that Europeans are what Béla Hamvas calls "people of wine," whose culture is founded on the myth of the Garden of Eden. The image on Draghi's *krater* depicts a liminal space—Europa's encounter takes place in a kind of "rural strip," an intermediate and transitional region between the polis and nature, the realm where the taming of satyrs, the cultivation of the vine, and the production of wine take place, an area on which the urban center of the ancient polis depends and which it needs to incorporate into its institutions (Isler-Kerényi 2007: 232). The supranational institutions seem to overlook Dionysus's civilizing function, the need to protect Europe, in a liminal situation, from regression. Nietzsche's argument that identifies in the Dionysian and the Apollonian drives, in the power of intoxicated frenzy and excesses (Dionysus), and in the power of visionary dreams of light, beauty, and pristine idyll (Apollo) the necessary conditions for the flourishing of all arts (1995), has not been felt as an inspiration. We have come to forget that the Dionysian *cannot* be banned; it is intrinsic in human nature.

According to Jean-Pierre Vernant and Pierre Vidal-Naquet, the lesson to be learned from the purgation of Bacchanalia by the Roman authorities in 186 BC is that attempts to completely eradicate the Dionysian from the *cosmion* will bring about a violent frenzy:

> If the world of the same refuses to absorb the element of otherness that every group and every human being unconsciously carry within themselves, … then all that is stable, regular, and the same tips over and collapses and the other, of hideous aspect, absolute otherness and a return to chaos, come to appear as the sinister truth, the other, authentic, and terrifying face of the same. (Vernant & Vidal-Naquet 1990: 402)

The biblical story of the Tower of Babel, which inspired the design of the building of the European Parliament in Strasbourg (the architecture evokes the oil paintings by Pieter Bruegel the Elder on this theme) and which is, in many senses, symbolic of European Union's internal architecture too, has several interpretations. One suggests that humans were driven by fear in their endeavors. They didn't want to be scattered over the whole earth but instead wished to put down deep roots into local soil and not go anywhere else. This reading sees in humans' decision a refusal to fulfill God's creational mandate addressed to them, which was to fill the earth and steward it. Joseph Weiler rightly argues that the argument that "we have to explain Europe better" to European citizens is "a morally repugnant argument": to argue that people do rush to cast their vote in an EP election "because they do not understand how important such a vote is, is both wrong and contemptuous of the very democracy on which these elections are predicated" (Viola 2015). This attitude, the structure of the governance system, and the populist rhetoric are all revealing of the authoritarian nature of the supranational elite and of their betrayal of their original plan. People's negative judgment on federalists' Tower of Babel is driven not by their alleged stupidity but by their protest to the refusal of the supranational elite to endeavor to fulfil their holy mandate—turn a technocratic elitist organization into a democratic *communitas*. The punishment is (also) constructive; it could be seen as a blessing and not as a curse: without renouncing the doctrine of the ever-closer union and the "there is no alternative" dogma, the supranational elite will not comply with the initial command of empowering people. What differentiates democracy from other political forms of society is the legitimization of conflict, the celebration of different conceptions of the good, and the refusal to eliminate diversity through the establishment of an authoritarian harmonious order. It is time to accept the in-between institutional character, the imperfect nature of the EU, and understand that it is neither desirable nor possible to reinvigorate the European project without further involving citizens.

Bibliography

Abdela, R., Y. Herrera, A. Johnston, and R. McDermott, eds. 2009. *Measuring Identity: A Guide for Social Scientists.* Cambridge: Cambridge University Press.

Abraham, N., and M. Torok. 1994. *The Shell and the Kernel.* Chicago: University of Chicago Press.

Abu-Lughod, L. E., and C. A. Lutz. 1990. "Language and the Politics of Emotion." In *Studies in Emotion and Social Interaction.* New York: Cambridge University Press.

Adams, L. 1990. "The Myth of Athena and Arachne: Some Oedipal and Pre-Oedipal Aspects of Creative Challenge in Women and Their Implications for the Interpretation of *Las Meninas* by Velazquez." *International Journal of Psychoanalysis* 71: 597–609.

Adams, V. 1982. "'Mommy and I Are One': Beaming Messages to Inner Space." *Psychology Today*: 24–36.

Adonnino, P. 1985. "A People's Europe: Reports from the Ad Hoc Committee." *Bulletin of the European Communities, Supplement 7/85.* Retrieved from http://aei.pitt.edu/992.

Agamben, G. 1999. "Aby Warburg and the Nameless Science." *Potentialities: Collected Essays in Philosophy*: 89–103.

Aiello, G. 2007. *The Appearance of Diversity: Visual Design and the Public Communication of EU Identity. European Union Identity: Perceptions from Asia and Europe.* Baden-Baden: Nomos.

Alberti, L. B. 1966. *On Painting.* Ed. and trans. John R. Spencer. New Haven, CT: Yale University Press.

Alexander, M. 2013. "Interview with Ton Roos, Director of Banknotes at the European Central Bank." 14 March. Retrieved from http://news.coinupdate.com/interview-with-ton-roos-director-of-banknotes-at-the-european-central-bank-1890.

Alford, C. F. 2001. "Leadership by Interpretation and Holding." *Organizational and Social Dynamics* 1(2): 153–73.

Allatson, P. 2007. "Antes cursi que sencilla: Eurovision Song Contests and the Kitsch-Drive to Euro-Unity." *Culture, Theory and Critique* 48(1): 87–98.

Almansi, R. J. 1960. "The Face-Breast Equation." *Journal of the American Psychoanalytic Association* 8: 43–70.

Almond, G., and S. Verba. 1963. *The Civic Culture: Political Attitudes and Democracy in Five Nations.* Princeton: Princeton University Press.

Alonso, A. M. 1994. "The Politics of Space, Time and Substance: State Formation, Nationalism and Ethnicity. *Annual Review of Anthropology* 23: 379–405.

Alvesson, M., and K. Sköldberg. 2010. *Reflexive Methodology. New Vistas for Qualitative Research.* 2nd ed. London: Sage.

Anderson, B. 1991. *Imagined Communities: Reflections on the Origin and Spread of Nationalism.* London: Verso.

Andrejevic, M., and Z. Volcic. 2011. "Nation Branding in the Era of Commercial Nationalism." *International Journal of Communication* 5: 598–618.

Archand, D. 1995. "Myths, Lies and Historical Truth: A Defence of Nationalism." *Political Studies* 43: 472–81.

Arlow, J. A. 1979. "Metaphor and the Psychoanalytic Situation." *Psychoanalytic Quarterly* 48: 363–85.

Arvanitakis, K. I. 1998a. "Some Thoughts on the Essence of the Tragic." *International Journal of Psychoanalysis* 79: 955–64.

———. 1998b. "A Theory of Theater: Theater as Theory." *Psychoanalysis and Contemporary Thought* 21: 33–60.

Aston, E. 2013. "Competing Femininities: A 'Girl' For Eurovision." In *Performing the 'New' Europe: Identities, Feelings, and Politics in the Eurovision Song Contest,* ed. K. Fricker and M. Gluhovic. 163–77. New York: Palgrave Macmillan.

Auer, S. 2013. "The End of the European Dream: What Future for Europe's Constrained Democracy?" *Eurozine* 22(2). Retrieved from http://www.eurozine.com/articles/2013-02-22-auer-en.html.

Augé, M. 1995. *Non-Places: Introduction to the Anthropology of Supermodernity.* Trans. J. Howe. New York: Verso.

Aumada, L. C. 2005. "From Mimesis to Agency: Clinical Steps in the Work of Psychic Two-ness." *International Journal of Psychoanalysis* 86(3): 721–36.

Backhaus, J. G. 1999. "Money and Its Economic and Social Functions: Simmel and European Monetary Integration." *American Journal of Economics and Sociology* 58(4): 1075–90.

Baier, S. 2006. "The History of Paneurope." *Paneuropa Union.* Retrieved from http://www.epaneurope.eu/tl_files/epaneurope2011/downloads/documents/Paneuropa%20History.pdf.

Bakhtin, M. M. 1968. *Rabelais and His World.* Trans. H. Iswolsky. Cambridge: Massachusetts Institute of Technology Press.

Balestrini, P. P., and R. Gamble. 2011. "Confronting EU Unpopularity: The Contribution of Political Marketing." *Contemporary Politics* 17(1): 89–107.

Balibar, É. 2004. *We, the People of Europe? Reflections on Transnational Citizenship.* Princeton, NJ: Princeton University Press.

Barchiesi, A., and W. Scheidel, eds. 2010. *The Oxford Handbook of Roman Studies.* Oxford: Oxford University Press.

Bargh, J. A., R. R. Hassin, and J. S. Uleman, eds. 2004. *The New Unconscious.* Oxford: Oxford University Press.

Barracco, A. 2011. "Into the Wild: Nelle terre selvagge." *Osservatorio Psicologia nei Media* 24(9). Retrieved from http://www.osservatoriopsicologia.com/2011/09/24/into-the-wild-nelle-terre-selvagge.

Barringer, J. M. 1991. "Europa and the Nereids: Wedding or Funeral?" *American Journal of Archaeology* 95: 657–67.

Barroso, J. M. D. 2012a. "Opening of 'Europe Meets the World.'" Copenhagen 12(1). Retrieved from http://europa.eu/rapid/press-release_SPEECH-12-7_en.htm.

———. 2012b. "State of the Union 2012 Address." Strasbourg, 12(9). Retrieved from http://europa.eu/rapid/press-release_SPEECH-12-596_en.htm.

———. 2012c. "Statement by President Barroso Following the Award of the 2012 Nobel Peace Prize." Brussels, 16(10). Retrieved from http://europa.eu/rapid/press-release_SPEECH-12-724_en.htm.

———. 2013. "A New Narrative for Europe." Brussels, 23(4). Retrieved from http://europa.eu/rapid/press-release_SPEECH-13-357_en.htm.
Barry, V. C. 2001. "Freud and Symbolism: Or How a Cigar Became More than Just a Cigar." *Annual of Psychoanalysis* 29: 51–65.
Barthes, R. 1972. *Mythologies*. Trans. A. Lavers. New York: Hill and Wang.
———. 1975. *The Pleasure of the Text*. Trans. R. Miller. New York: Hill and Wang.
———. 1977. "Rhetoric of the Image." In *Image, Music, Text,* trans. S. Heath, 152–63. New York: Hill and Wang.
Bassina, I., and M. Bas. 2002. *The United Europe as an Antidote to a Democratic Nation State in the Ideas of F. Nietzsche.* Retrieved from http://www.roepstem.net/nietzsche.html.
Baum, L. F. 1900. *The Wonderful Wizard of Oz.* Chicago: George M. Hill.
Bauman, Z. 2004. *Europe: An Unfinished Adventure.* Cambridge: Polity Press.
Beiner, R., ed. 1995. *Theorizing Citizenship.* Albany: State University of New York Press.
Bell, D. 2003. "Mythscapes: Memory, Mythology, and National Identity." *British Journal of Sociology* 54(1): 63–81.
———. 2008. "Agonistic Democracy and the Politics of Memory." *Constellations* 15(1): 148–66.
Bellah, R. 1967. "Civil Religion in America." *Daedalus* 96(1): 1–21.
———. 1970. *Beyond Relief Essays on Religion in a Post-Traditional World.* New York: Harper.
Belting, H. 1994. *Likeness and Presence: A History of the Image before the Era of Art.* Chicago: University of Chicago Press.
———. 2014. *Facce: Una storia del volto.* Rome: Carocci.
Benda, J. 2006. *The Treason of the Intellectuals.* New Brunswick, NJ: Transaction Publishers.
———. 1993. *Discours à la nation européenne.* Paris: Gallimard.
Benjamin, W. 1978. "One Way Street." In *One Way Street and Other Writings,* 61–94. London: Verso.
———. 1968. "The Work of Art in the Age of Mechanical Reproduction." In *Illuminations,* ed. Hannah Arendt. New York: Schocken Books.
Bennett, A. 2005. *Culture and Everyday Life.* London: Sage.
Bennett, W. L. 1979. "Imitation, Ambiguity, and Drama in Political Life: Civil Religion and the Dilemmas of Public Morality." *Journal of Politics* 41(1): 106–33.
Benveniste, E. 1969. *Il vocabolario delle istituzioni indoeuropee.* Ed. M. Liborio. Torino: Einaudi.
Berezin, M. 2000. "The Euro Is More than Money: Converting Currency, Exchanging Identity, and Selling Citizenship in Post-Maastricht Europe." *Center for Society and Economy Policy Newsletter* 1(1). Retrieved from http://www.bus.umich.edu/FacultyResearch/ResearchCenters/Centers/Cse/CseSite/Newsletter/Archives/IssueOne/Berezin.pdf.
Berger, J. 1972. *Ways of Seeing.* London: British Broadcasting Corporation and Penguin Books.
Berlin, I. 1990. *The Crooked Timber of Humanity.* Princeton, NJ: Princeton University Press.
Best, E., and F. Lambermont. 2011. *Citizen Involvement in EU Policies: Impos-*

sible Dream or Work in Progress? Maastricht: European Institute of Public Administration.

Bettelheim, B. 1976. *The Uses of Enchantment: The Meaning and Importance of Fairy Tales.* New York: Vintage Books.

Bhabha, H. K. 1994. *The Location of Culture.* New York: Routledge.

Biedenkopf, K. H., B. Geremek, and K. Michalski. 2005. *The Spiritual and Cultural Dimension of Europe: Reflection Group Initiated by the President of the European Commission and Coordinated by the Institute for Human Sciences; Concluding Remarks.* Luxembourg: Office for Official Publications of the European Communities. Retrieved from ftp://ftcordis.europa.eu/pub/citizens/docs/citizens_michalski_091104_report_annexes_en.pdf.

Bielby, D. D., and C. L. Harrington. 2005. "Flow, Home, and Media Pleasures." *Journal of Popular Culture* 38(5): 834–54.

Billig, M. 1995. *Banal Nationalism.* London: Sage.

Bion, W. R. 1959. *Experiences in Groups.* New York: Basic Books.

———. 1962. "A Theory of Thinking." In *Second Thoughts* 110-9. New York: Aronson.

Black, A., and C. Shore. 1994. "Citizens' Europe and the Construction of European Identity." In *Anthropology of Europe: Identities and Boundaries in Conflict,* ed. V. A. Goddard, J. R. Llobera, and C. Shore, 275–98. Oxford: Berg.

Bloch, E., and J. Derrida. 2008. "Psychoanalysis and Politics: The Theory of Ideology in Slavoj Žižek." *International Journal of Žižek Studies.* Retrieved from http://zizekstudies.org/index.php/ijzs/article/view/149/243.

Bloch, M., J. Casanova, J. Comaroff, and B. Kapferer. 2014. "Special Virtual Issue: Four Portraits." In *Religion and Society, Advances in Research.* New York: Berghahn Journals.

Blonsky, M. 1982. "The Body in Advertising." In *Social Text,* 73–85. Durham, NC: Duke University Press.

Bloom, W. 1990. *Personal Identity, National Identity and International Relations.* Cambridge: Cambridge University Press.

Blumenberg, H. 1985. *Work on Myth.* Trans. R. Wallace. Cambridge: MIT Press.

Bodner, E., and A. Gilboa. 2009. "What Are Your Thoughts When the National Anthem Is Playing? An Empirical Exploration." *Psychology of Music* 37(4): 459–84.

Bohlman, P. V., and D. Tragaki. 2013. "Europa Borealis: Reflections on the 2013 Eurovision Song Contest Malmö," 31 May, OUP Blog. Retrieved from http://blog.oucom/2013/05/europa-borealis.

Bolin, G. 2006. "Visions of Europe: Cultural Technologies of Nation-States." *International Journal of Cultural Studies* 9(2): 189–206.

Bollas, C. 1978. "The Aesthetic Moment and the Search for Transformation." *Annual of Psychoanalysis* 6: 385–94.

———. 1979. "The Transformational Object." *International Journal of Psychoanalysis* 60: 97–107.

Bonitzer, P. 1985. *Décadrages: Peinture et cinéma.* Paris: Éditions de l'Étoile.

Bornstein, R. F., and N. Becker-Matero. 2011. "Reconnecting Psychoanalysis to Mainstream Psychology: Metaphor as Glue." *Psychoanalytic Inquiry* 31(2): 172–84.

Bottici, C. 2007. *A Philosophy of Political Myth.* Cambridge: Cambridge University Press.

Bottici, C., and B. Challand. 2006. "Rethinking Political Myth: The Clash of Civilizations as a Self-Fulfilling Prophecy." *European Journal of Social Theory* 9(3): 315–36.

———. 2013. *Imagining Europe: Myth, Memory, and Identity.* Cambridge: Cambridge University Press.

Bouchard, G. 2007. "Le Mythe: Essai de définition." In *Mythes et sociétés des Amériques,* ed. G. Bouchard and B. Andrès. Montreal: Québec Amérique.

Bourdon, J. 2007. "Unhappy Engineers of the European Soul: The EBU and the Woes of Pan-European Television." *International Communication Gazette* 69(3): 263–80.

Brague, R. 1992. *Eccentric Culture: A Theory of Western Civilization.* South Bend, IN: St. Augustine's Press.

Braidotti, R. 2008. "Europe Does Not Make Us Dream: An Interview with Rosi Braidotti by Rutvica Andrijašević." 11 September. Retrieved from http://translate.eipcnet/strands/02/andrijasevicbraidotti-strands01en#redir.

———. 2011. *Nomadic Theory: The Portable Rosi Braidotti.* New York: Columbia University Press.

———. 1991. *Ethnicity and Nationalism: Theory and Comparison.* London: Sage.

Breckman, W. 2005. "Democracy between Disenchantment and Political Theology: French Post-Marxism and the Return of Religion." *New German Critique* 94: 72–105.

Bredekamp, H. 2015. *Immagini che ci guardano: Teoria dell'atto iconico.* Trans. S. Buttazzi. Milan: Raffaello Cortina Editore.

Breuilly, J. 1982. *Nationalism and the State.* Manchester: Manchester University Press.

Breuilly, J., and E. Gellner. 2008. *Nations and Nationalism.* Ithaca, NY: Cornell University Press.

Brey, M. 2014. "Conchita to 'Rise like a Phoenix' for Austria." *Eurovision* 18(3). Retrieved from http://www.eurovision.tv/page/news?id=conchita_to_rise_like_a_phoenix_for_austria.

Brion, R., and J. M. Moreau. 2001. *A Flutter of Banknotes: From the First European Paper Money to the Euro.* Antwerp: Mercatorfonds.

Brubaker, R. 1998. "Myths and Misconceptions in the Study of Nationalism." In *The State of the Nation: Ernest Gellner and the Theory of Nationalism,* ed. J. A. Hall, 272–306. Cambridge: Cambridge University Press.

Bruter, M. 2003. "Winning Hearts and Minds for Europe: The Impact of News and Symbols on Civic and Cultural Identity." *Comparative Political Studies* 36(10): 1148–79.

———. 2005. *Citizens of Europe? The Emergence of a Mass European Identity.* New York: Palgrave Macmillan.

———. 2009. "Time Bomb? The Dynamic Effect of News and Symbols on the Political Identity of European Citizens." *Comparative Political Studies* 42(12): 1498–1536.

Buber, M., and R. G. Smith. 1937. *Ich und Du. I and Thou.* Trans. R. G. Smith. Edinburgh: T. and T. Clark.

Buehler, A. 2011. "The Twenty-First-Century Study of Collective Effervescence: Expanding the Context of Fieldwork." *Fieldwork in Religion* 7(1): 70–97.

Burke, E. 1841. "Letters on a Regicide Peace." In *The Works on the Right Honourable Edmund Burke*. 12 vols. 2:275–352.

Burke, P. 2001. *Eyewitnessing: The Uses of Images as Historical Evidence*. Clerkenwell: Reaktion Books.

Burnett, J., S. Moriarty, and W. Wells. 2006. *Advertising: Principles and Practice*. 7th ed. Upper Saddle River, NJ: Pearson/Prentice Hall.

Butz, D. A. 2009. "National Symbols as Agents of Psychological and Social Change." *Political Psychology* 30(5): 779–804.

Caillois, R. 2000. *I giochi e gli uomini*. Milan: Bompiani.

Calogeras, R. C. 1973. "Levi-Strauss and Freud: Their 'Structural' Approach to Myths." *American Imago* 30: 57–79.

Campbell, J. 1993. *The Hero with a Thousand Faces*. London: Fontana Press.

———. 2002. *The Inner Reaches of Outer Space: Metaphor as Myth and as Religion*. New York: New World Library.

Caporaso, J. 1996. "The European Union and Forms of State: Westphalian, Regulatory or Post-Modern." *Journal of Common Market Studies* 34(1): 29–52.

Carey, S. 2002. "Undivided Loyalties: Is National Identity an Obstacle to European Integration?" *European Union Politics* 3(4): 387–413.

Carroll, M. 1981. "Lévi-Strauss, Freud, and the Trickster: A New Perspective upon an Old Problem." *American Ethnologist* 8(2): 301–13.

Cartwright, L., and M. Sturken. 2001a. *Practices of Looking: An Introduction to Visual Culture*. Oxford: Oxford University Press.

———. 2001b. "Images, Power, and Politics." In *Practices of Looking: An Introduction to Visual Culture*, 11–44. Oxford: Oxford University Press.

Cassirer, E. 1955. *The Myth of the State*. New York: Doubleday Anchor Books.

Castiglione, D. 2009. "Political Identity in a Community of Strangers." In *European Identity*, ed. J. T. Checkel and P. J. Katzenstein, 29–51. Cambridge: Cambridge University Press

Castoriadis, C. 1997a. "The Imaginary: Creation in the Social-Historical Domain." In *World in Fragments: Writings on Politics, Society, Psychoanalysis and the Imagination*, ed. D.A. Curtis, 3–18. Palo Alto, CA: Stanford University Press.

———. 1997b. "Psychoanalysis and Politics." In *World in Fragments: Writings on Politics, Society, Psychoanalysis and the Imagination*, ed. D.A. Curtis, 125–36. Palo Alto, CA: Stanford University Press.

Cavanagh, M., and J. Mitchell. 2001. "Context and Contingency: Constitutional Nationalists and Europe." In *Minority Nationalism, Globalization and European Integration*, ed. Michael Keating and John McGarry, 246–65. Oxford: Oxford University Press.

Cavicchiolo, A. 2002. *L'immagine moderna e antica del denaro-Incontro con Guido Crapanzano, tra i maggiori esperti mondiali di numismatica e di cartamoneta*. 13, 10–14. BVE institute. Retrieved from http://cont.ubibanca.it/cont/2/downloads/13immaginemoderna.pdf.

Centre Virtuel de la Connaissance sur l'Europe (CVCE). 2011. *The Currency of the European Union*. Retrieved from http://www.cvce.eu/obj/the_currency_of_the_european_union-en-de0d4ede-f55d-4610-b666-8ac20af880ab.html.

———. 2012. *The Flag of the European Union.* Retrieved from http://www.cvce.eu/en/education/unit-content/-/unit/eeacde09-add1-4ba1-ba5b-dcd2597a81d0/2b4e569f-9aa3-48dd-b877-13d0d5f1d177.

Cerulo, K. A. 1993. "Symbols and the World System: National Anthems and Flags." *Sociological Forum* 8(2): 243–71.

———. 1997. "Identity Construction: New Issues, New Directions." *Annual Review of Sociology* 23: 385–409.

Cerutti, F., S. Lucarelli, and V. A. Schmidt. 2011. *Debating Political Identity and Legitimacy in the European Union.* New York: Routledge.

Chabod, F., A. Saitta, and E. Sestan. 1961. *Storia dell'idea d'Europa.* Bari: Laterza.

Chamberlin, E. J. 2004. *If This Is Your Land, Where Are Your Stories? Reimagining Home and Sacred Space.* Cincinnati: Pilgrim Press.

Chambers, D., R. Johnson, P. Raghuram, and E. Tincknell. 2004. *The Practice of Cultural Studies.* London: Sage.

Checkel, J. T. 2005. "International Institutions and Socialization in Europe: Introduction and Framework." *International Organization* 59(4): 801–26.

Checkel, J. T., and J. Katzenstein. 2009. *European Identity.* Cambridge: Cambridge University Press.

Chianese D., F. Chianese, and A. Fontana. 2010. *Immaginando.* Milan: Franco Angeli.

Churchill, W. 1946. Speech delivered at the University of Zurich, 19(9). Retrieved from http://www.coe.int/t/dgal/dit/ilcd/Archives/selection/Churchill/ZurichSpeech_en.as.

Cieszynska B., J. E. Franco, and T. Pinheiro. 2012. *Ideas of/for Europe—An Interdisciplinary Approach to European Identity.* New York: Peter Lang.

Citrin, J., and J. Sides. 2004. "More than Nationals: How Identity Choice Matters in the New Europe." In *Transnational Identities: Becoming European in the EU,* ed. R. K. Herrmann, T. Risse, and M. B. Brewer, 161–85. Lanham, MD: Rowman and Littlefield.

Clark, C. 1997. "Forging Identity, Beethoven's 'Ode' as European Anthem." *Critical Inquiry* 23(4).

Cmeciu, C. M., I. Branch. 2012. "Insights into the European Years' Communication Toolboxes." *Styles of Communication* 4(1): 36–58.

Cohen, A. 1985. *The Symbolic Construction of Community.* London: Routledge.

Cohen, S. 1973. *Folk Devils and Moral Panic.* London: Paladin.

Coleman, S. 2008. "Why Is the Eurovision Song Contest Ridiculous? Exploring a Spectacle of Embarrassment, Irony and Identity." *Popular Communication* 6(3): 127–40.

Coman, J. 2001. "This Time It's Real: The Euro Conquers the Continent." *Telegraph* 30(12). Retrieved from http://www.telegraph.co.uk/news/worldnews/europe/1366693/This-time-its-real-the-euro-conquers-the-Continent.html.

Comte, A. 1957. *A General View of Positivism.* Trans. J. H. Bridges. New York: Robert Speller.

Conchita, W. 2014. *About Conchita Wurst.* Retrieved from http://www.eurovision.tv/page/history/year/participant-profile/?song=32263

Consultative Assembly of the Council of Europe (CACE). 1971. *Explanatory Memorandum by Mr. Radius.* 10(6), Archives of the European Commission,

Brussels. Retrieved from http://www.coe.int/t/dgal/dit/ilcd/Archives/selection/Anthem/PACE2978_en.pdf.

Cook, G. 2001. *The Discourse of Advertising.* 2nd ed. New York: Routledge.

Coudenhove-Kalergi, R. 1926. *Pan-Europe.* New York: Alfred A. Knopf.

Couldry, N. 2003. *Media Rituals: A Critical Approach.* New York: Routledge.

Council and Commission of the European Communities. 1992. *Treaty on European Union.* Maastricht, 7 February 1992. Retrieved from http://europa.eu/eu-law/decision-making/treaties/pdf/treaty_on_european_union/treaty_on_european_union_en.pdf.

Council of Europe. 1951. *Memorandum from the Secretariat General of the Council of Europe on the European Flag,* Strasbourg, 16 July 1951. Retrieved from http://www.cvce.eu/content/publication/2005/9/14/081673a8-1849-4930-a774-e23d0fbad413/publishable_en.pdf.

———. 1972. *Decision (71)187 of the Committee of Ministers of the Council of Europe.* Retrieved from http://www.cvce.eu/obj/Decision_71_187_of_the_Committee_of_Ministers_of_the_Council_of_Europe_12_January_1972-end8cea3a1-b065-4d1b-a6d7-6ab78a792bf4.html.

Cram, L. 2001. "Imagining the Union: A Case of Banal Europeanism?" In *Interlocking Dimensions of European Integration,* ed. Helen Wallace, 343–62. London: Palgrave.

———. 2009a. "Banal Europeanism: European Union Identity and National Identities in Synergy." *Nations and Nationalism* 15(1): 101–8.

———. 2009b. "Identity and European Integration: Diversity as a Source of Integration." *Nations and Nationalism* 15(1): 109–28.

———. 2012. "Does the EU Need a Navel? Implicit and Explicit Identification with the European Union." *Journal of Common Market Studies* 50(1): 71–86.

Craufurd Smith, R. 2006. "Tobias Theiler, Political Symbolism and European Integration." *Common Market Law Review* 43(6): 1757–58.

Cultural Committee. 2014. *A New Narrative for Europe: The Mind and Body of Europe.* Retrieved from http://ec.europa.eu/culture/policy/new-narrative/documents/declaration_en.pdf.

Cusa, N. 1988. *De Visione Dei.* In *Nicholas of Cusa's Dialectical Mysticism: Text, Translation, and Interpretive Study of De Visione Dei,* ed. J. Hopkins, 99–287. 2nd ed. Minneapolis: Press.

D'Angelo, F. J. 1986. "Subliminal Seduction: An Essay on the Rhetoric of the Unconscious." *Rhetoric Review* 4(2): 160–71.

Davin, A., and C. Ginzburg. 1980. "Morelli, Freud and Sherlock Holmes: Clues and Scientific Method." *History Workshop* 9: 5–36.

Dayan, D., and E. Katz. 1992. *Media Events: The Live Broadcasting of History.* Cambridge, MA: Harvard University Press.

De Clercq, W. 1993. "Reflection on Information and Communication Policy of the European Community: Report by the Group of Experts Chaired by Mr. Willy De Clercq Member of the European Parliament." Retrieved from http://aei.pitt.edu/29870.

Delzell, C.F. 1960. "The European Federalist Movement in Italy: First Phase, 1918–1947." *Journal of Modern History* 32(3): 241–50.

de Mendelssohn, F. 2001. "Building a Bridge to Heaven: Notes on the Construction, Destruction and Reconstruction of the Tower of Babel." *Free Associations* 8(3): 486–506.

Dean, J. 2006. *Žižek's Politics.* New York: Routledge.

Delanty, G. 1995. *Inventing Europe: Idea, Identity, Reality.* London: Palgrave Macmillan.

Delcourt, M. 1958. *Hermaphrodite: Mythes et rites de la bisexualité dans l'antiquité classique.* Paris: Presses Universitaires de France.

Della Sala, V. 2010. "Political Myth, Mythology and the European Union." *Journal of Common Market Studies* 48(1): 1–19.

Delors, J. 2013. "Rethinking the EMU and Making Greater Europe Positive Again." *Tribune, Notre Europe–Jacques Delors Institute,* 28.

Demiray, B. G. 2012. "The Avenging Females: A Comparative Analysis of *Kill Bill Vol. 1–2, Death Proof* and *Sympathy for Lady Vengeance.*" *CINEJ Cinema Journal* 1(2): 29–35.

Den Boer, P., P. Bugge, K. Wilson, J. Van der Dussen, and O. Waever 1995. *The History of the Idea of Europe.* Walton Hall: Open University.

Derrida, J. 2005. *Politics of Friendship.* London: Verso.

De Certeau, M. D. 1987. "The Gaze Nicholas of Cusa." *Diacritics* 17(3): 2–38.

Deutsch, K. 1953. "The Growth of Nations: Some Recurrent Patterns of Political and Social Integration." *World Politics* 5: 5–62.

———. 1966. *Nationalism and Social Communication.* Cambridge, MA: MIT Press.

Directorate-General for Communication and Education, Audiovisual and Culture Executive Agency. 2013. "Europe for Citizens Programme 2007–2013." Retrieved from http://eacea.ec.europa.eu/citizenship/programme/documents/2013/guide_2013_en_final%20.pdf.

Draghi, M. 2012. *Verbatim of the Remarks Made by Mario Draghi: Speech by Mario Draghi, President of the European Central Bank at the Global Investment Conference in London 26 July 2012.* Retrieved from https://www.ecb.europa.eu/press/key/date/2012/html/sp120726.en.html.

———. 2013a. *Unveiling of the 5 Euro Banknote of the New Europa series: Short Address by Mario Draghi, President of the ECB, at the Archaeological Museum in Frankfurt am Main, 10 January 2013.* Retrieved from https://www.ecb.europa.eu/press/key/date/2013/html/sp130110.en.html.

———. 2013b. *Address at the New Year's Reception of the Frankfurt Chamber of Commerce and Industry: Speech by Mario Draghi, President of the ECB, Frankfurt am Main, 22 January 2013.* Retrieved from https://www.ecb.europa.eu/press/key/date/2013/html/sp130122.en.html.

———. 2015a. *Draghi del BCE no ve sentido en especular sobre la salida de Grecia del euro.* 15 February. Retrieved from http://es.reuters.com/article/topNews/idESKBN0LJ0MZ20150215.

———. 2015b. *Address by Mario Draghi to Mark the Unveiling of the New €20 Banknote.* Frankfurt, 24 February. Retrieved from http://www.new-euro-banknotes.eu/News-Events/Press/SPEECHES-INTERVIEWS/ADDRESS-BY-MARIO-DRAGHI-TO-MARK-THE-UNVEILING-OF-THE-NEW-%E2%82%AC20-BANKNOTE.

Dryden, J., and S. Garth, trans. 2013. *The Metamorphoses by Ovid*. Retrieved from http://classics.mit.edu/Ovid/metam.mb.txt.

Duisenberg, W. F. 2001. *Euro 2002 Information Campaign: The EURO. OUR Money. Speech Delivered by Dr. Willem F. Duisenberg, President of the European Central Bank at the Conference Hosted by the Bank of Greece on 17 October 2001 in Athens.* Retrieved from https://www.ecb.europa.eu/press/key/date/2001/html/sp011017.en.html.

Durkheim, É. 1961. *The Elementary Forms of the Religious Life.* New York: Cottier-Macmillan.

Easton, D. 1975. "A Reassessment of the Concept of Political Support." *British Journal of Political Science* 5: 435–57.

Ebu News. 2014. "EBU President: 'Public Service Media Promote Values that Shape the EU.'" 16(9). Retrieved from http://www3.ebu.ch/contents/news/2014/09/ebu-president-public-service-med.html.

Eco, U. 1965. "Towards a Semiotic Enquiry into the Television Message." In *Communications Studies: An Introductory Reader,* ed. J. Corner and J. Hawthorn, 131–50. London: Edward Arnold.

———. 1981. "The Theory of Signs and the Role of the Reader." *Bulletin of the Midwest Modern Language Association* 14(1): 35–45.

———. 1984. *The Role of the Reader.* Bloomington: Indiana University Press.

Edelman, M. 1967. *The Symbolic Uses of Politics.* New York: Greenwood.

Efal, A. 2000. "Warburg's Pathos Formula in Psychoanalytic and Benjaminian Contexts." *Assaph-Studies in Art History* 5: 221–38.

Elbe, S. 2001. "We Good Europeans: Homo Europaeus beyond East and West-Genealogical Reflections on the Idea of Europe." *Millennium Journal of International Studies* 30(2): 259–84.

———. 2002. "'Labyrinths of the Future': Nietzsche's Genealogy of European Nationalism." *Journal of Political Ideologies* 7(1): 77–96.

———. 2003. *Europe: A Nietzschean Perspective.* Vol. 11. New York: Psychology Press.

Elgenius, G. 2005. "National Days and Nation-Building." In *Statehood Before and Beyond Ethnicity: Minor States in Northern and Eastern Europe 1600–2000,* ed. L. Eriksonas and L. Müller, 365–84. Brussels: Peter Lang.

Eliade, M. 1959. *Cosmos and History: The Myth of the Eternal Return.* New York: Harper and Brothers.

———. 1961. *Images and Symbols: Studies in Religious Symbolism.* Princeton, NJ: Princeton University Press.

———. 1965. *Rites and Symbols of Initiation.* New York: Harper and Row.

———. 1967. *Myths, Dreams, and Mysteries: The Encounter between Contemporary Faiths and Archaic Realities.* New York: Harper and Row.

———. 1978. *A History of Religious Ideas: From the Stone Age to the Eleusinian Mysteries.* Chicago: University of Chicago Press.

———. 1991. *Images and Symbols: Studies in Religious Symbolism.* Princeton, NJ: Princeton University Press.

Emery, E. 1995. "A Note on Sandor Ferenczi and the Dionysian Itinerary in Psychoanalysis." *Psychoanalytic Review* 82: 267–71.

———. 2000. "Facing 'O': Wilfred Bion, Emmanuel Levinas, and the Face of the Other." *Psychoanalytic Review* 87(6): 799–840.

Engel, P. 2009. "Julien Benda's Thoughtful Europe." *Monist* 92(2): 315–21.

Eriksen, T. H. 2007. "Some Questions about Flags." In *Flag, Nation and Symbolism in Europe and America,* ed. T. H. Eriksen and R. Jenkins, 1–13. New York: Routledge.

EurActiv. 2009.) "EU Official: 'New Narrative' Needed for Lisbon Agenda." Euractiv.com. Retrieved from http://www.euractiv.com/priorities/eu-official-new-narrative-needed-lisbon-agenda/article-183431.

European Broadcasting Union (EBU). 2012. *Empowering Society: A Declaration on the Core Values of Public Service Media.* Retrieved from https://www3.ebu.ch/files/live/sites/ebu/files/Publications/EBU-Empowering-Society_EN.pdf.

ECB (European Central Bank). 2002a. *The Euro, Our Money.* Retrieved from https://www.ecb.europa.eu/pub/pdf/other/eurobren.pdf.

———. 2002b. *The European Central Bank.* Retrieved from https://www.ecb.europa.eu/pub/pdf/infobr/ecbbren.pdf.

———. 2007. *How the Euro Became Our Money: A Short History of the Euro Banknotes and Coins.* Retrieved from https://www.ecb.europa.eu/pub/pdf/other/euro_became_our_moneyen.pdf.

———. 2011. *The First Ten Years of the Euro Banknotes and Coins.* Video. Retrieved from https://www.youtube.com/watch?v=o0YrRM7yee0.

———. 2012a. *Europa: The New face of the Euro.* Video. Retrieved from http://www.new-euro-banknotes.eu/Europa-Series/The-Myth-of-Europa.

———. 2012b. *The Second Series of Euro Banknotes.* Press kit on the Europa Series. Retrieved from http://www.neue-euro-banknoten.eu/press/Press_Kit_EN.pdf.

———. 2012c. *Announcement of Europa Series on 8 November 2012.* News release. Retrieved from http://www.new-euro-banknotes.eu/News-Events/Events/ANNOUNCEMENT-OF-EUROPA-SERIES-ON-8-NOVEMBER-2012.

———. 2013a. *Unveiling the New €5 Banknote.* Video. Retrieved from http://www.new-euro-banknotes.eu/News-Events/Events/UNVEILING-OF-THE-NEW-%E2%82%AC5-BANKNOTE.

———. 2013b. Press Kit for the Euro Exhibition in Riga and the Euro Information Campaign in Latvia. Retrieved from http://www.new-euro-banknotes.eu/press/pdfonline/Press_Kit_Riga-EN_Web/index.html.

———. 2014a. *Discover the New €10 Banknote.* Press kit on the Europa Series. Retrieved from http://www.new-euro-banknotes.eu/press/pdfonline/Press_Kit_10-Banknote-EN_Web/index.html.

———. 2014b. *Unveiling of the New €10.* Illuminating the Europa. Video. Retrieved from http://www.new-euro-banknotes.eu/News-Events/Events/UNVEILING-OF-THE-NEW-%E2%82%AC10.

———. 2015a. *Discover the New €20 Banknote.* Press kit on the Europa Series. Retrieved from https://www.ecb.europa.eu/euro/shared/files/150224_presskit_europa_en.pdf.

———. 2015b. *Unveiling of the New €20.* Illuminating the Europa. Video. Retrieved from http://www.new-euro-banknotes.eu/News-Events/Events/UNVEILING-OF-THE-NEW-%E2%82%AC20.

European Commission. 1983. *The Community and Culture. European File, 5/83, March.* Brochure. Luxembourg: Office for Official Publications of the European Communities. Retrieved from http://aei.pitt.edu/14648.

———. 1995. *Green Paper on the Practical Arrangements for the Introduction of the Single Currency.* Office for Official Publications of the European Communities. 31(5). Retrieved from http://aei.pitt.edu/1392/1/introduction_single_currency_COM_95_333.pdf.

———. 1998. *Report of the Expert Working Group "Euro-Education."* Brussels, 29(1). Retrieved from http://www.worldcat.org/title/report-of-the-expert-working-group-euro-education/oclc/245994115.

———. 2000. *Communication from the Commission to the Council, the European Parliament, the Economic and Social Committee and the Committee of the Regions: On Communications Strategy in the Last Phases of the Completion of Emu.* Brussels, 2(2). Retrieved from http://eur-lex.europa.eu/legal-content/EN/TXT/PDF/?uri=CELEX:52000DC0057andfrom=EN.

———. 2001. *European Governance: A White Paper.* Brussels. Retrieved from http://eur-lex.europa.eu/legal-content/EN/TXT/?uri=URISERV:l10109.

———. 2002. "Europe: Celebrating the Birth of the Euro." *Europe: Magazine of the European Union 412.* Retrieved from http://aei.pitt.edu/44847.

———. 2004. *Communication from the Commission to the Council, the European Parliament, the European Economic and Social Committee and the Committee of the Regions on the Implementation of an Information and Communication Strategy on the Euro and Economic and Monetary Union.* Retrieved from http://eur-lex.europa.eu/legal-content/EN/TXT/?uri=CELEX:52004DC0552.

———. 2005a. *Action plan to Improve Communicating Europe by the Commission.* Communication to the Commission. Brussels, 20(7). Retrieved from http://ec.europa.eu/dgs/communication/pdf/comm-initiatives/2005-action-plan-improve-communicating-europe-by-commission-sec2005-98n5_en.pdf.

———. 2005b. *Communication from the Commission to the Council, the European Parliament, the European Economic and Social Committee and the Committee of the Regions-The Commission's Contribution to the Period of Reflection and Beyond: Plan-D for Democracy, Dialogue and Debate.* Brussels, 16(10). Retrieved from http://eur-lex.europa.eu/legal-content/EN/TXT/PDF/?uri=CELEX:52005DC0494andfrom=EN.

———. 2006. *White Paper on a European Communication Policy.* Brussels, 1(2). Retrieved from http://europa.eu/documents/comm/white_papers/pdf/com2006_35_en.pdf.

———. 2007a. *Communication from the Commission to the European Parliament, the Council, the European Economic and Social Committee and the Committee of the Regions—on a European Agenda for Culture in a Globalizing World.* Brussels, 10(5). Retrieved from http://eur-lex.europa.eu/LexUriServ/LexUriServ.do?uri=COM:2007:0242:FIN:EN:PDF.

———. 2007b. *Communication from the Commission to the European Parliament, the Council, the European Economic and Social Committee and the Committee of the Regions.* Communicating Europe in Partnership, 3(10). Retrieved from http://eur-lex.europa.eu/legal-content/EN/TXT/PDF/?uri=CELEX:52007DC0568andfrom=IT.

———. 2008. *Standard Eurobarometer 69, Public Opinion in the European Union.* Spring 2008. Retrieved from http://ec.europa.eu/public_opinion/archives/eb/eb69/eb_69_first_en.pdf.

———. 2010. *EU Citizenship Report 2010: Dismantling the Obstacles to EU Citizens' Rights.* Retrieved from http://ec.europa.eu/justice/citizen/files/com_2010_603_en.pdf.

———. 2012. *Is the EU's Latest Enlargement Video Racist?* Video. Retrieved from https://www.youtube.com/watch?v=WQREDQjfzC4

———. *2013a. Co-Creating European Union Citizenship: Policy Review.* Retrieved from http://www.gppq.fct.pt/h2020/_docs/brochuras/society/co-creating_eu_citizenship.pdf.

———. 2013b. *EU Citizenship Report—EU Citizens: Your Rights, Your Future.* Retrieved from http://ec.europa.eu/justice/citizen/files/2013eucitizenshipreport_en.pdf.

———. 2013c. *Visual Identity Manual.* Retrieved from http://ec.europa.eu/dgs/communication/services/visual_identity/pdf/charter_en.pdf.

———. 2013d. *Europe: Your Vote Counts.* Video. Retrieved on 12 June 2016 from https://www.youtube.com/watch?v=U3gvH0lAbTs.

———. *2014a. Evaluation of the 2013 European Year of Citizens: Final Report.* Retrieved from http://europa.eu/citizens-2013/sites/default/files/content/publication/EYC%20evaluation%20final%20report%20FINAL_0.pdf.

———. 2015a. *The Mind and Body of Europe: A New Narrative* 12(5). Retrieved from http://ec.europa.eu/culture/library/publications/mind-body-europe_en.pdf.

———. 2015b. *Euro Banknotes.* Retrieved from http://ec.europa.eu/economy_finance/euro/cash/banknotes/index_en.htm.

European Convention. 2003. *Draft Treaty Establishing a Constitution for Europe.* Retrieved from https://www.ecb.europa.eu/ecb/legal/pdf/cv00850.en03.pdf.

European Council. 1973. "Declaration on European Identity." *Bulletin of the European Communities* 12: 118–22. Luxembourg: Office for official publications of the European Communities.

———. 1983. "Solemn Declaration on European Union." Stuttgart, 19 June 1983. *Bulletin of the European Communities* 6/1983: 24–29. Retrieved from http://aei.pitt.edu/1788.

———. 2007. "Final Act of the Lisbon Treaty." *Official Journal of the European Union* C 306. Retrieved from http://eur-lex.europa.eu/LexUriServ/LexUriServ.do?uri=OJ:C:2007:306:0231:0271:EN:PDF.

European Economic Community. 1957. *Treaty Establishing the European Economic Community.* Retrieved from http://eur-lex.europa.eu/legal-content/EN/TXT/?uri=URISERV:xy0023.

European Parliament. 2013a. "European Parliament Launches Information Campaign towards 2014 Elections." 10 September. Retrieved from http://www.europarl.europa.eu/news/en/news-room/content/20130906IPR18827/html/European-Parliament-launches-information-campaign-towards-2014-elections.

———. 2013b. *The Power to Decide What Happens in Europe.* 10 September. Retrieved from http://www.europarl.europa.eu/news/en/news-room/content/20130905STO18723/html/The-power-to-decide-what-happens-in-Europe.

———. 2013c. *Nine Months and Counting*. Video released by the European Parliament. Retrieved from https://www.youtube.com/watch?v=QBowgJA6LdY.

———. 2013d. *How It Works: Electing Europe's Future*. Video. Retrieved from http://www.europarltv.europa.eu/en/player.aspx?pid=4c478472-4fee-4eaa-b7df-a298014a1637.

———. 2013e. *Act. React. Impact.* Video. Retrieved from https://www.youtube.com/watch?v=v4PvZSGbd8E.

———. 2013f. *European Parliament Launches Elections Advertising Campaign*. Video. Retrieved from https://www.youtube.com/watch?v=UslDVJ2QSVM.

———. 2013g. *This Time It's Different. Act, React, Impact*. Retrieved from http://www.europarl.europa.eu/news/en/top-stories/content/20130902TST18451/html/This-time-it's-different.

———. 2014a. *Results of the 2014 European Elections*. Retrieved from http://www.europarl.europa.eu/elections2014-results/en/election-results-2014.html.

———. 2014b. *European Parliament Elections 2014—Official TV Spot*. Retrieved from https://www.youtube.com/watch?v=K5qghmYb5BA.

European Parliament and Council. 2012. "Decision No 1093/2012/EU of the European Parliament and of the Council on the European Year of Citizens (2013)." *Official Journal of the European Union* 21(11). Retrieved from http://eur-lex.europa.eu/legal-content/EN/TXT/PDF/?uri=CELEX:32012D1093andfrom=EN.

European Union. 1975. "Report by Mr. Leo Tindemans, Prime Minister of Belgium, to the European Council." *Bulletin of the European Communities* Supplement 1/76. Retrieved from http://aei.pitt.edu/942/1/political_tindemans_report.pdf.

———. 2007a. "Treaty of Lisbon: Amending the Treaty on European Union and the Treaty Establishing the European Community." *Official Journal of the European Union* Retrieved from http://eur-lex.europa.eu/legal-content/en/ALL/?uri=OJ%3AC%3A2007%3A306%3ATOC.

———. 2007b. "Final Act." *Official Journal of the European Union*. Retrieved from http://eurlex.europa.eu/LexUriServ/LexUriServ.do?uri=OJ:C:2007:306:0231:0271:EN:PDF.

———. 2013. *The European Union Explained: The Founding Fathers of the EU*. Retrieved from http://www.fh-vie.ac.at/var/em_plain_site/storage/original/application/a643b904714f130a8670e436ac463ebb.pdf.

Eurovision. 2015. "Nearly 200 Million People Watch Eurovision 2015." Retrieved from http://www.eurovision.tv/page/news?id=nearly_200_million_people_watch_eurovision_2015.

Fabietti, U. 2015. *Materia sacra: Corpi, oggetti, immagini, feticci nella pratica religiosa*. Milan: Raffaello Cortina.

Farber, A. 1974. "Segmentation of the Mother: Women in Greek Myth." *Psychoanalytic Review* 62(1): 29–47.

Farinelli, 2012. *Oltre il tempo attraverso il mito: Bontempelli e l'attualizzazione narrativa di un progetto teorico: da Eva ultima al Viaggio d'Europa*. Lubiana: Ars and Humanitas.

Fellerer, K. G., and M. Hadas. 1953. "Church Music and the Council of Trent." *Musical Quarterly* 39(4): 576–94.

Ferenczi, S. 1910. "The Psychological Analysis of Dreams." In *Contributions to Psycho-analysis,* trans. E. Jones, 80–111. Toronto: Badger R.G.

———. 1950. "The Symbolism of the Bridge." In *Further Contributions to the Theory and Technique of Psychoanalysis,* trans. C. M. Baines, 352–56. London: Hogarth Press.

Ferguson, M. J., T. Gross, R. R. Hassin, and D. Shidlovski. 2007. "Subliminal Exposure to National Flags Affects Political Thought and Behavior." *Proceedings of the National Academy of Sciences* 104(50): 19757–61.

Ferruta, A., and J. Parker. 2009. "Crossing the Bridge: Identity and Change." *Italian Psychoanalytic Annual* 3: 163–76.

Finizio, G., L. Levi, and N. Vallinoto, eds. 2011. *The Democratization of International Organizations.* International Democracy Watch. Retrieved from http://www.internationaldemocracywatch.org/attachments/454_EU-telo.pdf.

Fligstein, N. 2008. *Euroclash: The EU, European Identity, and the Future of Europe.* Oxford: Oxford University Press.

Flood, C. 2001. *Political Myth.* New York: Routledge.

Fontaine, P. 1991. *A Citizen's Europe.* Commission of the European Communities. Luxembourg: Office for Official Publications. Retrieved from http://aei.pitt.edu/15086/1/MOVE-ACITIZENSEUROPE-1991_1.pdf.

———. 2007. *Europe in 12 Steps.* Brussels: Commission of the European Union.

Foret, F., and P. Schlesinger. 2006. "Political Roof and Sacred Canopy? Religion and the EU Constitution." *European Journal of Social Theory* 9(1): 59–81.

Foret, F. 2009. "Symbolic Dimensions of EU Legitimization." *Media, Culture and Society* 31(2): 313–24.

———. 2010. "European Political Rituals: A Challenging Tradition in the Making." *International Political Anthropology* 3(1): 55–77.

Fornäs, J. 1995. *Cultural Theory and Late Modernity.* London: Sage.

———. 2011. *Signifying Europe.* Bristol: Intellect Press.

———. 2012. "European Identification: Symbolic Mediations of Unity and Diversity." *Global Media Journal-Australian Edition* 6(1).

———. 2014. "Mediatisation Times." Paper for the "Mediatization and Social Theory of Change" panel at ECREA Conference, Lisbon, 15(11). Retrieved from http://www.mediatization.eu/fileadmin/user_upload/pdf/conferences_calls/Mediatisation_Times_-_Johan_Fornaes.pdf.

Fossum, J. E. 2003. "The European Union: In Search of an Identity." *European Journal of Political Theory* 2(3): 319–40.

Foucault, M. 1978. *The History of Sexuality.* Vol. 1, *An Introduction.* Trans. Robert Hurley. New York: Pantheon Books.

———. 1986. "Of Other Spaces." *Diacritics* 16: 22–27.

Fourny, D. 1987. "Rousseau's Civil Religion Reconsidered." *French Review* 60(4): 485–96.

Freedman, H., and M. Simon. 1983. *The Midrash Rabbah.* Trans. H. Freedman. London: Soncino Press.

Freud, S. 1913. "Totem and Taboo." In *The Standard Edition of the Complete Psychological Works of Sigmund Freud,* ed. and trans. J. Strachey, 13: vii–162. London: Hogarth Press.

———. 1930. "Civilization and Its Discontents." In *The Standard Edition of the Complete Psychological Works of Sigmund Freud,* ed. and trans. J. Strachey, 1: 57–146. London: Hogarth Press.
———. 1937. "Analysis Terminable and Interminable." *International Journal of Psychoanalysis* 18: 373–405.
———. 2002. *The Joke and Its Relation to the Unconscious.* New York: Penguin.
Fricker, K. 2015. "Eurovision and the 'New" Europe.' In *Eurovision Song Contest: More Than Music?,* 8–15. Retrieved from http://zukunft.orf.at/rte/upload/download/15i0002.pdf.
Fricker, K., and M. Gluhovic, eds. 2013. *Performing the "New" Europe: Identities, Feelings, and Politics in the Eurovision Song Contest.* New York: Palgrave Macmillan.
Friedman, P. 1952. "The Bridge: A Study in Symbolism." *Psychoanalytic Quarterly* 21(1): 49–80.
Fuchs, M., M. Phillips, and K. Rieser. 2013. *ConFiguring America: Iconic Figures, Visuality, and the American Identity.* Bristol: Intellect Books.
Garrett S. 2012. "The Art of First Impressions: How to Cut a Movie Trailer." *Filmmaker Magazine,* 13 January. Retrieved from: http://filmmakermagazine.com/37093-first-impressions/#.V8bzLrnymM8.
Geertz, C. 1973. "Religion as a Cultural System." In *The Interpretation of Cultures: Selected Essays,* 87–125. New York: Basic Books.
———. 1977. "Centers, Kings, and Charisma: Reflections on the Symbolics of Power." In *Culture and Its Creators: Essays in Honor of Edward Shils,* 150–71. Chicago: University of Chicago Press.
———. 1986. *The Uses of Diversity.* University of Michigan: The Tanner Lectures on Human Values. 8(11). Retrieved from http://tannerlectures.utah.edu/_documents/a-to-z/g/geertz86.pdf.
Gell, A. 1998. *Art and Agency: An Anthropological Theory.* Oxford: Oxford University Press.
Gellner, E. 1964. *Thought and Change.* London: Weidenfeld and Nicolson.
———. 1997. *Nationalism.* London: Weidenfeld and Nicolson.
Gentile, E. 1990. "Fascism as Political Religion." *Journal of Contemporary History* 25(2/3): 229–51.
———. 1993. *Il culto del littorio: La sacralizzazione della politica nell'Italia fascista.* Bari: Laterza.
Giddens, A. 1990. *The Consequences of Modernity.* Cambridge: Polity Press.
Giesen, B. 2009. "The Three Cultural Projects of Modernity." *International Political Anthropology* 2(2): 239–50.
Gilbert, E. 1998. "'Ornamenting the Facade of Hell': Iconographies of Nineteenth-Century Canadian Paper Money." *Environment and Planning D: Society and Space* 16: 57–80.
———. 1999. "Forging a National Currency: Money, State Building and Nation-Making in Canada." In *Nation-States and Money: The Past, Present and Future of National Currencies,* ed. E. Gilbert, and E. Helleiner, 25–46. New York: Routledge.
Gilbert, E., and E. Helleiner. 1999. *Nation-States and Money: The Past, Present and Future of National Currencies.* New York: Routledge.

Ginsburg, L. M., and S. A. Ginsburg. 1992. "Paradise in the Life of Sigmund Freud: An Understanding of Its Imagery and Paradoxes." *International Review of Psycho-Analysis* 19(3): 285–308.
Ginzburg, C., and A. Davin. 1980. "Morelli, Freud and Sherlock Holmes: Clues and Scientific Method." In *History Workshop*, 5–36. Oxford: Ruskin College, Editorial Collective, History Workshop.
Girard R. 2005. *Violence and the Sacred.* New York: Continuum.
Gitter E. G. 1984. "The Power of Women's Hair in the Victorian Imagination." *PMLA* 99(5): 936–54.
Glynos, J., and Y. Stavrakakis. 2008. "Lacan and Political Subjectivity: Fantasy and Enjoyment in Psychoanalysis and Political Theory." *Subjectivity* 24(1): 256–74.
———. 2010. "Politics and the Unconscious: An Interview with Ernesto Laclau." *Subjectivity* 3(3): 231–44.
Gnath, K. 2006. "Guy Verhofstadt and the 'United States of Europe': The Eurozone as a New Core Europe?" *The Federal Trust for Education and Research—European Policy Brief* 22. Retrieved from http://fedtrust.co.uk/wp-content/uploads/2014/12/PolicyBrief22.pdf.
Goddard, V. A., J. R. Llobera, and C. Shore. eds. 1994. *The Anthropology of Europe: Identity and Boundaries in Conflict.* Oxford: Berg.
Golubock, D. G. 2014. "Conchita Wurst Prompts Calls for Russia to Leave Eurovision Song Contest." *Moscow Times* 11(5). Retrieved from http://www.themoscowtimes.com/art_n_ideas/article/conchita-wurst-prompts-calls-for-russia-to-leave-eurovision-song-contest/499889.html.
Gombrich, E. H. 1939. "Art and Propaganda." *The Listener* 1118–20. Retrieved from https://gombricharchive.files.wordpress.com/2011/04/showdoc66.pdf
———. 1966. "The Debate on Primitivism in Ancient Rhetoric." *Journal of the Warburg and Courtauld Institutes* 29: 24–38.
———. 1971. "Personification." In *Classical Influences in European Culture AD 500–1500,* ed. R. R. Bolgar, 247. Cambridge: Cambridge University Press. Retrieved from https://gombricharchive.files.wordpress.com/2011/04/showdoc20.pdf.
———. 1975. "Topos and Topicality Annual Lecture of the Society for Renaissance Studies." London: University College, 10(1). Retrieved from https://gombricharchive.files.wordpress.com/2011/04/showdoc21.pdf.
———. 1986. *Aby Warburg: An Intellectual Biography.* Oxford: Phaidon.
———. 1996. "Review of *Panofsky, Three Essays on Style and Perspective as Symbolic Form.*" *New York Review of Books* 15(2): 29–30.
———. 2002. *The Preference for the Primitive: Episodes in the History of Western Taste and Art.* London: Phaidon.
Goodwin, B., and K. Taylor. 2009. *The Politics of Utopia: A Study in Theory and Practice.* New York: Peter Lang.
Green, A. I. 2008. "Erotic Habitus: Toward a Sociology of Desire." *Theory and Society* 37(6): 597–626.
Green, D. M. 2007. *The Europeans: Political Identity in an Emerging Polity.* London: Lynne Rienner.
Greenstadt, W. M. 1991. "The Origin of the Gods: A Psychoanalytic Study of

Greek Theogonic Myth: By Richard S. Caldwell." *International Review of Psycho-Analysis* 18: 584–87.

Griffin R. 1996. "Staging the Nation's Rebirth: The Politics and Aesthetics of Performance in the Context of Fascist Studies." In *Fascism and Theater: Comparative Studies on the Aesthetics and Politics of Performance in Europe, 1925–1945*, ed. G. Berghaus. 11–29. New York: Berghahn Books.

Grigg, R. 2006. "Beyond the Oedipus Complex." In *Jacques Lacan and the Other Side of Psychoanalysis: Reflections on Seminar XVII*, ed. J. Clemens and R. Grigg. 50–68. Durham, NC: Duke University Press.

Gripsrud, J. 2007. "Television and the European Public Sphere." *European Journal of Communication* 22(4): 479–92.

Grotstein, J. S. 1997a. "Why Oedipus and not Christ? A Psychoanalytic Inquiry into Innocence, Human Sacrifice, and the Sacred—Part I: Innocence, Spirituality, and Human Sacrifice." *American Journal of Psychoanalysis* 57(3): 193–220.

———. 1997b. "Klein's Archaic Oedipus Complex and Its Possible Relationship to the Myth of the Labyrinth: Notes on the Origin of Courage." *Journal of Analytical Psychology* 42(4): 585–611.

———. 1998. "The Numinous and Immanent Nature of the Psychoanalytic Subject." *Journal of Analytical Psychology* 43(1): 41–68.

Guarascio, F. 2015. "Two-Speed Europe is the Future of Enlarged EU, Juncker Says." *Reuters*, 18 November.

Guibernau, M. 1998. *Nations without States*. Cambridge: Polity Press.

Haas, E. 1958. *The Uniting of Europe: Political, Social and Economic Forces, 1950–1957*. Palo Alto, CA: Stanford University Press.

Habermas, J. 1987. *The Theory of Communicative Action*. Vol. 2, *Lifeworld and System: A Critique of Functionalist Reason*. Cambridge: Polity Press.

———. 1989. *The Structural Transformation of the Public Sphere*. Trans. Thomas Burger. Cambridge, MA: MIT Press.

———. 1992. "Citizenship and National Identity: Some Reflections on the Future of Europe." *Praxis International* 12(1): 1–19.

———. 2001. "Why Europe Needs a Constitution." *New Left Review* 11(17). Retrieved from http://newleftreview.org/II/11/jurgen-habermas-why-europe-needs-a-constitution.

———. 2006. *The Divided West*. Cambridge: Polity Press.

Hagman, G. 2002. "The Sense of Beauty." *International Journal of Psychoanalysis* 83: 661–74.

———. 2005. *Aesthetic Experience: Beauty, Creativity, and the Search for the Ideal*. New York: Rodopi.

Hall, S. 1973. *Encoding and Decoding in the Television Discourse*. Birmingham: Centre for Cultural Studies, University of Birmingham.

Hamvas, B. 1983. *A világválság*, Budapest: Magvető Könyvkiadó.

———. 2007. "A bor filozofiája." In *A magyar Hüperion*, 2:201–84. Budapest: Medio.

Hansen, L., and M. C. Williams 1999. "The Myths of Europe: Legitimacy, Community and the 'Crisis' of the EU." *Journal of Common Market Studies* 37(2): 233–49.

Harap, L. 1938. "Some Hellenic Ideas on Music and Character." *Musical Quarterly* 24(2): 153–68.

Harries, K. 1978. "Metaphor and Transcendence." *Critical Inquiry* 5: 73–90.

Havel, V. 1994. *Speech Delivered at the European Parliament,* 8(3). Retrieved from http://www.vaclavhavel.cz/showtrans.php?cat=projevyandval=221_aj_projevy.htmlandtyp=HTML.

Heald, S., and A. Deluz, eds. 1994. *Anthropology and Psychoanalysis: An Encounter through Culture.* London: Psychology Press, Routledge.

Hedetoft, U. 1995. *Signs of Nations: Studies in the Political Semiotics of Self and Other in Contemporary European Nationalism.* Aldershot: Dartmouth.

Heffernan, M. 1998. *The Meaning of Europe: Geography and Geopolitics.* London: Arnold.

Heidegger, M. 1971. "The Thing." In *Poetry, Language, Thought,* trans. Albert Hofstadter. New York: Harper and Row.

Heinonen, A. 2015. *The First Euros: The Creation and Issue of the First Euro Banknotes and the Road to the Europa Series.* European Central Bank. Retrieved from https://www.ecb.europa.eu/pub/pdf/other/the_first_euros_2015en.pdf.

Helleiner, E. 1997. "One Nation, One Money: Territorial Currencies and the Nation-State." *Working Paper,* 17. Oslo: Arena.

———. 2003. *The Making of National Money: Territorial Currencies in Historical Perspective.* Ithaca, NY: Cornell University Press.

Heller, A. 1988. "Europe: An Epilogue?" In *The Postmodern Political Condition,* ed. A. Heller and F. Fehér, 146–60. New York: Columbia University.

———. 2001. "Cultural Memory, Identity and Civil Society." *Internationale Politik und Gesellschaft* 2: 139–43.

Henare, A., M. Holbraad, and S. Wastell, eds. 2007. *Thinking through Things: Theorising Artefacts Ethnographically.* London: Routledge.

Herrero-Tejedon, L. 2006. *Report on the White Paper on a European Communication Policy.* European Parliament, Committee on Culture and Education. 16(10). Retrieved from http://www.europarl.europa.eu/sides/getDoc.do?pubRef=-//EP//NONSGML+REPORT+A6-2006-0365+0+DOC+PDF+V0//EN.

Herrmann, F. 1993. "The Rani of Chitor: The Face." *International Journal of Psychoanalysis* 74: 101–12.

Herrmann, R. K., T. Risse, and M. B. Brewer, eds. 2004. *Transnational Identities: Becoming European in the EU.* Lanham, MD: Rowman and Littlefield.

Hill, J. 1996. "At Home in the World." *Journal of Analytical Psychology* 41: 575–98.

Hills, M. 2007. "Essential Tensions: Winnicottian Object-Relations in the Media Sociology of Roger Silverstone." *International Journal of Communication* 1(1): 37–48.

Hobbes, T. 1994. *Leviathan: With Selected Variants from the Latin Edition of 1668.* Indianapolis: Hackett.

Hobsbawm, E. 1990. *Nations and Nationalism since 1780: Programme, Myth, Reality.* Cambridge: Cambridge University Press.

Hobsbawm, E., and T. Ranger, eds. 1983. *The Invention of Tradition.* Cambridge: Cambridge University Press.

Hocart, A. M. 2004. *The Life-Giving Myth and Other Essays.* New York: Routledge.

Horvath A., and B. Thomassen. 2008. "Mimetic Errors in Liminal Schismogenesis: On the Political Anthropology of the Trickster." *International Political Anthropology* 1(1): 3–24.

Hosking, G., and G. Schopflin, eds. 1997. *The Myths of Nationhood.* London: Hurst and Company.

Hoy, M. 1992. "Bakhtin and Popular Culture." *New Literary History* 23(3): 765–82.

Hugo, V. 2007. *Les Miserables.* Vol. 5. Fairfield, IA: 1st World Library.

Hülsse, R. 2006. "Imagine the EU: The Metaphorical Construction of a Supra-Nationalist Identity." *Journal of International Relations and Development* 9, 396–421.

Husserl, E. 1965. *Phenomenology and the Crisis of Philosophy.* Trans. Q. Laurer. New York: Harper Torche Books.

———. 1970. *The Crisis of European Sciences and Transcendental Phenomenology: An Introduction to Phenomenological Philosophy.* Evanston, IL: Northwestern University Press.

Hyde, L. 1998. *Trickster Makes This World: Mischief, Myth, and Art.* New York: Farrar, Strauss and Giroux.

Hymans, J. E. 2004. "The Changing Color of Money: European Currency Iconography and Collective Identity." *European Journal of International Relations* 10(1): 5–31.

———. 2006. "Money for Mars? The Euro Banknotes and European Identity." In *The Year of the Euro: The Cultural, Social, and Political Import of Europe's Common Currency,* 15–36. Notre Dame, IN: University of Notre Dame Press.

Ifversen, J., and C. Kølvraa. 2011. *Myth and History Politics in European Integration: The Myth of the Fathers.* Paper presented at the EUSA Conference, Boston. March 3–5.

Irigaray, K. 1991. *Philosophy in the Feminine.* New York: Routledge.

Isin, E. F., and M. Saward. 2013. *Enacting European Citizenship.* Cambridge: Cambridge University Press.

Isler-Kerényi, C. 2007. "Dionysos in Archaic Greece: An Understanding through Images." In *Religions in the Graeco-Roman World,* ed. H. S. Versnel, D. Frankfurter, and J. Hahn. Leiden: Brill.

Ivic, S. 2011. "European Commission's Plan D for Democracy, Dialogue and Debate: The Path towards Deliberation?" *Journal of Law and Conflict Resolution* 3(2): 14–19.

Jauk, W. 2015. "The Unity of Plurality." In ORF (2015b) *Eurovision Song Contest: More than Music?,* 20–26. Retrieved from http://zukunft.orf.at/rte/upload/download/15i0002.pdf.

Jensen, K. B., ed. 2002. *A Handbook of Media and Communication Research: Qualitative and Quantitative Methodologies.* New York: Routledge.

Jo, S.-S. 2007. *European Myths: Resolving the Crises in the European Community/European Union.* Lanham, MD: University Press of America.

Johnson, C. 2005. "Savage Civil Religion." *Numen* 52(3): 289–324.

Johnston, W. M. 1991. *Celebrations: The Cult of Anniversaries in Europe and the United States Today.* New Brunswick, NJ: Transaction Publishers.

Jones, E. 1948. "The Theory of Symbolism." In *Papers on Psycho-Analysis.* 5th ed. London: Baillière, Tindall and Cox.

Jones, J. W. 1996. *Religion and Psychology in Transition: Psychoanalysis, Feminism, and Theology*. New Haven, CT: Yale University Press.

Jordan, P. 2014. *The Modern Fairy Tale: Nation Branding, National Identity and the Eurovision Song Contest in Estonia*. Tartu: University of Tartu Press.

———. 2015. "Best Practice in Public Broadcasting." In ORF (2015b) *Eurovision Song Contest: More than Music?*, 31–34. Retrieved from http://zukunft.orf.at/rte/upload/download/15i0002.pdf.

József, A. 1999. *The Iron-Blue Vault: Selected Poems*. Trans. Zs. Ozsváth and F. Turner. Newcastle upon Tyne: Bloodaxe.

Judt, T. 1996. "The Past Is Another Country: Myth and Memory in Postwar Europe." *Daedalus* 121(4): 83–118.

———. 2011a. *A Grand Illusion? An Essay on Europe*. New York: NYU Press.

———. 2011b. *Postwar: A History of Europe since 1945*. Munich: Random House.

Juncker, J. C. 2014. *A New Start for Europe: My Agenda for Jobs, Growth, Fairness and Democratic Change*. European Commission document, Strasbourg, 15(7). Retrieved from http://www.eesc.europa.eu/resources/docs/jean-claude-juncker—-political-guidelines.pdf.

Jung, C.G. 1979. *The Collected Works of CG Jung*. Princeton: Princeton University Press.

Jussen, B. 2009. "The King's Two Bodies Today." *Representations* 106(1): 102–17.

Kaelberer, M. 2004. "The Euro and European Identity: Symbols, Power and the Politics of European Monetary Union." *Review of International Studies* 30: 161–78.

Kahn, V. 2009. "Political Theology and Fiction in *The King's Two Bodies*." *Representations* 106(1): 77–101.

Kantorowicz, E. H. 1957. *The King's Two Bodies: A Study in Mediaeval Political Theology*. Princeton, NJ: Princeton University Press.

Katsambekis, G., and Y. Stavrakakis 2013. "Populism, Anti-populism and European Democracy: A View from the South." 23 July, Open Democracy. Retrieved from: https://www.opendemocracy.net/can-europe-make-it/giorgos-katsambekis-yannis-stavrakakis/populism-anti-populism-and-european-democr.

Kellas, J. 1991. *The Politics of Nationalism and Ethnicity*. New York: St Martin's Press.

Kerenyi, K. 1956. "The Trickster in Relation to Greek Mythology." In *The Trickster: A Study in American Indian Mythology*, 173–91. New York: Schocken Books.

Kertzer, D. I. 1988. *Ritual, Politics, and Power*. New Haven, CT: Yale University Press.

Kitzinger, B. 2014. "Review of *Theorie des Bildakts* by Horst Bredekamp," 10 September. Retrieved from http:/www.caareviews.org/reviews/2162.

Klebanow, S. 1989. "Power, Gender and Money." *Journal of American Academy of Psychoanalysis* 17: 321–28.

Klein, M. 1929. "Personification in the Play of Children." *International Journal of Psychoanalysis* 10: 193–204.

———. 1975. *Love, Guilt and Reparation and Other Works: 1921–1945*. London: Hogarth Press.

Knoblauch, S. H. 2006. "The Apollonian Eye and the Dionysian Ear." *Psychoanalytic Inquiry* 26(3): 326–43.

Kohut, A. 2013. *The New Sick Man of Europe: The European Union. French Dispirited; Attitudes Diverge Sharply from Germans.* Washington DC: Pew Research Center

Kølvraa, C. 2013. "The Father on Display: The House of Jean Monnet and the Construction of European Identity." *Culture Unbound: Journal of Current Cultural Research* 4(4): 747–65.

Kristeva, J. 2000. *Crisis of the European Subject.* New York: Other Press.

Kromm, J. 1987. "'Marianne' and the Madwomen." *Art Journal* 46(4): 299–304.

Krueger, D. W. 1990. "Money Meanings and Madness: A Psychoanalytic Perspective." *Psychoanalytic Review* 78(2): 209–24.

Kukkonen, K., and M. Stocchetti, eds. 2011. *Images in Use: Towards the Critical Analysis of Visual Communication.* Amsterdam: John Benjamins Publishing.

Kylstad, I. 2010. "Turkey and the EU: A 'New' European Identity in the Making?" *LEQS Paper* 27.

Kymlicka, W., and W. Norman. 1994. "Return of the Citizen: A Survey of Recent Work on Citizenship Theory." *Ethics* 104(2): 352–81.

La Rocca, E., ed. 2013. *Augusto.* Rome: Electa.

Lacan, J. 1949. "The Mirror Stage as Formative of the Function of the I as Revealed in Psychoanalytic Experience." In *Écrits: A Selection* (2001), trans. A. Sheridan, 1–8. New York: Routledge.

———. 2001. *Écrits: A Selection.* Trans. A. Sheridan. New York: Routledge.

Laffan, B. 2004. "The European Union and Its Institutions as Identity Builders." In *Transnational Identities: Becoming European in the EU*, ed. R. K. Herrmann, T. Risse, and M. B. Brewer, 75–96. Lanham, MD: Rowman and Littlefield.

———. 2006. "The Politics of Identity and Political Order in Europe." *Journal of Common Market Studies* 34(1): 81–102.

Larat, F. 2005. "Present-ing the Past: Political Narratives on European History and the Justification of EU Integration." *German Law Journal* 6(2): 273–90.

Larsen, G., and D. O'Reilly. 2009. *Festival Tales: Utopian Tales.* Bradford: Bradford University School of Management.

Lasswell, H. 1936. *Politics: Who Gets What, When, How.* New York: Whittlesey House.

Lears, J. 1994. *Fables of Abundance: A Cultural History of Advertising in America.* New York: Basic Books.

Lefort, C. 1986. *The Political Forms of Modern Society: Bureaucracy, Democracy, Totalitarianism.* Cambridge: Polity Press.

———. 1988. "The Permanence of the Theologico-Political?" In *Democracy and Political Theory*, ed. C. Lefort and D. Macey. 213–55. Minneapolis: University of Minnesota Press.

Lehtonen, M. 2000. *The Cultural Analysis of Texts.* London: Sage.

Letta, E. 2013. *Lavoriamo per gli Stati Uniti d'Europa.* Retrieved from http://www.enricoletta.it/proposte/lavoriamo-per-gli-stati-uniti-deuropa.

Levine, S. Z. 1995. "Virtual Narcissus: On the Mirror Stage with Monet, Lacan, and Me." *American Imago* 53(1): 91–106.

Lichtenstein, D. 2009. "Born in Exile: There Is No Place Like Home." *Psychoanalytic Psychology* 26(4): 451–58.

Lim, M., and M. Moufahim. 2009. "Towards a Critical Political Marketing Agenda?" *Journal of Marketing Management* 25(7/8): 763–76.

Lindholm, C. 1990. *Charisma*. Basil: Blackwell.
Littlefield, H. M. 1964. "*The Wizard of Oz*: Parable on Populism." *American Quarterly* 16(1): 47–58.
Long, K. 2006. *Hermaphrodites in Renaissance Europe*. Aldershot: Ashgate.
Lord, B. 2006. "Foucault's Museum: Difference, Representation, and Genealogy." *Museum and Society* 4(1): 1–14.
Lukes S. 1975. "Political Ritual and Social Integration." *Sociology* 9(2): 289–308.
Maas, W. 2007. *Creating European Citizens*. Lanham MD: Rowman and Littlefield.
MacDonald Cornford, F. 1997. *Plato's Cosmology: The Timaeus of Plato*. Indianapolis, IN: Hackett.
Mach, Z. 1993. *Symbols, Conflict, and Identity: Essays in Political Anthropology*. New York: State University of New York Press.
Maman, D., and G. Yair 1996. "The Persistent Structure of Hegemony in the Eurovision Song Contest." *Acta Sociologica* 39(3): 309–25.
Mangion, C. 2003. "Nietzsche's Philosophy of Myth." *Humanitas* 2: 1–11.
Manners, I. 2006. "The Symbolic Manifestation of the EU's Normative Role in World Politics." In *The European Union's Roles in International Politics*, ed. O. Elgström and M. Smith, 66–84. New York: Routledge.
———. 2010. "Global Europa: Mythology of the European Union in World Politics." *Journal of Common Market Studies* 48(1): 67–87.
———. 2011. "Symbolism in European Integration." *Comparative European Politics* 9(3): 243–68.
Martin, J. 1995. *Sounds and Society: Themes in the Sociology of Music*. Manchester: Manchester University Press.
Matynia, E. 2009. *Discovering Performative Democracy*. New York: New School for Social Research. Retrieved from http://www.societasethica.info/past-conferences-papers/2009-warsaw/1.334531/Matynia.pdf
Mauss, M. 1954. *The Gift: Forms and Functions of Exchange in Archaic Societies*. Trans. W. D. Halls. New York: W. W. Norton.
McDaniel, J. 1993. "Impossible Inventions: A Review of Jacque Derrida's *The Other Heading: Reflections on Today's Europe*." *Iowa Journal of Cultural Studies* 12: 176–79.
McGowan, T. 2003. "Looking for the Gaze: Lacanian Film Theory and Its Vicissitudes." *Cinema Journal* 42(3): 27–47.
McKinney, R. 2007. "The Trickster as Comic Hero." *Philosophy Today* 51(2): 176–85.
McLaren, L. M. 2006. *Identity, Interests and Attitudes to European Integration*. London: Palgrave.
McLuhan, M. 1954. *Counterblast*. Berkley: Gingko Press.
McNamara, K. 2010. "Constructing Authority in the European Union." In *Who Governs the Globe?*, ed. D. Avant, M. Finnemore, and S. K. Sell, 153–79, Cambridge: Cambridge University Press.
Mersch, Y. 2014. "Address by Yves Mersch to Mark the Unveiling of the New €10 Banknote." ECB—Our Money. 13 January 2014, Frankfurt. Retrieved from http://www.new-euro-banknotes.eu/News-Events/Press/SPEECHES-INTERVIEWS/ADDRESS-BY-YVES-MERSCH-TO-MARK-THE-UNVEILING-OF-THE-NEW-%E2%82%AC10-BANKNOTE.

Miettinen, T. 2013. *The Idea of Europe in Husserl's Phenomenology: A Study in Generativity and Historicity, Philosophical Studies.* Helsinki: Multiprint.
Miłosz, C. 1990. *The Captive Mind.* New York: Vintage International.
Milward, A. 1992. *The European Rescue of the Nation-State.* New York: Routledge.
Mitchell, W. J. T. 2005. *What Do Pictures Want? The Lives and Loves of Images.* Chicago: University of Chicago Press.
Modell, A. H. 2009. "Metaphor: The Bridge between Feelings and Knowledge." *Psychoanalytic Inquiry* 29(1): 6–11.
Morales, X. 2003. "*Kill Bill*: Beauty and Violence." *The Record: The Independent Newspaper of the Harvard Law School* 16: 34–35.
Moravcsik, A. 2005. "The European Constitutional Compromise and the Neofunctionalist Legacy." *Journal of European Public Policy* 12(2): 349–86.
Morgan, D. 1997. *Visual Piety: A History and Theory of Popular Religious Images.* Los Angeles: University of California Press.
———. 2005. *The Sacred Gaze: Religious Visual Culture in Theory and Practice.* Los Angeles: University of California Press.
Morley, D. 2000. *Home Territories: Media, Mobility and Modernity.* New York: Routledge.
———. 2001. "Belongings: Place, Space and Identity in a Mediated World." *European Journal of Cultural Studies* 4(4): 425–48.
Moro, G., ed. 2013. *The Single Currency and European Citizenship: Unveiling the Other Side of the Coin.* London: A & C Black.
Moro Tornese, S. 2013. "Musical Aesthetics and the Transformation of the Soul in Neoplatonism." In *Philosophy and Art in Late Antiquity,* ed. D. Iozzia, 31–65. Rome: Bonanno Editore.
Moschus. 1912. *The Poems of Moschus and the Greek Bucolic Poets.* Trans. J. M. Edmonds. Vol. 28. Cambridge: Harvard University Press.
Mourelatos, A. D. 1970. *The Route of Parmenides.* New Haven, CT: Yale University Press.
Müller J. W. 2006. "Benda's Anti-passionate Europe." *European Journal of Political Theory* 5(2): 125–37.
Mulvey, L. 1975. "Visual Pleasure and Narrative Cinema." *Screen* 16(3): 6–18.
Nanz, I. 2000. "In-between Nations: Ambivalence and the Making of a European Identity." In *Europe and the Other and Europe as the Other,* ed. B. Stråth, 279–310. Brussels: Peter Lang.
Newman, M. 2001. *Allegiance, Legitimation, Democracy and the European Union.* Working paper 5. San Domenico: European University Institute.
Nicolaïdis, K., and J. Pélabay. 2009. "One Union, One Story? In Praise of Europe's Narrative Diversity." *Reflections on European Integration* 50: 175–94.
Niederland, W. G. 1956. "River Symbolism—Part I." *Psychoanalytic Quarterly* 25: 469–504.
———. 1957. "River Symbolism—Part II." *Psychoanalytic Quarterly* 26: 50–75.
Nietzsche, F. 1995. *The Birth of Tragedy.* Trans. C. Fadiman. New York: Dover.
Nobel Prize. 2012. *The Nobel Peace Prize for 2012,* 12(10). Retrieved from http://www.nobelprize.org/nobel_prizes/peace/laureates/2012/press.html.
Nussbaum, M. C. 2011. "Reinventing the Civil Religion: Comte, Mill, Tagore." *Victorian Studies* 54(1): 7–34.

———. 2013. *Political Emotions: Why Love Matters for Justice*. Cambridge, MA: Belknap Press.

Oakeshott, M. 1975. *Hobbes on Civil Association*. Oxford: Blackwell.

Ober J. 2005. *Athenian Legacies: Essays on the Politics of Going on Together*. Princeton, NJ: Princeton University Press.

Obradovic, D. 1996. "Policy Legitimacy and the European Union." *Journal of Common Market Society* 34(2): 191–221.

Oostlander, A. 1993. *Report of the Committee on Culture, Youth, Education and the Media on the Information Policy of the European Community*. Session Documents, European Parliament, 14(6).

Österreichischer Rundfunk (ORF). 2015a. *Eurovision Song Contest: Media Handbook. Building Bridges*. Retrieved from https://www.eurovision.tv/upload/press-downloads/2015/MediaHandbook_ESC2015.pdf.

———. 2015b. *Eurovision Song Contest: More than Music?* Retrieved from http://zukunft.orf.at/rte/upload/download/15i0002.pdf.

Orluc, K. 2010. "Decline or Renaissance: The Transformation of European Consciousness after the First World War." In *Europe and the Other and Europe as the Other*, ed. B. Stråth, 123–57. Brussels: Peter Lang.

Orr, C. 2013. "Why *Her* is the Best Film of the Year." *Atlantic*, 20 December. Retrieved from http://www.theatlantic.com/entertainment/archive/2013/12/why-em-her-em-is-the-best-film-of-the-year/282544.

Orr, R. 1992. "A Double Agent in the Dream of Michael Oakeshott." *Political Science Reviewer* 2: 44–62.

Otto, R. 1958. *The Idea of the Holy: An Inquiry into the Non-rational Factor in the Idea of the Divine and Its Relation to the Rational*. 2nd ed. Oxford: Oxford University Press.

Otto, W. F. 1973. *Dionysus: Myth and Cult*. Trans. R. B. Palmer. Bloomington: Indiana University Press.

Packard, V. 1957. *The Hidden Persuaders*. New York: David McKay.

Pagden, A., ed. 2002. *The Idea of Europe: From Antiquity to the European Union*. Cambridge: Cambridge University Press.

Panofsky, E. 1972. *Studies in Iconology: Humanistic Themes in the Art of the Renaissance*. New York: Harper and Row.

Panofsky, E., and C. Wood. 1991. *Perspective as Symbolic Form*. New York: Zone Books.

Papagaroufali, E. 2008. "Of Euro-symbols and Euro-sentiments: The Case of Town and School Twinning." *Historein* 8: 72–82.

Parsons, C. 2002. "Showing Ideas as Causes: The Origins of the European Union." *International Organization* 56: 47–84.

Passerini, L. 2000. "The Last Identification: Why Some of Us Would Like to Call Ourselves Europeans and What We Mean by This." In *Europe and the Other and Europe as the Other*, ed. B. Stråth, 45–67. Brussels: Peter Lang.

———. 2002a. *Il mito d'Europa: Radici antiche per nuovi simboli*. Firenze: Giunti Editore.

———. 2002b. "Il triplice destino del mito di Europa nella contemporanità." In *Il mito di Europa: Da fanciulla rapita a continente*, ed. C. Pescio, 157–62. Firenze: Giunti Editore.

———. 2003a. "Dimensions of the Symbolic in the Construction of Europeanness." In *Figures d'Europe: Images and myths of Europe,* ed. L. Passerini, 21–34. Brussels: Peter Lang.

———, ed. 2003b. *Figures d'Europe: Images and Myths of Europe?* Brussels: Peter Lang.

Patočka, J., E. V. Kohák, and J. Dodd. 1996. *Heretical Essays in the Philosophy of History.* Chicago: Open Court.

Philippot, J-C. 2014. "EBU President: 'Public Service Media Promote Values That Shape the EU.'" EBU News, 16 September. Retrieved from http://www3.ebu.ch/contents/news/2014/09/ebu-president-public-service-med.html.

Phinnemore, D., and A. Warleigh-Lack. 2009. *Reflections on European Integration: 50 Years of the Treaty of Rome.* London: Palgrave Macmillan.

Pizzorno, A. 1986. "Some Other Kinds of Otherness: A Critique of 'Rational Choice' Theories." In *Development, Democracy, and the Art of Trespassing: Essays in Honor of Albert O. Hirschman,* 355–73. Notre Dame, IN: University of Notre Dame Press.

———. 1987. "Politics Unbound." In *Changing Boundaries of the Political: Essays on the Evolving Balance between the State and Society, Public and Private in Europe,* ed. C. S. Maier, 27–62. Cambridge: Academic.

———. 2010. "The Mask: An Essay." *International Political Anthropology* 3(1): 5–28.

Pointon, M. 1998. "Money and Nationalism." In *Imagining Nations,* ed. G. Cubitt, 229–54. Manchester: Manchester University Press.

Poirion, D., and C. Weber. 1999. "Mask and Allegorical Personification." Yale French Studies, No. 95, *Rereading Allegory: Essays in Memory of Daniel Poirion,* 13–32. New Haven, CT: Yale University Press.

Prager, J. 1993. "Politics and Illusion." *Psychoanalysis and Contemporary Thought* 16: 561–95.

Prodi, R. 2002. *More Europe.* Speech to the European Parliament in Strasbourg, 16(1). Retrieved from http://europa.eu.int/comm/commissioners/prodi/speeches/index_en.htm.

———. 2003. "Europe: The Dream and the Choices." *Bulletin Quotidien Europe,* 21 November, No. 2339/2340.

Propp, V. 1968. *The Morphology of the Folktale.* Austin: University of Texas Press.

Quintilian. 1920. *Institutio oratoria.* Trans. H. E. Butler. London: William Heinemann.

Rabier, J.-R. 2003. "Tradition et résurgences d'un mythe: Le ravissement d'Europe." In *Figures d'Europe: Images and myths of Europe,* ed. L. Passerini, 65–76. Brussels: Peter Lang.

Radin, P. 1956. *The Trickster: A Study in Native American Mythology.* New York: Philosophical Library.

———. 2002. *Primitive Man as Philosopher.* New York: Courier Corporation.

Rappaport, R. A. 1999. *Ritual and Religion in the Making of Humanity.* Cambridge: Cambridge University Press.

Raykoff, I., and R. D. Tobin, eds. 2007. *A Song for Europe: Popular Music and Politics in the Eurovision Song Contest.* Aldershot: Ashgate.

Reding, V. 2012. "Why We Need a United States of Europe Now." European Commission Speech. Passau, 8(11). Retrieved from http://europa.eu/rapid/press-release_SPEECH-12-796_en.htm.

———. 2013a. "2014: Time to Make a Choice." KPN's New Year's reception/Brussels, 7(1). Retrieved from http://europa.eu/rapid/press-release_SPEECH-14-1_en.htm.

———. 2013b. "EU Citizenship—Anno 2013." Dialogue with Rik Torfs, Rector of KU Leuven/Kortrijk. Campus of the University of Leuven, 2(12). Retrieved from http://europa.eu/rapid/press-release_SPEECH-13-1003_it.htm.

———. 2013c. "Towards a Federal Europe: What We Can Learn from Our Central Banks." 25th Anniversary of the Österreichische Nationalbank/Austrian Central Bank Representative Office in Brussels, 3(12). Retrieved from http://europa.eu/rapid/press-release_SPEECH-13-1007_en.htm.

———. 2014. "The United Kingdom and the EU—Inevitably Drifting Apart?" Cambridge, 17(2). Retrieved from http://europa.eu/rapid/press-release_SPEECH-14-137_en.htm.

Remotti, F. 1996. *Contro l'identità.* Bari: Laterza.

Renan, E. 1990. "What Is a Nation?" In *Nation and Narration,* ed. H. K. Bhabha, 9–22. New York: Routledge.

Renault, J. M. 2002. *Les fées de la République.* Montpellier: Créations du Pélican.

Rensmann, L. 2006. "Europeanism and Americanism in the Age of Globalization: Hannah Arendt's Reflections on Europe and America and Implications for a Post-national Identity of the EU Polity." *European Journal of Political Theory* 5(2): 139–70.

Riall, L. 2008. *Garibaldi: Invention of a Hero.* New Haven, CT: Yale University Press.

Ricoeur, P. 1974. *The Conflict of Interpretations: Essays in Hermeneutics.* Evanston, IL: Northwestern University Press.

———. 1984. *Time and Narrative.* Vol. 1. Chicago: University of Chicago Press.

———. 1996. "Reflections on a New Ethos for Europe." *Philosophy and Social Criticism* 21(5/6): 3–13.

———. 2004. *Memory, History, Forgetting.* Chicago: University of Chicago Press.

Riedl, M. 2012. "The Containment of Dionysos: Religion and Politics in the Bacchanalia Affair of 186 BCE." *International Political Anthropology* 5(2): 113–33.

Riklin, F., and W. White. 1915. "Wishfulfillment and Symbolism in Fairy Tales." *Psychoanalytic Review* 2: 203–18.

Ringmar, E. 1998. "Nationalism: The Idiocy of Intimacy." *British Journal of Sociology* 49(4): 534–49.

Risse-Kappen, T. 2003. "The Euro between National and European Identity." *Journal of European Public Policy* 10(4): 487–505.

———. 2010. *A Community of Europeans: Transnational Identities and Public Spheres.* Ithaca, NY: Cornell University Press.

Roba, A. 2010. *Princess Europa Exhibition.* Retrieved from http://www.eutrio.be/princess-europa-exhibition.

Roberts, H. E., ed.. 2013. *Encyclopedia of Comparative Iconography: Themes Depicted in Works of Art.* London: Routledge.

Roberts, R. H. 2006. "Gaia and Europa: Religion and Legitimation Crisis in the 'New Europe.'" In *The Shape of the New Europe,* ed. R. Rogowski and C. Turner, 146–66. Cambridge: Cambridge University Press.

Robertson, M. 1965. "Attic Red-Figure Vase-Painters." *Journal of Hellenic Studies* 85: 90–101.

Roche, M. 2001. "Citizenship, Popular Culture and Europe." In *Culture and Citizenship,* ed. N. Stevenson, 74–98. London: Sage.

Rodari, G. 2010. *Grammatica della fantasia.* Trieste: Edizioni EL.

Rogowski, R., and C. Turner, eds. 2006. *The Shape of the New Europe.* Cambridge: Cambridge University Press.

Róheim, G. 1932. "Animism and Religion." *Psychoanalytic Quarterly* 1: 59–112.

———. 1942. "The Origin and Function of Culture." *Psychoanalytic Review* 29: 131–64.

Roth, N. 1959. "The Face-Genital Equation." *Psychoanalytic Quarterly* 28: 493–500.

Ruby, J. 1980. "Exposing Yourself: Reflexivity, Anthropology, and Film." *Semiotica* 30: 1–2.

Rutter, N. K., and B. A. Sparkes. 2000. *Word and Image in Ancient Greece.* Vol. 1. Edinburgh: Edinburgh University Press.

Salgó, E. 2014. *Psychoanalytic Reflections on Politics: Fatherlands in Mothers' Hands.* New York: Routledge.

Sandvoss, C. 2008. "On the Couch with Europe: The Eurovision Song Contest, the European Broadcast Union and Belonging on the Old Continent." *Popular Communication* 6(3): 190–207.

Scheipers, S., and D. Sicurelli. 2007. "Normative Power Europa: A Credible Utopia?" *Journal of Common Market Studies* 45(2): 435–57.

Schianchi, F. 2014. "Renzi: realizziamo il sogno degli Stati Uniti d'Europa." *La Stampa* 30(6). Retrieved from http://www.lastampa.it/2014/06/30/italia/politica/renzi-realizziamo-il-sogno-degli-stati-uniti-deuropa-c2cHYZKBll9w5RZOsGSXJJ/pagina.html.

Schmid, J. 2001. "Etching the Notes of a New European Identity." *New York Times* 3(8). Retrieved from http://www.nytimes.com/2001/08/03/news/03iht-euro_ed3_.html.

Schmiel, R. 1981. "Moschus' Europa." *Classical Philology* 76(4): 261–72.

Schöpflin, G. 1997. "The Functions of Myth and a Taxonomy of Myths." In *The Myths of Nationhood,* ed. G. Hosking and G. Schöpflin. 19–35. London: Hurst and Company.

Schroeder, J. 2014. "Could It Be Her Voice? Why Scarlett Johansson's Voice Makes Samantha Seem Human." *Culture, Society, Technology,* 28 February. Retrieved from http://thepsychreport.com/culture/could-it-be-her-voice-why-scarlett-johanssons-voice-makes-samantha-seem-human.

Segal, H. 1978. "On Symbolism." *International Journal of Psychoanalysis* 59: 315–19.

Seiden, H. M. 2009. "On the Longing for Home." *Psychoanalytic Psychology* 26(2): 191–205.

Seldin, J. 1955. "Selling to the Id: Freud Writes the Ads." *The Nation* 180, 21(5): 442–43.

Sels, N. 2011. "Myth, Mind and Metaphor: On the Relation of Mythology and Psychoanalysis." *Journal of the Jan van Eyck Circle for Lacanian Ideology Critique* 4: 56–70. Retrieved from https://biblio.ugent.be/publication/1983963/file/6741297.pdf.

Sendler, E. 1988. *The Icon, Image of the Invisible: Elements of Theology, Aesthetics, and Technique.* Redondo Beach, CA: Oakwood Publications.

Shacklock, G. and Smyth, J. 1998. *Being Reflexive in Critical Educational and Social Research.* London: Falmer.

Shanahan, S. 2003. "Currency and Community: European Identity and the Euro." In *Figures d'Europe-Images and Myths of Europe,* ed. L. Passerini, 159–79. Brussels: Peter Lang.

Shils, E., and M. Young. 1955. "The Meaning of the Coronation." *Sociological Review* 3: 63–81.

Shore, C. 1993. *Inventing the People's Europe: Critical Approaches to European Community Cultural Policy.* London: University of London.

———. 2000. *Building Europe: The Cultural Politics of European Integration.* New York: Routledge.

———. 2001. "European Union and the Politics of Culture." In *The Bruges Group,* Paper 43, 15(12).

Shuker, R. 1998. *Key Concepts in Popular Music.* New York: Routledge.

———. 2013. *Understanding Popular Music.* 4th ed. New York: Routledge.

Silver, D. 1985. "Mirror in Dreams: Symbol of Mother's Face." *Psychoanalytic Inquiry* 5(2): 253–56.

Silverstone, R. 1994. *Television and Everyday Life.* New York: Routledge.

Simmel, G. 1909/1994. "Bridge and Door." *Theory, Culture and Society* 11(2): 5–10.

Slavtcheva-Petkova, V. 2014. "Rethinking Banal Nationalism: Banal Americanism, Europeanism, and the Missing Link between Media Representations and Identities." *International Journal of Communication* 8: 43–61.

Smismans, S. 2010. "The European Union's Fundamental Rights Myth." *Journal of Common Market Studies* 48(1): 43–64.

Smith, A. 1964. *The Ethnic Origins of Nations.* Oxford: Blackwell.

———. 1991. "The Nation: Invented, Imagined, Reconstructed?" *Millennium—Journal of International Studies* 20(3): 353–68.

———. 1992. "National Identity and the Idea of European Unity." *International Affairs* 68(1): 55–76.

———. 1995. *Nations and Nationalism in a Global Era.* Cambridge: Polity Press.

———. 2004. *The Antiquity of Nations.* Cambridge: Polity Press.

Smith, A. C. 2005. "The Politics of Weddings at Athens: An Iconographic Assessment." *Leeds International Classical Studies* 4(1): 1–32.

———. 2011. *Polis and Personification in Classical Athenian Art.* Leiden: Brill.

Smith, G., and R. Speed. 2011. "Cultural Branding and Political Marketing: An Exploratory Analysis." *Journal of Marketing Management* 27(13/14): 1304–21.

Solbes, P. 2001/2002. "Europe Interview with European Pedro Solbes, Commissioner to Economic and Monetary Affairs." *Europe,* December/January: 16–17.

Sonntag, A. 2011. "False Expectations: The Counterproductive Side Effects of the EU's Use of Political Symbols." In *Debating Political Identity and Legitimacy in the European Union,* ed. S. Lucarelli, F. Cerutti, and V. A. Schmidt, 115–50. London: Routledge.

Sorel, G. 1999. *Reflections on Violence.* Cambridge: Cambridge University Press.

———. 2012. *Remarks at the Festival of Economics.* Trento, 2(6). Retrieved from http://www.georgesoros.com/interviews-peeches/entry/remarks_at_the_festival_of_economics_trento_italy.

Stadin, K. 2005. "The Masculine Image of a Great Power." *Scandinavian Journal of History* 30(1): 61–82.

Stavrakakis, Y. 1999. *Lacan and the Political.* New York: Routledge.

———. 2009. "Psychoanalysis and Ideology: Comment on RD Hinshelwood." *Psychoanalysis, Culture and Society* 14(2): 149–63.

———. 2015. "Populism in Power: Syriza's Challenge to Europe." *Juncture* 21(4): 273–80.

Steen, M. 2012. "Super Mario Reaches the Last Level—German Politics." *Financial Times,* 7 September. Retrieved from http://www.ft.com/intl/cms/s/0/44d6ccbe-f81e-11e1-bec8-00144feabdc0.html#axzz3nua3ZDNG.

Stillman, R. E. 1995. "Hobbes's Leviathan: Monsters, Metaphors, and Magic." *ELH* 62(4): 791–819.

Stocchetti, M., and K. Kukkonen. 2011. *Images in Use: Towards the Critical Analysis of Visual Communication.* Amsterdam: John Benjamins Publishing.

Storvik-Green, S. 2015. "Nearly 200 Million People Watch Eurovision 2015." *Eurovision* 3(6). Retrieved from http://www.eurovision.tv/page/news?id=nearly_200_million_people_watch_eurovision_2015.

Stowers, S. 2007. "The Concepts of 'Religion,' 'Political Religion' and the Study of Nazism." *Journal of Contemporary History* 42(1): 9–24.

Stråth, B. 2000a. *Myth and Memory in the Construction of Community: Historical Patterns in Europe and Beyond.* New York: Peter Lang.

———, ed. 2000b. *Europe and the Other and Europe as the Other.* Brussels: Peter Lang.

———. 2005. "Methodological and Substantive Remarks on Myth, Memory and History in the Construction of a European Community." *German Law Journal* 6(2): 255–71.

Stratulat, C., and J. A. Emmanouilidis. 2013. *The European Parliament Elections 2014: Watershed or, again, Washed Out?* Brussels: European Policy Center.

Streeter, C. A. 2003. "The Hazards of Visibility: 'Biracial' Women, Media Images, and Narratives of Identity." In *New Faces in a Changing America: Multiracial Identity in the 21st Century,* ed. L. I. Winters and H. L. DeBose. Thousand Oaks, CA: Sage Publications.

Szakolczai, A. 2001. "In a Permanent State of Transition: Theorising the East-European Condition." *Limen* 2. Retrieved from http://limen.mi2.hr/limen1-2001/arpad_szakolczai.html.

———. 2008a. "The Spirit of the Nation-State: Nation, Nationalism, and Inner-worldly Eschatology in the Work of Eric Voegelin." *International Political Anthropology* 1(2): 193–212.

———. 2008b. "Citizenship and Home: Political Allegiance and its Background." *International Political Anthropology* 1(1): 57–76.
Szondi, G. 2008. *Public Diplomacy and Nation Branding: Conceptual Similarities and Differences.* Clingendael: Netherlands Institute of International Relations.
Tannen, D. 2007. *Talking Voices: Repetition, Dialogue, and Imagery in Conversational Discourse.* Cambridge: Cambridge University Press.
Taylor, Q. 2005. "Money and Politics in the Land of Oz." *Independent Review* 9(3): 413–26.
Tešan, J. 2013. "Liminality and Democratic Imagination." *International Political Anthropology* 6(1).
Thomassen, B. 2008. "Mimetic Errors in Liminal Schismogenesis: On the Political Anthropology of the Trickster." *International Political Anthropology* 1(1): 3–24.
Time. 1993a. Special Issue—The New Face of America. 18(11). Retrieved from http://content.time.com/time/covers/0,16641,19931118,00.html.
———. 1993b. "Rebirth of a Nation, Computer Style." Special Issue—The New Face of America. 18(11). Retrieved from http://content.time.com/time/magazine/article/0,9171,979738,00.html.
Toennies, F. 1955. *Community and Society.* New York: Routledge.
Torresi, I. 2010. *Translating Promotional and Advertising Texts.* Manchester: St. Jerome Pub.
Tragaki, D., ed. 2013. *Empire of Song: Europe and Nation in the Eurovision Song Contest.* Lanham, MD: Scarecrow Press.
Tuckett, D. 2011. *Minding the Markets: An Emotional Finance View of Financial Instability.* London: Palgrave MacMillan.
Tudor, H. 1972. *Political Myth.* London: Macmillan.
Turner, B. S. 2011. *Religion and Modern Society: Citizenship, Secularisation and the State.* Cambridge: Cambridge University Press.
Turner, E. 2012. *Communitas: The Anthropology of Collective Joy.* New York: Palgrave Macmillan.
Turner, V. 1967. *The Forest of Symbols: Aspects of Ndembu Ritual.* Ithaca, NY: Cornell University Press.
———. 1968. "Myth and Symbol." In *International Encyclopedia of the Social Sciences,* ed. D. Sills. Vol. 10. New York: Macmillan.
———. 1969. *The Ritual Process: Structure and Anti-structure.* Ithaca, NY: Cornell University Press.
———. 1975. *Dramas, Fields, and Metaphors: Symbolic Action in Human Society.* Ithaca, NY: Cornell University Press.
———. 1982. *From Ritual to Theatre: The Seriousness of Human Play.* New York: Performing Arts Journal Publications.
———. 1987. *The Anthropology of Performance.* New York: Performing Arts Journal Publications.
United Nations 2014. "Secretary-General's remarks at meeting with Conchita Wurst." Vienna, 3(11). Retrieved from http://www.un.org/sg/statements/index.asp?nid=8160.
Uždavinys, A. 2008. "Metaphysical Symbols and Their Function in Theurgy." *Eye of the Heart: A Journal of Traditional Wisdom* 2: 37–59.

Van de Putte, T. 2014. *Discourses on Democracy: The European Year of Citizens 2013 and the Public Sphere.* Central European University. Retrieved from www.etd.ceu.hu/2014/putte_thomas.pdf.

Van Straten, R. 1994. *An Introduction to Iconography.* Vol. 1. New York: Psychology Press.

Varoufakis, Y. 2011. *The Global Minotaur.* New York: Zed Books.

Verba, S. 1965. "The Kennedy Assassination and the Nature of Political Commitment." In *The Kennedy Assassination and the American Public,* ed. E. Parker and B. Greensberg. Palo Alto, 348–60. CA: Stanford University Press.

Verdery, K. 1999. *The Political Lives of Dead Bodies: Reburial and Postsocialist Change.* New York: Columbia University Press.

Vernant, J. P. and P. Vidal-Naquet. 1990. *Myth and Tragedy in Ancient Greece.* New York: Zone Books.

Vico, G. 1948. *The New Science.* Translated from the third edition (1744) by T. Goddard Bergin and M. H. Fisch. Ithaca, NY: Cornell University Press.

Vigna, E. 1996. "Shakespeare? Scartato perchè antisemita. Mozart? Troppo massone." *Corriere della Sera* 17(12).

Villanueva, D. C. 2005. "Richard von Coudenhove-Kalergi's Pan-Europa as the Elusive 'Object of Longing.'" *Rocky Mountain Review of Language and Literature.* 59(2): 67–80.

Viola, D. M., ed. 2015. *Routledge Handbook of European Elections.* London: Routledge.

Voegelin, E. 1987. *The New Science of Politics: An Introduction.* Chicago: University of Chicago Press.

———. 1997. "History of Political Ideas: Hellenism, Rome, and Early Christianity." In *The Collected Works of Eric Voegelin.* Vol. 19. Columbia: University of Missouri Press.

———. 1998. "History of Political Ideas: Religion and the Rise of Modernity." In *The Collected Works of Eric Voegelin.* Vol. 23. Columbia: University of Missouri Press.

———. 2000. "Modernity without Restraint: The Political Religions, the New Science of Politics, and Science, Politics, and Gnosticism." In *The Collected Works of Eric Voegelin.* Vol 5. Columbia: University of Missouri Press.

Vogler, V. 2007. *The Writer's Journey: Mythic Structure for Writers.* 3rd ed. Studio City, CA: Michael Wiese Productions.

Wæver, O. 2004. "Discursive Approaches." In *European Integration Theory,* eds. A. Wiener and T. Diez. Oxford: Oxford University Press.

Wallace, H. 2009. "Some *Reflections* on 50 Years of Experience since the Signature of the Treaties of Rome." In *Reflections on European Integration—50 Years of the Treaty of Rome,* eds. D. *Phinnemore* and A. Warleigh-Lack 11–21. London: Palgrave Macmillan.

Wallström, M. 2007. "Europe's Public Relations: The EU Lacks a Story." *Spiegel International* 19(1). Retrieved from http://www.spiegel.de/international/europe-s-public-relations-the-eu-lacks-a-story-a-460540.html.

Walzer, M. 1967. "On the Role of Symbolism in Political Thought." *Political Science Quarterly* 82(2): 191–204.

Waterfield, B. 2014. "We Want a United States of Europe Says Top EU official." *Telegraph* 8(1). Retrieved from http://www.telegraph.co.uk/news/world

news/europe/eu/10559458/We-want-a-United-States-of-Europe-says-top-EU-official.html.

Weber, M. 1946. *Essays in Sociology.* New York: Oxford University Press.

Webster, T. B. L. 1954. "Personification as a Mode of Greek Thought." *Journal of the Warburg and Courtauld Institutes* 17(1/2): 10–21.

Weiler, J. H. 1997. "To Be a European Citizen: Eros and Civilization." *Journal of European Public Policy* 4(4): 495–519.

———. 2011. *On the Political and Legal DNA of the Union and the Current European Crisis.* Retrieved from https://www.hertie-school.org/fileadmin/images/Downloads/media_events/weiler_rede.pdf.

———. 2012. "Europe in Crisis—On Political Messianism, Legitimacy and the Rule of Law." *Singapore Journal of Legal Studies*: 248–68.

Weiss, E. 1985. *Elementi di psicoanalisi.* Pordenone: Edizioni Studio Tesi.

Wernick, A. 2001. *Auguste Comte and the Religion of Humanity: The Post-theistic Program of French Social Theory.* Cambridge: Cambridge University Press.

White, H. 2000. "The Discourse of Europe and the Search for a European Identity." In *Europe and the Other and Europe as the Other,* ed. B. Stråth, 67–87. Brussels: Peter Lang.

Williams, W. 2003. "David Morgan, Visual Piety: A History and Theory of Popular Religious Images." *Journal of American Studies* 37(1): 135–77.

Wilson, B., G. J. Buelow, and A. Hoyt. 2001. "Rhetoric and Music. *NG* 2(21): 260–75.

Winnicott, D. W. 1956. "Primary Maternal Preoccupation." In *Through Paediatrics to Psychoanalysis: Collected Papers,* 300–305. London: Tavistock.

———. 1960. "The Theory of the Parent-Infant Relationship." *International Journal of Psychoanalysis* 41: 585–95.

———. 1967. "Mirror-Role of Mother and Family in Child Development." In *The Predicament of the Family: A Psycho-analytical Symposium,* ed. P. Lomas. London: Hogarth Press and the Institute of Psycho-Analysis.

———. 1971. *Playing and Reality.* London: Tavistock Publications.

Winter, B. 2009. "Marianne goes Multicultural: Ni putes ni soumises and the Republicanisation of Ethnic Minority Women in France." French History and Civilization: Papers from the George Rudé Seminar, 2:228–40.

Wintle, M. 2004. *Europa and the Bull, Europe, and European Studies: Visual Images as Historical Source Material.* Amsterdam: Amsterdam University Press.

———, ed. 2008. *Imagining Europe: Europe and European Civilisation as Seen from Its Margins and by the Rest of the World, in the Nineteenth and Twentieth Centuries.* New York: Peter Lang.

———. 2009. *The Image of Europe: Visualizing Europe in Cartography and Iconography throughout the Ages.* Cambridge: Cambridge University Press.

Wolf, E. R. 1958. "The Virgin of Guadalupe: A Mexican National Symbol." *Journal of American Folklore* 71(279): 34–39.

Wydra, H. 2008. "Democratisation as Meaning-Formation–Insights from the Communist Experience." *International Political Anthropology* 1(1): 113–32.

———. 2009. "The Liminal Origins of Democracy." *International Political Anthropology* 2(1): 91–109.

———. 2011a. "In-Betweenness: The Extraordinary as the Ground of Social Reality." *International Political Anthropology* 4(2): 185–94.
———. 2011b. "The Politics of Transcendence." *Cultural Politics* 7(2): 265–88.
———. 2012. "Victims and New Wars." *Cambridge Review of International Affairs* 13(11).
———. 2015a. "Spells of the Sacred in a Global Age." *Journal of International Political Theory* 11(1): 95–110.
———. 2015b. *Politics and the Sacred.* Cambridge: Cambridge University Press.
Yair, G. 1995. "'Unite Unite Europe': The Political and Cultural Structures of Europe as Reflected in the Eurovision Song Contest." *Social Networks* 17(2): 147–61.
Zaiotti, R. 2011. "Performing Schengen: Myths, Rituals and the Making of European Territoriality beyond Europe." *Review of International Studies* 37(2): 537–56.
Zakaria, F. 1999. "Money for Mars." *Newsweek* 11(1).
Zigelyte, L. 2012. "Gazing at Fiction in Brussels: Europe as Forgery in David Černý's Entropa." *European Review* 20(1): 54–67.
Ziolkowski, T. 2008. *Minos and the Moderns: Cretan Myth in Twentieth-Century Literature and Art.* Oxford: Oxford University Press.
Žižek, S. 1989. *The Sublime Object of Ideology.* New York: Verso.
———. 1992. *Everything You Always Wanted to Know about Lacan but Were Afraid to Ask Hitchcock.* New York: Verso.
———. 1993. *Tarrying with the Negative: Kant, Hegel, and the Critique of Ideology.* Durham, NC: Duke University Press.
———. 1994. *The Metastases of Enjoyment: Six Essays on Woman and Causality.* New York: Verso.
———. 1997. *The Plague of Fantasies.* New York: Verso.
———. 2006. *The Universal Exception.* New York: Continuum.
———. 2007. "Ode to Joy,' Followed by Chaos and Despair." *New York Times* 24(12). Retrieved from http://www.nytimes.com/2007/12/24/opinion/24zizek.html?_r=0.
Žižek, S., and G. Daly. 2004. *Conversations with Žižek.* Cambridge: Polity Press.
Zweig, S. 1943. *The World of Yesterday: An Autobiography by Stefan Zweig.* New York: Viking Press.

Index